The only reason conspiracies remain shrouded in theory...

is that their fullness eludes the imagination

of those outside the plot.

This book is dedicated to the eradication of relativism,
all of its false promises,
and all of its many poisonous ideologies
that have pervaded our world.
May this book be a thumb in the eye
of the worshippers of relativism,
chief among them the father of lies,
who cherishes relativism as his first and most precious lie

Contents

PART I

IT'S THE ECONOMY, STUPID

1. Welcome to the Reset Event Horizon
2. Who Rules the World?
3. The 0.000001%
4. The New World Order & How We Got Here
5. Their Ultimate End: The Great Reset

PART II

POLITICS IS DOWNSTREAM OF CULTURE (YOU KNOW, EXCEPT WHEN IT'S NOT)

6. The Soul of America
7. The Soul of the Global Communist Movement
8. Why There Are No Communist Governments
9. The Marxists: The Ultimate Useful Idiots
10. Whose Future Will We Live In?

PART III

ALL HUMAN CONFLICT IS ULTIMATELY THEOLOGICAL

11. The Greatest Conspiracy: The Denial of the Satan Adjacent

12. The Death of Relativism and All of its False Promises

13. He Places Before You Life or Death; Choose Life

14. What Can I Do? And What Must Be Done.

15. In Conclusion: Reset Wisely

PART I

IT'S THE ECONOMY, STUPID

CHAPTER 1

Welcome to the Reset Event Horizon

WORD TO THE READER

This book will either become forgotten or obsolete in time. It will either be burned and erased from history by a rising regime, or it will serve as (at least one) guide out of the madness in which we are descending. History does not repeat itself but like a poem, it flows ever onward ... still managing to rhyme with itself. There are timeless principles in this book, and therefore, as an echo of days gone by, some future reader might find solace here as they face what a future age holds. But this book is not written for some future age or to address some past abuse; it is written for our age. I want to directly address the poison that we don't even realize is already destroying our minds. In doing so, it is important that you understand the harm that is being inflicted upon us—on you—is being done by design. Stop to make sure you have wrapped your head around that before reading on.

When an enemy lays siege and declares war on you, you are not at leisure to deny your enemy their war. You must either surrender or fight, which means there are a few ways to lose but only one way to win. War was waged long ago, before many of us ever came to the fight. In fact, the war has been going on for so long that the enemy's siege has worked. Now they hold the keys to the kingdom. If you are still fighting for this country, you are now the insurgent, the new rebellion, who now must get creative in laying your own siege. Choose to do nothing about your enemy or yourself, and you will most certainly be controlled. Fight with frail weapons and a small mind, and you will be humiliated first and then controlled. Rather, choose your weapons of war wisely, prepare for the battle, and outmaneuver your enemy.

I am not exactly sure when the wisdom of the ages will be officially declared contraband, but your enemy has taken great strides to make sure it is dying in the court of public opinion. If it is allowed to be snuffed out, forgotten, or erased from the memory of this age, you will have forfeited the only thing that can defeat the enemy, who, make no mistake, controls the citadel now. You must realize that the country we once had is controlled by your declared enemy. Now, we are the resistance fighters who must take it back.

In The Art of War, Sun Tzu says something profound about the nature of war. The book that delves deeply into the strategies and tactics of war begins by shifting the reader's mindset about the mission and goal the tactician should be striving for. Lesson 1 is that war is not about war; it is not about military might, nor is it even inherently about the conflict at hand. Fundamentally, we understand that there are winners and losers in war. But understanding how to get into the winner's circle requires a different and more foundational way of thinking; one cannot simply wish or will themselves into it. Winners in war are not declared; they are proven by their enemy's defeat; winners win by controlling and overcoming the loser. Sun Tzu recognized that control of the situation is an inestimable asset in any conflict.

It is out of this concept that tacticians must operate as they approach any conflict that they hope to win. Sun Tzu goes into detail on how to maximize one's control over terrain, situational strategy, mental and physical preparations, and even controlling the enemy's perception and morale. What is a foregone conclusion in his writing is that you will not always be the stronger force. The inevitability of victory or defeat is based not in any perception or reality but rather in who commands control of the conflict. And this, my friends, leads to perhaps the keenest insight of the book: control of the conflict begins long before you find yourself toe-to-toe with the enemy on the battlefield. If your strategy begins after the first shot is fired, you have deeply misunderstood the necessary elements to win a war. So egregiously that you may have lost the war before it has ever had a chance to begin.

If you understand that conflict is won or lost by who commands control, then you can understand what Sun Tzu means when he says, "All warfare is based on deception."[1] Paraphrasing now: 'If you are strong, appear weak; if you are weak, appear strong.' This is akin to the advice given to trial lawyers: when you are questioning someone on the stand, do not ask a question that you do not know the answer to. While everyone might be surprised by the revelation, no one will be surprised that you lost the case. It is also similar to effective negotiation: begin by negotiating to terms well beyond your point of compromise, and always be able to walk away from the table. The wise man knows not to reveal everything about his position when it comes to dealing with conflict. In fact, by practicing the art of deception and appearing to be the opposite of what you are, you can often get your enemy to unknowingly reveal his own position and thus give you greater control of the conflict. If you think that sounds too Machiavellian or harsh, just remember: we aren't talking about your friends; we are talking about your enemies. Transparency and authenticity are the most likeable and admirable human traits. Common sense and neuroscience both tell us that we are far more attracted to authentic people. But when you find yourself in a conflict, you must operate by a different set of rules, or you will be overcome by an enemy who will use anything and everything against you in their pursuit to command control (including your authenticity, your transparency, and your good will).

This is why it is paramount for you to understand that what is happening is not an accident of circumstance. It is being deliberately done to you by an enemy who wants to control you. If you fail to understand this, you will continue to fumble through life, treating your enemies and your friends as equals until you have neither. You will end up in the lonely place of being a loser, not worth befriending or defeating. You will continue to float in a sea of gray where right and wrong, good and evil, chaos and meaning are all just insignificant outcomes of losing a war you can't even see is being waged on you. A war that you are forfeiting by doing nothing—a war you are losing by thinking you can deny your enemy their war.

There is one last juxtaposition that I want to draw from the wisdom of The Art of War. Sun Tzu says, "to fight and conquer ... is not supreme excellence; supreme excellence consists in breaking the enemy's resistance without fighting."[2] Winning a war without ever engaging in kinetic battle was, in Sun Tzu's estimation, the greatest victory; to win merely by tactic and not physical defeat on the battlefield. Conversely, there is only one scenario in The Art of War where Sun Tzu recommends direct engagement in kinetic war with your enemy, and it is this: when there is no advantage to be gained from the weather or environment–and you are strategically disadvantaged and trapped by the terrain–and, most importantly, when your enemy strikes, you find yourself in what Sun Tzu deemed 'desperate ground.' And his advice? "In desperate ground, fight." [3] Damn the torpedoes, fix bayonets, draw steel, or whatever the call to arms is, you have no choice but to put down the tactician's lens and fight to the death.

We are not quite there yet, thankfully. However, in desperate times, we must be willing to not only entertain the idea but be willing and prepared for it. If we continue to deny our enemy their war, if we continue to give up ground and allow ourselves to be backed into a corner, if our plan is to start strategizing when the first punch is thrown, we will lose. And any method of our ever winning again will be destroyed by the enemy. This book and any others that even give hints on how to defeat their ideology will be burned. Do not expect your enemies to be your friends once they have complete control over this conflict.

Recognize you are in a conflict, recognize your enemy, and recognize that what is happening is happening because your enemy has brought this conflict to your door. Denying your enemy their war is no longer an option, and choosing to do nothing is forfeit. It is time that we put on the tactician's armor and outmaneuver our enemy. Only one of us is going to command control of this conflict in the end. To win is a necessity, because our enemy will certainly not transform into a benevolent victor once they are completely established. We must ultimately be better in victory, but let us not talk about the spoils of war before the war has been won. So let us prepare for war by knowing our enemy first and then by knowing ourselves. Then, let us be unafraid to do what is necessary to command complete control of the conflict that is being waged upon us. There is only one way to win; any other path taken is merely some form of defeat ... and only the victor gets the spoils.

THE PREMISE

There is a stirring in the West and indeed throughout the world. It is like the unease of beholding an approaching storm that does not come in its season or upon its usual bearing. We live in interesting times, whether we want to acknowledge it or not. These times feel both common and foreign, sometimes easy to understand and sometimes too baffling to comprehend. We are at a precipice in history, a seminal moment whereupon the end of an age will close and the world will never be the same. An event horizon is the point of no return; it is the place where things are forever changed. History is not yet written because you have not lived it yet and your descendants (or those that have defeated you) have not written it about you. You will shape the outcome of the end of this age, and your thoughts, your actions, and your character will decide whether the next age begins in freedom or slavery.

In this moment—our moment—there is much unrest and violence, and there seems to be an endless cacophony of competing ideologies. Today's politics seem disjointed and polarized as the positions of both the right and left shift under our very feet. All of it can make sense, but not through the old paradigmatic lenses of politics, society, and culture. We are not living in times that can harken back to previous decades for grounding; if we think we can navigate the next decade by mimicking the last, we do so to our own peril. The world in the information age has shifted so far beyond most people's imaginings that they have no idea what they are up against. Even those who believe in a conspiracy or three might be caught flat-footed when what looms before us comes into full view. The upheaval of information–who has it and who hides it–is an elaborate scheme being manipulated, sometimes exposed, but always orchestrated to a very precise end by a very particular group of people. They are at the center of all of this, and the rest of the noise is manufactured or allowed to exist for the purpose of making a fog so thick that the true nature of what they are doing is never exposed. That is, until they have achieved their end, and nothing that we failed to notice will have mattered anyway.

If you want this book to be a Democrat or a Republican manifesto, you will end up disappointed. If you want it to be a defense of our current purple establishment, you will be sorely disappointed. I won't pretend to be a moderate either; people who stand in the middle during this time are going to be hit by a truck going one way or the other. You will come to know my biases and my viewpoint of the world throughout this book. I hope by the end of this book our differences on religion, politics, or social issues will be properly couched in light of what will be required to conquer our common enemy. I am under no false pretenses: I am in this fight, I have chosen my side, and I damn sure plan to win.

However, my side is not going to conveniently line up with partisan politics. No matter where you are on the political spectrum, just wait; I'm sure I'll get to your pet issue and piss you off with my perspective. I joke, but pretending that we can interpret what is going on in the world today through these old lenses is a huge part of the problem; it's why we cannot see more clearly what is going on. Worse, it is causing a massive delaying action by which the people who wish to see America's demise are gaining ground while most of our elected officials are still trying to figure out what time it is. Worse of all, it is making us think that we are enemies and on opposite sides of their game. But it's their game, a game they fully anticipate winning and a game that requires all of us to be losers. What game, you might say? The one that is being played in plain sight, if only we have eyes to see. Here is my case in the simplest terms I can distill it down to. Theoretically, it's a conspiracy theory. This is the lens that you must look through for the chaos of the West and the world to make sense. Here is my elevator pitch.

THE ELEVATOR PITCH

The owners of the Federal Reserve (the Fed), the World Bank, and the International Monetary Fund (the IMF) have gained a plurality of ownership of the world's wealth. They have done so by establishing a debt-based monetary system for the world's reserve currency (the USD), as well as adopting the roll of 'the house' in their international casino enterprise known as 'stock markets.' Their influence over world economies and therefore world politics is unparalleled and incomparable to any regime in history. We are now at the precipice where their influence and power are stronger than any other force on earth, and they are mobilizing it in a radically new way. They have formed a Political Action Committee (PAC) called the World Economic Forum (WEF) and have declared that they will achieve their political vision by 2030. That is to establish a centrally-planned one world government with complete global hegemony, and they will achieve this end by any means necessary.

THE GAME AFOOT

Who are these villains, you might ask? You don't know them. The faces of the World Economic Forum are the new initiates. Sure, Klaus Schwab is the founder, but he does not provide the organization's legitimacy. He is there to appear as an intellectual figurehead and do the public work and the bidding of the people whose wealth makes him blush. The people that run the WEF don't count their wealth; they weigh their wealth in influence and power. As comedian JP Sears puts it, 'money is a poor man's currency.' You can look back at the historical record and find the names of the people who own the Fed and the IMF. These families have been established wealth for generations, and you rarely hear from any of them. And why would we? They live in places that are more luxurious than any king's or dignitary's palace. They vacation in places that you have never heard of. Because those places only exist for their enjoyment; the hoi polloi can't make reservations on a travel site. They want for nothing materially and live in such a lap of luxury that it would dumbfound modern kings and queens. If the royalty of antiquity were able to peer into this state of wealth, they would think that they were seeing a vision of Mount Olympus! The lower ranks of these families go to Oxford or Harvard, but the direct descendants and heirs are even too elite to attend these lowly schools and rub shoulders with that upper echelon. It is not surprising then, having no real contact with the humanity they feel a sovereign godship over, that they see the world as theirs and people as nothing more than chattel to be manipulated and controlled.

And it stands to reason that their political action committee, the WEF, attracts bond villains, intellectual psychos, and autistic computer nerd billionaires who are equally out of touch with humanity and reality. I don't know if they are lizard people, but that particular conspiracy does capture at least one true element: they are so far removed from humanity and so insulated from the common experience of man that they might as well be a different species. It may not be their conscious thought, but it is certainly an underlying feature of how they view the world. The real power behind the WEF is not a corporate CEO, your rich neighbor down the street, or even the eccentric jet setters of the world. This echelon of elites doesn't consider billionaires in their class and probably mocks people like Elon Musk at their dinner parties. It is a very small ring of influence that finds themselves in the precarious position of being on top, looking down at all of us, and navigating how best to control us for the sake of their power.

So, for the sake of this book and open dialogue, let's define this upper echelon of the elite of the world. These are the people of such unimaginable wealth that they consider themselves the kingmakers of the world. Thus, they believe themselves to sit upon the throne of the world itself. So, in all fairness, let us call our would-be sovereign overlords the Thrones of Davos (or T.O.D.s for short). This would be the very small, interconnected group of people who have gained an outsized plurality of the world's wealth through their banks and their own stock positions in the companies that are financed through their banks. This small group consists of fewer than a hundred families (and perhaps far fewer) from around the world that have outsized sway of nearly every global system, and thus the global population of eight billion people. This cabal is now seeking to use their economic power to reign in the governments of the world and pull them under their tutelage. That is the driving force behind the madness that we are seeing in the world today.

How do you know this, you might ask? The sign posts are everywhere. Until it gets banned, there is a video floating around the internet that compares the opening statements of local news channels across the country. If you type 'this is a danger to our democracy' into your search bar, you will find the eerie video of local broadcasters throughout the United States repeating the exact same diatribe from 2016. It is clearly a word-for-word script, warning of the dangers of 'fake news,' online media companies 'spreading misinformation,' and how this is a 'danger to our democracy.' And it is repeated nearly verbatim; the producer of the video did a good job cutting the broadcasts together so that you could see the lock-step. Every newscaster in the country, on every single local TV station, read the same propaganda. Who has the power to orchestrate that? The network, sure, but who can orchestrate all of the networks to say that? The people who control not just one, but all of the media companies. Six corporations pump out over ninety percent of the media that is consumed–everything you watch, listen to, or read. That is scary enough, but who owns those six companies? That's who I am talking about. That's who runs the WEF. The WEF has made a 'prediction' that by 2030, you will own nothing and be happy. You owning nothing does not eliminate ownership; de facto, it means that we own nothing, and the owners of the WEF go from owning a majority of everything to owning everything—everything.

You can go to the WEF website and read all of this for yourself; I encourage you to do so. On their website, you will find all kinds of cool articles on their so-called philanthropic work, technology, and societal advancements through the collaboration of countries. All of it is designed to look benign, to appear that they themselves are consultants and collaborators on the world stage, and to suggest that they just want what's best for humanity. But it is all designed as a mechanism to hide their plans in plain sight. If you can listen to their arguments, read their 'predictions' for 2030, and parse fact from fiction, a different picture begins to emerge. They have plans for the world, that's for sure. Their plans would require a total upending of societies around the world, and we are seeing just the tip of the spear in our modern chaos.

Eventually, the goal is to destroy the countries of the world, beginning with the most powerful: America. They will do this by imposing the global communist movement. That self-loathing hatred of Western heritage, and an economy driven by virtue signaling that will drive the prosperity of the West into a ruin. A ruin from which those economies, and thus those countries, cannot return. It is a manufactured anno-cyclosis–the cycle of regimes. Anno-cyclosis says that monarchy decays into oligarchy, oligarchy decays into democracy, and then democracy decays into a chaos requiring a strong man to rule it; hence, the cycle begins over with monarchy. We are in the chaos now, but in this timeline, we have an oligarchy manufacturing the chaos that will legitimize their right to rule.

Global communist movement: The global collection of people who espouse the Marxist form of communism and actively bring these ideas into their academic, intellectual, and political pursuits. This group is cohesive in Marx's own call for this idea to rule over every political and economic system of the world, thus bringing 'the revolution' to its end.

(Source: The author intends to define this as a unique term for the purposes of this book, regardless of similar usage of the words or phrases by any other person who would define it differently.)

HOW RELATIVISM IS INVOLVED (AND CENTRAL TO THE PLOT)

As I said in my introductory note, this book is for our time. It is for this age, and I want to address the pitfalls we encounter, overcome our failures, and use the strategies we must use to reclaim our country. As this book seeks to expose the people who pose the most radical threat to our way of life, I feel it is equally necessary to also expose their ideology and their modes of operation. Therefore, this book will also seek to expose the dangerous philosophy of relativism and why it is the most radical threat that we face in the world today. This is the decoder ring, if you will, to defeating the WEF and saving America. You encounter the phenomenon of relativism in countless different ways, and you most likely do so without knowing it. You have certainly experienced relativism, even if you had no means of identifying it.

Relativism is romanticized by our modern culture as the wise, more understanding, and more 'woke' point of view and is a hero in the modern narrative. The villains of the story of the modern narrative are many. Relativism stands opposed to almost every aspect of historical civilization, and therefore its enemies are ... most (if not all) civil institutions (like civil law, basic moral conduct, social contract, religion, etc.). Because relativism is out to blame and destroy all of that which has come before, it leaves me wondering if an 'Oedipus

Complex' does justice in describing the modern narrative. For it makes a villain out of the order that bore it while making a hero out of the chaos and destruction it produces. And that is where the rubber meets the road; relativism is the devolution of human thought. It is the unraveling of civil society and the destruction of human decency. Relativism is savagery, plain and simple. It is tribal warfare, clan bickering, simple bullying, and downright brutishness. It destroys human relationships and makes human flourishing impossible, for the user or the used. By its very nature, relativism cannot build anything up.

relativism /rĕl′ə-tĭ-vĭz″əm/ **(noun)** - The theory that value judgments, as of truth, beauty, or morality, have no universal validity but are valid only for the persons or groups holding them.
(Source: The American Heritage® Dictionary of the English Language, 5th Edition)

What is this terrible beast? Simply put, it is a denial of truth. It is the principal position that nothing is absolute—that everything is relative. Of course, we can all have our differences of opinion; social and cultural diversity should be fostered. As long as it is a circumstance where the truth is not being discerned. We all have our likes and dislikes, and for trivial things like cultural tastes, we are entitled to our 'relative' opinions. When it comes to sandwiches, relativism is good. Where it becomes the destroyer of worlds is when it becomes the prevailing life ideology of a society and the decider of morals and justice. To approach the whole of life in this way is to do nothing less than pretend one's preference for mustard is just as trivial as their distaste for murder.

Relativism is barbarism; it is a world where there is no right or wrong, and the one with the biggest stick, the loudest mouth, and the smoothest tongue wins. Relativism will eat through the philosophy, reason, and logic that built the comfortable home it gladly devours. Know well the beast of relativism, for it is the beam in our generation's eye as we poke at the splinters of generations past. This book will revisit relativism often and shed light on the myriad of ways this self-refuting premise truly is the destroyer of worlds. G.K. Chesterton, in his book Orthodoxy, points to a key insight into relativism. He describes 'a thought that stops thought' and rightly concludes that this is 'the only thought that ought to be stopped.' Relativism is by nature dismissive; it is deconstructionist. Relativism is the basis for all thoughts that stop thought. Today, it goes by many names: liberalism, collectivism, socialism, communism, critical theory, critical race theory, gender theory, etc. The list is practically unlimited and so intertwined with our social norms that it becomes maddening to try and make sense of it all. At the heart of all of these evil ideologies is the theology of relativism. They all rest on the evil premise that it is impossible to discern good ideas and actions from evil ones. And that those who would insist on a shared reality and a common truth are therefore evil as well.

All of these ideologies are entangled together for many reasons, and none of these reasons are for the benefit of society, the betterment of your life circumstances, or the good of your soul. In the end, it is about manipulation and control. People who are confused are easier to deceive. People without a strong moral sense are easy to lead astray. People who have lost the ability to reason for themselves are easier to manipulate. People who cannot draw distinctions or see nuance are easier to bully. People who are afraid of threats are easier to coerce into acting against their own interests. People who are addicted to pleasures are easier to distract from higher things. People who are morally compromised are easier to blackmail. People who are addicted to modern conveniences are easier to extract loyalty from. People whose government provides them with sustenance will also come to provide their rights, and those people are subjects, not citizens. And the more of these crutches that can be foisted on society, the easier the people will be to control. It is not a mistake that we live in this madness; that we live in a world that cannot see right from wrong—or even define the two. It is by design that prominent people express their opinions and call it 'my truth.' It is an orchestrated chaos that asserts that the words 'my lived experience' trump all reason or data to the contrary. It all stems from the pernicious theology of relativism. An ideology that requires you to possess such an open mind that, ultimately, your brain falls right out of your head ... and the world descends into madness.

CHAPTER 2

Who Rules the World?

Disclaimer: This chapter is not pretty; it is designed to explain to you how we got into the political and economic situation we find ourselves in. If it feels like a violent ripping off of the blinders, just know there is hope. The rest of the book is going to explain these themes much deeper, find solutions and answers in how to win this fight, and provide a roadmap out of the path that lies ahead. But there is only one way out. You must know what you are up against to have any hope of defeating it.

Alexander the Great once conquered the world. Well, the caveat was that it was 'the known world,' but we were taught that he was a world ruler. At its height in 323 B.C., the Alexandrian Empire covered roughly two million square miles. That may sound like a lot, but in context, that is about half the size of the United States. Alexander the Great's story is fascinating to us, especially when you couch it not as the Macedonian conquest of the world but rather the conquest of the world by a single person. Genghis Khan was another person from antiquity that we deemed a 'world ruler.' At the height of its power (the latter half of the thirteenth century), the Mongol Empire held lands from the Mediterranean to the Pacific, roughly equivalent to the land mass of Africa.

These two rulers muddle the lines between personal wealth and political power because they were the leaders of great armies that so embodied the empires they created, they can hardly be separated. The claiming and holding of land usually go hand in hand with wealth. But there are circumstances when the wealth of an empire or a country can outpace the sheer wealth that they have by virtue of their land holdings. For example, the height of the land holdings of the Roman Empire came in A.D. 117, almost a century after it reached its height in overall wealth. At the time of his death in 44 B.C., Julius Caesar was purported to be worth trillions of dollars in today's money. Arguably the greatest empire of all time was the British Empire. It could be rightly said that the sun never set on it. It was both the largest in land mass (they controlled twenty-five percent of the land mass of Earth), and because of the industrial revolution and their mercantile economy, they were also the wealthiest. It is almost impossible to calculate these things, but many sources put the value of the British Empire north of seven trillion dollars in today's money.

So, the best example of someone ruling the world is King George V of Britain, and he only held a quarter of it. A height reached after 850 years of (mostly uninterrupted) kingship since the Norman Conquest, mostly due to the world being radically re-economized by the industrial revolution. It may sound crazy to assert that there could be a shadow empire out there with more money, more power, and the potential to claim the whole world for itself. Well, there is.

By now, you might see where I am going with this. The wealthiest people in history have been world leaders, leaders of government. They are 'top tier' if you will, in the hierarchy of wealth, influence, and power. Beneath them are the second-class citizens of the wealth scale: the aristocrats and oligarchs. Their wealth is contingent upon the monarch's good graces. The third class are the military leaders, traders, and mercantilists. The generals do the dirty work of nation-building, while the traders do the dirty work of wealth-building. The classless hoi polloi at the bottom do all the living, working, and dying in the country–the dirty work of system maintenance. And they were all paid accordingly! This is how the world was and how all history can be defined until the end of the eighteenth century. If someone became wealthier than the king, then they usurped and became the king (or died in the ensuing and inevitable conflict that arose). This went down all the way to the tribal clans and chieftains, who fought in their own diminutive realms for power. Even the banking cartels of antiquity, although wealthy, were not more powerful than the countries in which they operated.

The modern idea of the global economy is a true anomaly of world history that has not before existed. The idea that a business tycoon or tech entrepreneur could have wealth that is outside of (or not accountable to) a monarch or government leader does not have any real, pound for pound, historical comparisons. Trying to view the modern economy in terms of historical references is a natural human tendency, but we cannot hope to do so and see the world for what it is today. And once we get outside of that traditional lens and see the global economy for what it is, we still have one more step to go. The development of the modern economy is not an organic development of capitalism, nor has it been an undirected mistake. The global economy, in theory and in a vacuum, is not necessarily a bad thing. However, if someone (or a small group of people) were to somehow control the world economy, then they would have unparalleled power over all the principalities and governments of the world. They would become the de facto rulers of the world by virtue of being able to destroy the economy and livelihood of any country that dared to defy them. I hate to break it to you, but this isn't a terrible 'what-if' scenario; it's simply the fact of how the world is today.

SUBSECTION I

Here are some things that happened that may or may not have been part of a larger, broader conspiracy but got us to the point that the conspiracy became nakedly obvious.

Second Disclaimer: If I am fortunate enough to have this book lambasted by the mainstream financial community, they will run to their mainstream shows and pretend to 'destroy this chapter with facts and logic.' And although they might be technically right in their assertion that I got this or that iota wrong, it will not detract from the overall point of this chapter. I am not a financial advisor or expert in the field. I do have common sense, though, and can recognize a system when I see one. And even if I'm imprecise in my wording or lack clarity on the intricacies, that will not negate the meta story brewing under the surface. This chapter is not meant to be an exact, bean-counting, academically precise explanation. The following is a large-scale explanation, like describing a city's water distribution system. It might not address the leak on Third Street, but the city will still get its water.

During the time of the industrial revolution (1760-1840), the world was drastically changed. This event gave rise to our modern notions of cities and urbanization that had previously been unknown. It also gave rise to the modern idea of a 'job,' working hours, hourly wages, time off, weekends, and many of the things that we take for granted today as just 'the way the world works.' It also raised the class of the mercantilists and opened an avenue of opportunity that did not exist mere generations before. Still, the greatest empire ever to exist held its economy in control; there were no tycoons of industry in England that rivaled the wealth and prestige of the King. But in the early days of the industrial revolution, there was a tiny corner of the globe that found itself with no king. It was once a colony of the great empire, but the citizens of the colony revolted and won their freedom. They founded a constitutional republic and declared that all citizens had the right to life, liberty, and the pursuit of happiness. The government would not reign over the economy as it had in other nations. Instead, the people would engage in free trade and have the right to property over what they owned, produced, and sold. It was early days in the industrial revolution, and the complete upending of the concept of economy had not yet been realized.

This little country could not imagine what was to come as the world was absolutely industrialized (and it certainly could not fathom the Information Revolution that was on a distant horizon in its future). Thus, the country saw a boom in commerce—but all on the local level. Even the most illustrious businessmen had two factories or three general stores. It was a far simpler time economically, and the citizens of America were much more principled back then. They were far less likely to abuse a system or allow their fellow countrymen to do so. What's more, your name was tied to everything you did, and the legal system in America was one of the best in the world. So even if a rich man tried to swindle a poor one, they had equal recourse under the law. Unfortunately, this little country was like all its predecessors in one way: it accepted the evil, yet globally normalized, practice of slavery. These rights would not extend to those brought to its shores as slaves. This needs to be mentioned here and pointed out as a deep hypocrisy. Slavery in America could only be hypocrisy because the legal system America set up was good; it was hypocrisy because the union that they founded held itself to a higher standard than the rest of the world ... and yet denied participation to some. Thank God we have rectified that injustice in this country. America remains the only country in the world to have fought a civil war to unite races of people in equality and justice. As the industrial revolution came to a close and the Civil War ended, the era of Reconstruction (1861-1900) began and ushered in a new age with a new feature of wealth consolidation. It was the dawning of the age of the personal corporation.

The economy before the industrial revolution was highly personal. You had a craft or a trade in which you traded for the goods and services of other skilled workers in your community. You took on apprentices to teach the next generation, and the cycle roughly repeated this way and had done so for quite some time. I am quite convinced that America's nickname as the 'land of opportunity' came from this sentiment: that as a skilled tradesman, you need only find a small, burgeoning village that needs your services. Your name backed your product, your name backed your service. If you were a crappy cooper, you'd soon find yourself replaced by one who could make a proper barrel. If you were constantly short on payment or proved untrustworthy, you lost out on business. As I said before, someone who was a good businessman might have a few stores in different towns, a larger farm than his neighbor, or even two ferry exchanges. But the idea that a man would own a business that he could not operate or manage himself would have been a ridiculous notion. The idea that a 'board' of men would 'invest' in an idea, and then 'incorporate' a company to be run by other men simply so the original group of men could make a 'return on investment' would have been beyond the pale of the common man. Although this type of arrangement did exist, it was for large-scale projects and for those wealthy enough to 'gamble' that money on a relative or trusted associate; it certainly wasn't the modus operandi of the economy or the common man. I can't imagine what a shop owner in 1850 would think about Alphabet, the parent company of Google ... a company worth $1.64 trillion as of 2023 (not including the value of the personal information they have on all of us).

Corporations have been around since America's earliest days, but they were institutions of the elite and their lawyers, and they were used primarily in establishing family trusts, trusts for the multi-party purchase of land, large-scale construction projects, and very large industrial businesses. Unlike today, where almost every business is at least an LLC, past precedent was that the average American didn't have the foggiest idea what a corporation was. That is, unless you wore ascots and owned the horses that everyone else was betting on at the race track. So, it comes as no shock that the court case that would change the landscape of business irrevocably went almost entirely unnoticed by the American people in 1886.

In Santa Clara County v. Southern Pacific Railroad, the Supreme Court upheld a decision that the Fourteenth Amendment applied to corporations. It would make little to no splash at the time of the decision, but it would become very important after the establishment of the Federal Reserve, the IRS, and the assignment of Tax IDs. As you remember from history class, the Thirteenth, Fourteenth, and Fifteenth amendments were passed by the Northern States in January of 1865. This was roughly four months before the end of the Civil War, and the reunion of the states. It is worth noting that they barely passed the needed two-thirds vote in the House, despite not a single Confederate state being allowed to vote. The Thirteenth abolished slavery. The Fourteenth protected the rights of the recently freed slaves, who had just become newly formed citizens of the United States. And the Fifteenth protected those citizens' right to vote. I do not know what mental voodoo the lawyers brought into the courtroom that day in 1886, but to think that any aspect of the Fourteenth Amendment was written for the protection of a corporation or to enumerate the right for people to form companies and that those companies should be treated like people is beyond me. Alas, it is 'precedent' now. In case you were wondering, the answer is no. No one sees the hypocrisy of the fact that slavery was once 'precedent' too.

In the wake of the industrial revolution, there were factories everywhere. This dislodged many people from their rural homes and relocated them into cities. This was a boon for many industries, as housing and other necessities were required. For the most part, the industrialization of America still remained somewhat local; there were not manufacturing corporations with locations throughout the country. There were rare exceptions like GE, which by 1900 had plants in twenty-three cities. The 'nationwide' industries were those like Vanderbilt's railroads and later Rockefeller's Standard Oil. It is in the late nineteenth and early twentieth centuries that you see the wealth of these tycoons being compared to the wealth of kings and queens. By the height of the roaring twenties, the wealth of most of

Europe's monarchs was not comparable to the wealth of magnates like J.P. Morgan, Rockefeller, and Carnegie. There was clearly social angst at the time concerning this matter. Congress passed the Sherman Anti-Trust Act in 1890. Sadly, it would be over twenty years later before it was actually put to use.

Even during this time, there was a very common theme for the American corporation: they did something. Something was manufactured, some service was provided, there was a widget or a gadget that could be produced, bought, and sold. We had a real economy whose value was tangible, and the American corporation employed AMERICANS at every level of the company. Today, things are much different. Modern corporations are nothing more than a conglomeration of companies. Hundreds of businesses that otherwise would operate independently, being managed by the same c-suite team and delegated over by the same board. All of the opportunities and jobs are shipped overseas, and now Americans are just consumer customers to be exploited. I don't begrudge the business owners of smaller corporations for selling to the multinational corporations in their 'diversification' schemes. I don't suppose that I necessarily begrudge the larger corporations who can make such moves. I certainly am not arguing for collectivism, nor am I coming from a place of grievance policy. I believe that markets should be free. I also believe that this version of corporatism is designed to stifle the market; it is an anti-capitalist wrench in the free-market system.

There is nothing inherently wrong with a 'board' coming together to 'incorporate' their holdings. Given our modern legal system, I would say that it is a crucial part of protecting yourself from the nastiness of the business world, the convolution of the tax code, and anyone looking to exploit you by lawsuit. The real problem with corporate law in America is that there is no limiting principle. No limiting principle means that, in many respects, there is no distinction between the incorporation of the corner deli— and Wal-Mart. No limiting principles or distinctions means, ultimately, no accountability. Even in that court case in 1886, I don't believe this was an accident. Whether it was a convenient power grab at the time whose complications weren't fully reasoned out or if it was part of a broader vision, no one knows. But we are now coming to the precipice, a breaking point, where it is beginning to matter in cataclysmic ways.

We are beginning to deal with corporations that have outgrown any allegiance to our country, have no accountability to their customers, and are treated no differently in the eyes of corporate law than small businesses or even individual people. Because there is no legal limiting principle written into corporate establishment, it is theoretically possible that 'MegaCorp' could continue to 'diversify' itself until it had incorporated every other company in the world. At that point, the value of the company is only limited by the value of Planet Earth itself! 'Oh no,' you say. Congress would break them up! Well, that ship sailed a long time ago. Now, most of the S&P 500 are global corporations who don't need Congress' approval to do a damn thing. Closing down their American-based corporate offices would only hurt our economy in the end. It is a hurt that we are going to have to endure someday and a reckoning that is long overdue. I digress; the corporation, as a mechanism to create outsized wealth, is a huge part of how we got here. But even these multinational corporations are not the big players in the game. There is a central turning point that makes our problem with crony corporatism pale in comparison: the creature that emerged from Jekyll Island.

I am trying to deal with each of these things in turn, and it makes the most sense to me to introduce them chronologically. We are not done with crony corporatism, but it is time to introduce the event that changed everything and accelerated the whole system in its downward spiral. This is the last part of "Subsection I: Here are some things that happened that may or may not have been part of a larger, broader conspiracy but got us to the point that the conspiracy is nakedly obvious." It is the bridge because I think that this was a paradigmatic moment for our monetary system and our economy. Perhaps at the time it was the conspirators 'coup de gras.' In their mind's eye, they knew that this would forever set them apart as the truly wealthy above even the super-rich, the very well off, the rich, and then everyone else at the bottom whose wealth bracket is wholly incomparable. I don't think that, at the time, they saw it as laying the foundation for anything; it was just the next (albeit very large) step in enriching themselves and gaining more power. Regardless of whether the conspiracy is this deep, the creature of Jekyll Island was a necessary part of how we got here (this play on words comes from a book that I would highly recommend: The Creature from Jekyll Island: A Second Look at the Federal Reserve, by G. Edward Griffin).

A meeting took place on Jekyll Island, which is just off the coast of southeastern Georgia. The Federal Reserve website has no issues declaring the names of the six men who met and that they did so in November of 1910. They pushed for a national banking system and got the men of industry to support their plan as well. They dolled up the creature of Jekyll Island to look like it was good for the American people and that it would stabilize our banking system, and most perniciously, they gave it the guise that the Federal Government would have ownership of it by way of "oversite." Regardless of any check or balance that the government may or may not have, the Federal Reserve was made our official national banking system on December 23, 1913, by a narrow, party-line vote in Congress. It was done very late, at the end of the session after many members of Congress had returned home. It was also signed into law by Woodrow Wilson the same day. It is very odd for the president to be on standby at the eleventh hour to sign legislation. That is usually done days later at the hokey pen ceremony. Politics aside, the Federal Reserve is not federal; it is a private banking institution that works in conjunction with the U.S. Department of Treasury. Despite the 'fact checks' on the Fed website, you can see a list of who owns the Fed at: facts-are-facts.com/news/the-federal-reserve-is-privately-owned. I saved a screenshot for my own records, but suffice it to say, the six men who met at Jekyll Island, their crony magnates from America and abroad, and the private banks that all these men own are on the list. This means that the monetary policy of the United States is ultimately in the hands of the T.O.D.s. It is also oddly suspicious that the Sixteenth Amendment went into effect the same year, in February of 1913, giving the Federal Government the right to impose and collect taxes—not on income from investments but on workers' wages. Prior to this amendment, the government did not have the right to lay taxes without regard to census or enumeration; simply put, this amendment allowed the federal government to act unilaterally in its enforcement of and collection of taxes.

Prior to its passage, income was categorized as money derived from the sale of assets, such as buying or selling a stock, building and selling a home or business, or manufacturing and selling products. Your wages were not considered income; in all fairness, wages are a zero-sum game. You are trading your talent and time for money.

However, the Sixteenth Amendment forever changed tax laws in our country. For the first time in American history, workers would have to pay taxes on their wages. In fact, the government had the right to withdraw those taxes before the wages were ever given to the employee! The creation of the Federal Reserve, done under Wilson's radically 'progressive' administration, no doubt created the environment of immense wealth and opulence during the 'roaring twenties' but also set up the roller coaster and the crash into the Great Depression in the next decade. What these men did in making their banks underwrite the U.S. dollar was to set themselves up as 'the house.' Now all they needed was a casino.

SUBSECTION II

Now there are too many coincidences.

The convenient thing about a corporation is that you can offer 'shares' for sale to other people. So, people 'buy' shares, which simply means that they give their money to a corporation, and in exchange, you receive a 'certificate of quasi-ownership' in the company. From the time you hand them your money, this share, or stock certificate, will have a perpetually fluctuating value known as the 'market price.' The market price is the speculative value of the entire company divided by the number of issued shares. So basically, it is whatever the corporation thinks that they can inflate its value to by making it seem valuable. The corporation promises that you can come back to them anytime and cash out your stock certificates, and they will be happy to pay 'market value,' the arbitrary speculative value of the share at the time. Small-time owners of shares don't have any control or carry any weight in the running of the business, so they will get what they will get, and that will be that. The gamble comes from hoping the stock is at a higher market value when you sell it. The only thing that you own one-hundred percent of ... is your risk. The corporation moves along doing its thing, 'diversifying' every now and again, and as long as you have a strong position, you can weather the storms of good times and bad and cash out your stocks for a profit someday.

That is what 'stock markets' used to be. They were places of purchase and exchange, where real companies produced real goods and services, and investors could see the vision of those companies, what they would produce, and what they would sell, and be able to make a grounded decision as to whether the company would succeed and pay back a return on investment. It was a place for only people of means, and after you purchased your stocks in the company, you could physically go and see the new factory they were building with your investment, or you could see the railroad or bridge with your own eyes. What's more, if a company went belly up, you personally knew the slouch that lost your money! It was nothing like what we see today, a hoard of hyenas buying and selling in a purely speculative arena, with God knows how many side bets and chicanery under the table.

In 1901, J.P. Morgan was the most powerful banker in America. He convinced an aging Carnegie (magnate of the Carnegie Steel Corporation) to sell up. The long and intricate back story can be found in the book Think and Grow Rich by Napoleon Hill. Long story short, Carnegie Steel was purchased at the same time as nine other steel companies (all unbeknownst to each other), and they were all merged into the United States Steel Corporation. Because of the merger, US Steel was able to double its value in the form of consolidating its assets and then selling new stocks to prospective investors. It was successful because, lo and behold, operations were much more efficient after the consolidation, and again, they were a corporation that produced something. I don't think the selling of these stocks was wrong, and good on them for seizing the opportunity of a lifetime. The investors who purchased that stock speculated that things would look up for the company, so they invested. And that was the 'speculation' aspect of stock markets and exchanges from its earliest days.

Interest in the stock market increased, and with this increased interest came the outright speculators. They began to buy stocks simply for the purpose of 'flipping' them days or weeks later when the stock price increased. Buy low, sell high. I'm sure it seemed sleazy to the early traders, but not for long. Throughout the late 1800s and early 1900s, there were many regional stock exchanges that served a variety of different investor needs. The NYSE was the largest in the country, and by 1929, it had become the premier in the country. Today, that and the NASDAQ are the only two in the whole country. Somewhere along the way, there was an orchestrated move to begin speaking of 'the market' as its own entity. No longer would a company show up to the exchange and sell its individual value to the investor. When you think about it, if a company is worth the dollar amount that they have collected in stocks, they don't care what the 'market' looks like. Ostensibly, when they look at the strength of the market, they are also looking at the strength of their competition! If Wal-Mart were to go under tomorrow due to the discovery of gross mismanagement, why should that cause a panic in 'the market' or a decrease in the stock value of any other company? Although we know it would cause market upheaval, the common-sense answer is that it shouldn't affect the value of GE or any other Fortune 500 company. If the value being traded in the stock market equals the actual market value and forces, then there would not be bubbles, panics, or depressions. But it's not; by converting the conversation to 'the market,' you shift the entire game.

The idea of speculation as a means to get rich by buying and selling stocks necessarily means that you no longer care about the company's position or the stock's actual value. This was certainly the case in the 1920s, as people were watching the collective rise and fall of millions of stocks that were being traded on the stock exchange, trending mostly in the 'up' direction. Throughout the 1920s, the stock exchange grew sixfold. Monday, October 28, 1929, was the tipping point. Instead of new stocks flooding the market for suckers to buy, the smartest suckers started selling what they had. Over nine million stocks were sold off on that Monday by the stockholders. That is to say, these were not new stocks issued by a corporation. They were people who wanted out completely, selling stocks already in circulation, asking for their cash back. On Black Tuesday, sixteen million more stocks were sold off. The run on the stock market had begun. The average Joe panicked and tried to sell whatever he had in the stock market, now at a much lower price, just to get something back out. Almost every small bank in the country had a run on it as well, and the country was plunged into the Great Depression.

But here is a dirty little secret that no one on Wall Street wants you to know: the number of stocks in circulation never decreased; they simply lost value. Sure, the overall net worth of the corporations on the exchange decreased, but ownership never changed hands. The board and the founders own at least fifty-one percent of the company's stock, so even if all forty-nine percent of stocks in circulation in the market went to one cent, as long as the board bought all of the shares back, the company would still be solvent. In fact, corporations would much rather buy stock back in a depression than a recession! The worse the collapse, the better the buy-back deal. The corporation that sold the stocks at the initial offering never has to pay the money back they collected because the wealth transfer happens on the front end. So yes, those that sold first were paid 'market value,' and that market value might even have been at a profit. But as the market continued to decline, the 'market value' of the stocks declined in turn. Meaning that if the company wanted to stay solvent, they had to buy back the stocks. But what a deal! You sell a stock for one hundred dollars, the market tanks, and now the stock is worth twenty dollars. The corporation took the one hundred dollars and only had to pay back twenty to stay solvent! I'm no mathematician, but I do know who came out upside-down on that bargain.

Again, I want to reiterate: if the value of the stock was real, then that company would do just fine no matter what was going on around them. The only reason that anyone would view the strength of a company through the lens of 'the market' is if that company was just one of many in their 'portfolio' of holdings. Defining the economy as 'a market' means that someone sees the entire economy as their portfolio, regardless of your individual stake in it. The T.O.D.s that own the banks and the majority of stocks in these large corporations are so wealthy that they don't care what the value of the stock is or what the value of a dollar is. If the U.S. dollar collapsed tomorrow, they wouldn't give a damn. Because they don't count their wealth by counting the number of dollars in their bank account, they weigh their wealth in terms of percent control of 'the market,' a.k.a., the global economy.

The goal of the market going up and down is a simple equation: your money transfers into their increased percent ownership every time you "lose" money in the stock market. They buy the shares that the desperate are selling, and they are buying at a premium to boot! Sure, there are many winners, just like there are many people who leave Vegas with more money than they came with. But everyone knows that the ultimate winner is always the house. Even if they win just fifty-one percent of the time, they have successfully increased their market share by one percent. Over enough time and enough dips, bubbles, and recessions, those small percentages start to add up. In a depression, they add up even faster.

This is what happened to Average Joe Stock Investor in the leadup to the Depression. Joe was holding his stock certificates in his hands that he bought from the corporation. They promised him that if things went well, the stocks would go up in value, and one day he could resell them to some buyer in the future for more than he paid for them. Then they took Joe's money. They let it go up in value and let Joe sell it to some other idiot for even more money. Joe made a little, but the corporation made way more when they cut another million shares (saving back fifty-one percent, of course) and then sold those at the new price that Joe had just helped them inflate it to. Then they took all of those other people's money. When they had taken so much money and couldn't possibly justify the price of the stock any longer, they sold just enough of their own stock to make the price drop (or people got wise to the fact that the money the corporation so willingly took never translated to a position of equal corporate value). The people holding the pieces of paper that were never worth what they bought them for started to panic. Then 'the market' overall goes down, and everyone begins to question the validity of everything. In just a few days' time, nearly every piece of paper all of the Average Joes are holding has become simultaneously worthless and up for sale to the highest bidder. And the corporations still have all their money. When their stocks became worthless, it didn't decrease the money in the pockets of the people who owned the companies. It didn't reduce their assets, and it only gave them more power and control. Sure, a few banks collapsed and a few members of the exchange had to declare bankruptcy, but the vast majority of businesses owned by wealthy people stayed afloat and did just fine.

Remember this: money is never lost in the stock market; it simply changes hands. Corporations never go under during a crash; they are simply 'diversified' into their competitors' portfolios.

If you are very wealthy, you have extra cash no matter how bad things get. If you are a Regular Old Joe, you have to sell everything when things get bad, including your investments. The price of the stocks will drop until the wealthy (the only ones with money to spend in hard times) are willing to buy the shares that they sold you in the first place on the very same exchange, except instead of paying you what you paid them, they buy back their piece of paper for pennies on the dollar. They buy your worthless stocks back with only a fraction of the money they took from you in the first place! Warren Buffet has admitted as much; he says things such as, 'keep your head in a recession' and that 'the smart investors buy in during a recession.' Those are paraphrases of his advice he has given so many times before that there are countless cuts of it all over the internet. His advice may be useful to those who can buy stocks during a recession, but his advice can't be said without saying the quiet part out loud. This advice is given so that a few of us can fly home from Vegas with money in our pockets. But our winnings will be a drop in the bucket of the overall take, and we all know the house wins the majority of the take.

The WEF is currently pushing for The Great Reset. We may think of this as a singular item, but this is not true. The stock market crash of 1929 was just one of many lesser resets, a smaller move toward their ultimate agenda. It ushered in the era of Social Security, pensions, and retirements, but it was never about caring for the downtrodden. It just set up a system by which the government could 'tax' people even more and put those pensions in the new stock market with special security labels. Now, almost every employee's retirement is tied up in some aspect of the NYSE. Imagine how bad it will be this time around when they 'reset' the market.

After the Fed was formed and in the aftermath of the Great Depression, a new elite class of wealthy people was created that the world had previously never seen. It is a type of wealth and power that is not controlled by a single government nor could be controlled by a federation or union of nations. We cannot compare this shift to previous historic peoples, or collections of wealth. As said earlier, if someone became wealthier than the king, it meant that he would become the new king (or die in the ensuing and inevitable conflict). These men now controlled the wealth of the most powerful nation and economy on Earth! Arguably, they had become the kings of America. And, in many respects, they are. This is not an officious title, nor do they want it to be! They are much happier and more powerful as the inapparent kings of America.

Shortly after the formation of the Fed, the markets coalesced, and the overall number of corporations began to shrink as well as the distribution of their shares. We also started seeing market fluctuations that were never depression-level events, but every recession and bubble resulted in a dip while the market continued to climb and climb and climb. Never mind that pensions were always the first to be eaten away in the bad times, and the economic reality of the average American seemed to become worse and worse and worse. The house has always seemed to come out on top, especially in this new age of 'modern monetary theory.' MMT can best be summed up by the slogan of the old slapstick show Whose Line is it Anyway?: 'where everything is made up and the points don't matter.' We live in an economy and an age where the dollars are made up and the value doesn't matter.

It is now time to pick back up on our riff about crony corporatism. It is speculated that Wilson ran on an isolationist platform only because he had a silent handshake deal with the titans of American industry. The agreement was that he would most certainly enter WWI after being reelected during a well-financed campaign. It is a convenient conspiracy theory because that is exactly what happened. Despite the average American being against entering the European war, we somehow found ourselves entangled in it shortly after Wilson was reelected (on an isolationist platform). Perhaps an observer of facts who can see plainly might be considered a conspiracy theorist by those trying to conceal a conspiracy.

The truth is, our industry moguls and magnates had international holdings, many of which were older than their American holdings. Go look at the list of the people who own the Fed; some are names you will recognize from American business that are tied to international banks around the world. War has always been good for business, and that is an easy trope, so I won't spend time trying to trace the allegiances of finance around war. Needless to say, there were many American business interests that were deeply concerned about the war and its outcome. They did not want to see the Kaiser achieve world dominance, but they also did not want their German holdings seized by the Kaiser or lost to the dustbin of history. It was a legitimate concern that a re-writing of the European map without the consent of the inapparent kings of America could prove detrimental to the weight of their wealth.

The wealthiest men in the world had just orchestrated the formation of the Fed and the imposition of the wage tax (most unjustly called an 'income' tax). Is it truly too hard to believe that these same men did not have the power to finance the presidential campaign of a radical progressive to achieve their ends (a radical who was elected the first time due solely to the split of the Republican vote by Teddy Roosevelt)? The saving of Europe in WWI was not for the noble cause of saving our comrades in the Western sphere. It was an unholy alliance between Woodrow Wilson, a true believer and collectivist, and the new inapparent kings of America. They both gladly accepted the Faustian bargain. Wilson thought that he had finally achieved the socialist economy that every collectivist leader wants: complete control over the means of production, beginning with what he thought was government control of the money supply via the newly formed Fed.

The inapparent kings of America gladly accepted the bargain; they would relent to a 'voluntary socialism,' but one they knew they would ultimately control. They knew they would be able to act far more unilaterally through the Fed than the Congress would ever be able to muster. Wilson got the illusion of control, and they got to save their European assets and keep up the slow march of ticking up their wealth, percentage point by percentage point. Because the Americans had joined WWI late, they got the simultaneous privilege of being deemed savior/heroes while having the least skin in the game. They were also given the privilege of a seat at the table of post-war negotiations. The Great War, as it was called at the time, resulted in the decolonization of the world through Wilson's great insistence. That is a subject all its own whose content fills the tomes of history and the dissertation of many a radical, and the merits will be debated right up to the moment of the Second Coming. What this did ensure is that the best Europe would ever be able to muster was a league of nations, or a European Union, that would never rival the power or influence of the inapparent kings of America. There would be no rival kingly class to ever rise out of the West again. They could, however, form a loose global alliance of countries that could serve as a loose central sphere of global influence. Perhaps even in time, as the independent economies of countries mattered less and less, it could serve as a means of establishing ... a new world order.

A decade after the Great War, the Great Depression saw a transfer of wealth never before seen in the history of the world. Conveniently, to save us from the Depression, came WWII. But not before we saw a new radical take the reins of power in America. Franklin D. Roosevelt was the bold leader who would stagnate the American economy for a decade and ensure that the inapparent kings of America would have an ultimate say in the goings on–and again, the outcome–of the war. FDR would also institute many federal projects that would give rise to what we now know as the fourth branch of government–the alphabet soup mafia of federal organizations that centrally plan our lives. We will continue to explore the unholy alliance between the collectivists and the T.O.D.s because it is a fascinating dynamic that needs to be properly understood.

As the U.S. emerged on the world stage as a global superpower whose economy had no rival and no means of being rivaled, the Great Depression struck, and it affected the entire world. The

T.O.D.s did not care that the market was down; they were able to increase their market share! It also pleased their allies in the federal government, who got to centrally plan and implement their collectivist schemes in the name of protecting the downtrodden. But in the fall of 1939, the T.O.D.s again found themselves face to face with their nightmare scenario: losing market share. There were much more legitimate reasons for us to be involved in WWII than the Great War, but when it was all said and done, we did find ourselves ultimately in the position of savior/heroes to our comrades in the West. The Paris Peace Treaties of 1947 attempted to end WWII on much more agreeable terms than those in the Treaty of Versailles, which ended the Great War, and only mildly succeeded. After the war, the world would never be the same. The collectivists in government had to go into hiding after the fascists and socialists of Europe were defeated. the American people had a bad taste in their mouth for collectivism. Not to mention, the previous alliance with Russia was barely tenable at best and rapidly deteriorated shortly after the war.

By the 1950s, we were bitter enemies with communist Russia and would remain so until the collapse of the U.S.S.R. in 1992. Our stateside communists burrowed deeply into the institutions created under FDR and encouraged the growth of the fourth branch of government. They do hold hegemonic power over our modern institutions because of this focus, conceding the spotlight of elected office to non-collectivist Democrats and an occasional Republican, all hand-selected by the inapparent kings of America, of course. It was also a new age of opportunity; many industries would arise from the technology developed during the war and in the decades following. The nuclear revolution, the chemical revolution, and the technology revolution would produce unimaginable wealth for America during this time. It would take a second tycooning of all these industries for the T.O.D.s to rebalance the scales of market share. But slowly, from agriculture to energy, the balance of power was wrestled back into the hands of those who could raise the capital (from their own banks) to incorporate, diversify, and then siphon control back into their corner.

There was also a huge counter revolution in America that occurred during the 1960s that forever changed the landscape of American politics and political discourse. All of these we will discuss in later detail because they are important topics. For now, we are almost through the gauntlet.

The world greatly modernized in the last half of the twentieth century, but there was a pivotal moment that flew mostly under the radar at the time and is not even talked about in the modern day. In August of 1971, President Nixon made an announcement the U.S. would implement wage and price controls to battle inflation. Oh, and by the way, you could no longer convert your dollars into gold. Our currency before this time was backed, by a large degree, by gold. This meant that, theoretically, there was enough gold in Fort Knox to match every dollar. This reserve backing is nothing new; the abandonment of it is not new either. There are clear outcomes that happen from abandoning it, and it never ends well. That is why the BRICS nations are demanding their member nations use local currency, and that currency has to be backed by gold. This move was made semi-stable by making a deal with OPEC that oil would only be traded in U.S. dollars. So as long as GDP ticked up steadily, there would not be a collapse of the economy or a collapse of the dollar.

What ensued over the next thirty years was a complete selling out of the American economy. Factories, jobs, and resources were shipped overseas to willing participants like China. We would no longer be a real economy; we would become an economy that produces nothing real and only consumes. What resulted was another giant shift of wealth as people became poorer, while the T.O.D.s continued to grow their divide. But GDP ticked up! The multinational corporation became the norm of business, and millions of corporations were 'diversified' into behemoth globo-corps whose stock price would tick up because of mergers. But at least the market was up!

Every real economic standard decreased after this monumental decision, and the U.S. economy became completely beholden to the global economy and 'the market.' The T.O.D.'s market share continued to creep up, and as their holdings continued to be internationalized, they had less oversite from Congress and anti-trust law, and fewer and fewer allegiances to the government or the American people. I encourage you to look at the website: WTFhappenedin1971.com. It has tracked America's real economy since 1971 in multiple categories. Be prepared to be made angry by what you find at WTFhappenedin1971.com. Each graph and chart that you look at are 'illustrations' to the playbook of how a generation of American politicians and businessmen sold us down the river for a price that we could never repay. As the political pressure of the progressives has slowly decayed our government and way of life, the money that has flooded out of our economy was not lost; it has merely changed hands. The progressives got what they wanted: hegemonic control of the levers of government and the destruction of America for the sake of rebuilding it in their image. And the T.O.D.s got what they wanted: more percent ownership of the global economy.

The final chapter in the story of how we got here is the revolution that is now happening: the transition of the technology revolution into the information revolution. In the past thirty years, there have been many new tycoons on the world stage. Tech entrepreneurs are the 'new money' on the scene and have created companies and industries that are currently going through 'The Third Great Tycooning.' The technology revolution has provided advanced forms of global communication that have only sped up during the information revolution. The T.O.D.s have always been able to control the narrative; it used to be buying off the newspaper men in the olden days, but their schemes have advanced with the technology. More than tycooning and controlling the market share, the T.O.D.s are much more interested in the usefulness of technology to advance their goals and distribute their narrative. They are also deeply disillusioned about their own potential power over life through the use of technology. This is one of their great weaknesses that we can exploit against them. Even with the advent of AI, be assured that the T.O.D.s are investing heavily, controlling market share, and trying to use the information revolution as a way to gain outsized control; it is a new method by which they can weigh their wealth. Information has never been more decentralized and readily available in human history. And yet, the levers of power seem to keel in one direction still, don't they? It is not an accident or a mistake. Technology is a modern weapon, like it or not. Whoever wields the public square and his motives will determine much of this fight. A knife can be used to destroy life in a botched mugging or to save it through surgery. Technology, properly understood and bent toward good ends, can be the undoing of much of this madness. This, too, will be revisited.

To truly get a sense of the power that the T.O.D.s wield, you have to look at the money that they are willing to gamble in their own casino. Every publicly traded company must divulge their financial records and ownership. Likewise, public hedge funds and money managers have to be transparent as well. But private hedge funds (those owned by individuals investing their own money) do not. There are three private hedge funds that are wholly incomparable to the rest in their sheer magnitude. Think about what percent of your wealth or earnings are invested in the stock market as compared to your overall wealth or earnings. Then consider that in terms of the amount of money that these private hedge funds have invested in the stock market.

ACCORDING TO DATA PULLED FROM THE S&P 500 PROFILE PAGES FROM CNN BUSINESS

(SEPTEMBER 2023)

Total stock market value **$ 48 trillion**

(The total net worth of all of the companies traded in the stock market)

Total value of the S&P 500: **$40 trillion**

(The largest 500 globo-corps on the stock market exchange)

Value of the Big 3 Portfolio **$ 7 trillion**

(Total value of all of the shares that are held by State Street, Black Rock, and Vanguard, the three private hedge funds of the T.O.D.s; this does not include any of their public offerings.)

The Big 3 S&P Market Share **17.16%**

Translation: a fifth of the stock market is owned by a very small group of people: the T.O.D.s. All of the companies that produce things, entertain us, inform us, and provide crucial goods and services are beholden to this group of people by threat of destroying not just their company but their entire industry! This does not include the corporations, publicly traded and privately owned, that the T.O.D.s own themselves, thus providing more heft to that market share. Oh, and by the way, this is just a fraction of the weight of their wealth. These same people own the banks that finance these corporations and the other four-fifths of the market. Their stock holdings are just one part of their game for control. Not to mention that they control the monetary supply for America and countries all over the world. They literally own governments by servicing their national debts. Whether you are a government, a public corporation, a private company, a public figure, or a private citizen, they have the power to put you in your place.

The inapparent kings of America are the inapparent kings of what is now a global economy that they finance, place for sale in their markets, and have a majority share in. I wanted to set up this 30K-foot view so that you can see that these people are playing an entirely different game. They own somewhere between a fifth and a third of the global economy, and there are no rivals or methods of rivaling them in their ownership of the world. These are the types of people that can make every media company in the mainstream parrot their talking points. These are the type of people that can lean hard enough on Google to make them 'memory hole' information (the company that controls the flow of ninety percent of information on the internet). Information is censored on social media platforms at their request or the request of their crony collectivists that they have placed in governments throughout the world. These are the types of people that can 'epstein' dissidents ... if you know what I mean. And these are the types of people who would implement ESG: environmental, and social governance policies on the corporations that they either own or are the largest shareholders in. Of course, it will hurt these companies, drive up prices, and make things worse—that's the plan! They don't care that you will lose your pension or private investments; all they care about is the market share they will gain and the power that it will allow them to wield.

So, who rules the world? Well, economically speaking, it is clear: the formerly nameless elite group of puppet masters, the Thrones of Davos (T.O.D.s). The inapparent kings of the world who are politically represented by their political action committee: the World Economic Forum. Who rules the cultural sphere? Well, unfortunately, that would be the Marxists, whose rhetoric is supported by the inapparent kings of the world. Marx himself said that communism must be a global endeavor and that if free market alternatives remained, people might choose them instead! The inapparent kings of the world know how powerful communism is; it is an amazingly destructive force. It requires literal religious adherence to believe in and appeals to the lesser wills and baser passions of mankind in such a visceral way that it is almost impossible to remove once implemented.

The grievance policies of communism make it a perfect force to tear down Western civilization and destabilize it to the point that a strong man will have to show up to save the day. How convenient a plan for an inapparent king looking to be crowned! Who rules the political sphere? Well, at least here in this country, the American arm of the global communist movement! And the political allies of the inapparent kings of the world: the Progressives. They take the grievance rhetoric of the communists and do the destroying, manipulating, and twisting of the American form of government into an unrecognizable mess, ruling over disenfranchised and downtrodden people who will be happy to elect a 'strong man' of their own, one that will ultimately be picked by the inapparent kings, of course. The unholy alliance of the communists and the T.O.D.s will become very apparent as we explore it further in future chapters.

Ultimately, the overlapping Venn diagram between the two reveals what both sides are after and what it is that they worship. For there is an ultimate ruler over all of these people who are personal relativists with soulless ideologies. This ruler was given dominion over the whole earth by God himself. I am speaking, of course, of Satan, who has made deals with them all. I am not saying that they worship Satan, mind you; for all I know, they might, but that is not my point. Satan is the first relativist, the first one to reject the service of God for service of self through the false god of relativism. The false idea that you are the arbiter and ultimate controller of your reality, your present, and your future. That you can change the very nature of things by simply thinking or wishing it so. To think that you can recreate yourself not in Imago Dei, but in Imago Me.

Relativists abandon all morality, goodness, decency, and every other human virtue for the sake of power and money and to build for themselves a kingdom apart from God. In doing so, they become Satan's children, or at least his disciples. Satan is not God, nor is he a lesser god or competitor to God. His proclamation at The Fall was non-serviam; I will not serve (God). This made him the de-facto Chief Priest of Relativism. His back is facing his followers because he is facing the same way they are: toward the false god of relativism.

It is his example that they follow, and he shepherds them. As we get closer to the fruition of the WEF's schemes in the Great Reset of 2030, their evil will continue to become more apparent. Satan is dangerous because evil is dangerous. But his ultimate goals are futile in the end. At the end of time, even his knee will bend and his tongue will proclaim the glory of God (no matter how reluctant that admission is). All his children, despite their hissing, wailing, and gnashing of teeth, will do the same. But I don't want to wait until the end times to see justice served. Do you? We do not have to let the children of Satan enslave us and rule over the world in the meantime.

I hope you will stand with me, friend. Because we don't have a rural vs. urban divide here; we don't have a left vs. right, black vs. white, or a coke vs. pepsi/team red vs. team blue problem. We have a top-down problem. A tiny number of people have built up a great heft with which to crush us. A heft never before seen in world history, and a heft that, if we don't act, has the power to crush humanity into whatever form of domination they please. But it doesn't have to end this way. We do not have to live in the world they are trying to manifest. So, let's begin fighting back by knowing our enemies and how we might come to defeat them. You are already well on your way, and I salute you.

CHAPTER 3

The 0.000001%

'It's the Economy, Stupid' is a paraphrase of the popular slogan coined by James Carville in 1992 while he worked on the Clinton campaign. I thought it would be the most appropriate title for this section of the book, as it is the economy of America, which has become the global economy, that is the mechanism by which our sovereignty and freedom are being stolen. Bernie Sanders, who is a true believer in his crazy ideas, used to always rail against the 'millionaires and billionaires.' By his estimation, these were the greedy people who were to blame for poverty in this country. After he published several books full of his claptrap, he became a millionaire himself. So, after that, he just continued to rail against the 'billionaires.' But I don't begrudge billionaires. I certainly don't begrudge millionaires.

There is a sad but true sarcastic scene from the Austin Powers movies that illustrates just how little a million dollars is. After being cryogenically frozen in 1967 (right before '71), Dr. Evil is reawakened in 1997, does his evil plot, and is at the shakedown meeting with the U.S. government. He promises to relent from his plans for ... (pinkie poised) one—million—dollars. The fake movie president then laughs in his face and accepts his terms. This is sad (and true) because the government spent one million dollars every five seconds last year in 2022. According to the Treasury.gov website, total government spending in the calendar year 2022 was a staggering $6.27 trillion dollars. It only took in $4.89 trillion in taxes, according to Statista.com, meaning that you and I will one day have to pay the $1.38 trillion difference. The $6.27 trillion is an incredible amount of money to think about. When you really break down how much money that is for an annual budget, it is downright infuriating.

$6.27 Trillion per Year
$522.5 Billion per Month
$17 Billion per Day
$715 Million per Hour
≈$12 million per Minute
≈$200,000 per SECOND

Mind you, the median household income (most households having two incomes) was $75k for the calendar year 2022, according to the Census.gov website. Less than seven percent of people made $200k a year, a salary that the vast majority of Americans would kill for, and that is barely worth a second to the government. The comparison is sad but true; a million dollars is a drop in the bucket. But for who? A million dollars would change my life, and I'm sure it would change yours as well. This radical divide between the wealth of the government and the wealth of the common man is one that should be causing much more pause and stirring many more people to action. If someone is making a billion dollars a year on a great venture they founded, good on them! They could fund government spending for an hour and a half. The millionaire's money wouldn't last five seconds even if we took every last penny. The truth is, successful people who have made millions and billions of dollars are not the problem. In fact, those of us whose salaries are much closer to the median should aspire to be as successful as these people. To argue that millionaires and billionaires are the problem is to pretend that the guy who won money at the card table next to you in the casino is the reason that you lost yours. Until you start looking at the casino as the rightful taker of your money, you are going to continue to be angry, comrade.

This is one of the reasons that I find Bernie Sanders so disingenuous and out of touch with reality. He has no concept of the realm of wealth that is actually to blame—or maybe he does. Maybe he is a good little puppet who is spouting his talking points. Talking points that purposely obfuscate the point and make the employee hate the employer, make the poor hate the middle class, or make those who are struggling to make ends meet blame a wealthy business owner for their problems. Like I said, I think that Bernie is a true believer, I don't think that he is so sinister that he is parroting these talking points for the purpose of advancing the elite's interests. But his squawking does get amplified by the media and the powers that be, doesn't it? It is by design to set us against each other without realizing we are trapped on a side quest within the elite's larger simulation; a side quest designed to burn our own resources and energy while at the same time keeping us from beating their game.

I made the comparison of wealth in terms of government spending for a reason. This country is supposed to be by us and for us, and yet how much power do we really have over the regulatory state? How much power do our elected officials have in fighting omnibus spending or taking on entities like the CIA? To riff off of the simulation/game analogy, how much power does the character ultimately have over the game that he has been written into? It is ridiculous that our country collects this much money from the American people, even the millionaires and billionaires that pay the lion's share. But it is downright shameful that we have to go even further into debt in order to cover the government's spending.

If the government had just evenly divided its 2022 spending and given it out equally to the American people, they could have written every American a $20,000 check. A fortune runs through our government every year to all destinations around the world, but mostly into the regulatory agencies, charitable foundations, research hubs, and shadow agencies all over our government (that does God knows what). Whatever they are doing, they are not doing the bidding of the American people, I can promise you that. And this fortune is only part of the fortune that the T.O.D.s are willing to gamble on America and launder through its system. Let me ask you, are you getting your money's worth? Is a family of four in this country seeing $80K worth of value, services, and perks by virtue of living under this government?

There is a connection between why our government spends so irresponsibly, why there are open communists up and down our government, and why this all points back to the WEF. Remember, destabilization is the name of the game. In 1965, if you divided total federal spending by the U.S. population, the government spent $4,333 per person (adjusted for inflation). Today, that same number is almost $20,000. Why? The numbers are inflation-adjusted, so this isn't a sleight of hand. The number of bureaucracies has grown drastically since then, and that is certainly part of it. Social programs have been piled on, and the Great Society programs were just getting ramped up in 1965. But the real answer is that the T.O.D.s have lobbied the government for decades and have found out how to funnel tax money into their own pet projects and corporations. They form NGOs (non-governmental organizations) that function as a proxy for the government, providing goods and services to people all over the world in exchange for their loyalty to our government. These organizations operate tax-free, controlled by the T.O.D.'s and the people they place in charge of them, and as long as they can feign benevolence, the tax breaks and tax dollars keep pouring in. The common people have their taxes taken out of their paycheck, and it goes to the IRS without our consent on how it is spent (we're supposed to, but let's be honest, the American people don't really have any control over the fourth branch of government that our trillions of tax dollars go to). It is only the rich who can tax shelter their dollars and fund what they want to fund.

Bill Gates, through his foundation, has contracts with USAID, the CDC, the NIH, and the Department of Defense, just to name a few. Bill does pour billions of his own dollars into his foundation, but you pour money into his foundation, too, every payday. How about that? George Soros is another example of someone with a fancy foundation. Privately, he gives millions in political contributions. Lately, he has been funding local district attorney races. He has been targeting the DA post in urban areas and funding the campaigns of people who are openly hostile to the justice system. He puts people in a law enforcement and prosecution role who believe that the justice system is racially motivated or completely wrong-headed about what justice for criminals should look like. His foundation is the Open Society Foundation. Do you remember the giant migrant caravan in 2021, where they were all wearing matching shirts? They were white t-shirts with the words 'Biden, please let us in.' The name Biden, of course, was spelled out in his 2020 campaign font. After some independent journalism began to scratch the surface, the organization of the caravan and the t-shirts were allegedly funded by the Open Society Foundation. These foundations, as well as many others, give out taxpayer money in the form of grants as well. Guess who gets the grants? You guessed it–the ones who get in line and are on board with the globalist vision.

You pay for countless NGO organizations, many whose values are contrary to yours, because your government gave them the money they took from your wages. As I said before, people like Soros and Gates are the junior partners, or the 'new money' in the cabal. They have to be out in the open, doing the public work of the WEF. However, all these pet projects of the elite are fueled by the federal spending of the U.S. It is all designed to funnel tax money into what they deem important, their way of thinking and doing and central planning. That should make every red-blooded American angry. But all the tax money isn't enough! They cause the government to go into debt to pay for the world to be run in their image. The fact that they are indebting our nation to fund their pet projects and globalist vision should cause you to go into a rage. It should cause a national march on Washington and a complete dismantling of the interloping beast that has body-snatched our government.

Remember, every trillion we borrow will have to be paid back. They are indebting our nation's children—your children—with a debt that they may never be able to repay. And that, my friends, is not their threat, but their promise. While they basically fund their global government through our tax dollars, they know it will collapse our government. And the thirty trillion-plus in debt will only be able to be serviced through their banks! The Federal Reserve will collapse, but that will be fine; they'll 'diversify' the nation's debt into their financial institutions and be the willing 'strong men' to take over from a broken and impotent President, Congress, and Supreme Court. They don't intend for this debt to be repaid by the American people, or the American government. They don't intend for the debts of any nation to be repaid by its sovereign government. They intend to declare debt forgiveness by declaring a jubilee year in 2030. All they ask for in return ... the assent of the world's population to their Great Reset.

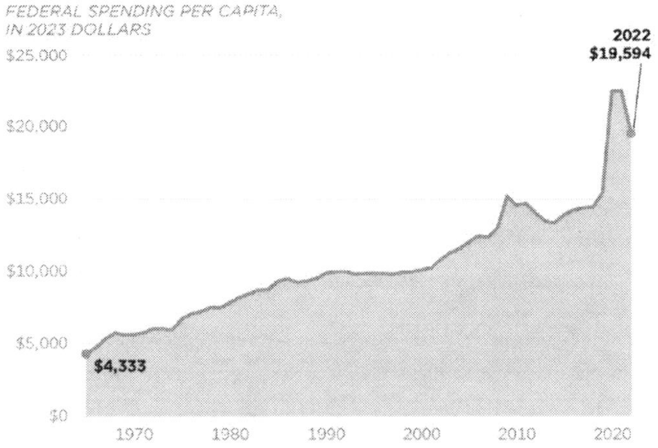

Image compliments of: federalbudgetinspending.com

About a decade ago, I was having a conversation with a friend about the Federal Reserve. I rarely get to have real conversations about the Fed—that is to say, having a candid conversation about a private cartel of banks that lobbied the government to underwrite the U.S. currency. We were discussing how much power these underwriting banks actually had in shaping U.S. economic policy and, in general, how much pressure they could put on the government.

I remember shocking my friend by saying that the owners of the Fed had the power to take over the government if they truly wanted to. I was shocked by his being shocked, which is why the encounter has stuck in my mind. I did make the caveat that it would have been a hostile takeover, it wouldn't end pretty, and that between a third and half the nation would most likely die from the fallout, conflict, and ensuing economic hardship. But I still stand by what I said: the Fed had piled up a significant amount of American debt by 2012.

It also could have pressured China and other American debt holders to call in their loans as well. After the U.S. defaulted, the Fed could rightly start re-possessing, beginning with the U.S. military, their equipment, and the weapons programs that the government had been funding. Then, they would guarantee the salaries of the military and promise housing and care for their families. They would also guarantee the support and funding of the President, the Congress, and the Supreme Court. After holding an outright majority of the Fed, they would siphon the economic control of the country and the IRS out of the government and under their direct control. In the name of peace and security, they would do the same to the military until the President or Congress had no control over it. They would make the military 'federal' in the same way that they made the Fed 'federal,' claiming it was under the control of the American people. Then, they would begin a program of allegiance, cutting off funding to members of the government who in any way opposed them. Slowly, they would gain hegemonic control of the government and slowly begin to reshape it into a parliament or whatever was most convenient for them to control. This would have been the pathway of least resistance, without conflict breaking out. However, if conflict had broken out, it only meant they had to crack a few more eggs to make their omelet.

I still believe that if the members of the Fed followed this plan, there would be little to nothing that the government could do to stop it. Outside of declaring our independence in regional or local areas, there would be little we could do as well (and then we'd have to have the ability to hold our positions, a strategy I do not advocate for and would only consider as an absolute last resort). It was 2012 when my friend and I were having this conversation. As you remember, the Mayan calendar said we were all going to die anyway that year, so this conversation was somewhat in the realm of normalcy. In 2012, after the Obama administration, the national debt was $16.05 trillion. That was up from the $7 trillion Bush had racked up to that point since 2004. The national debt has now more than doubled, and it has no downward trajectory in sight. You know what's also up? The chances that the scenario I laid out in 2012 would actually become a real pathway to resetting the world.

I have admittedly been talking quite a bit about the U.S. government and debt for a chapter that is supposed to reveal who makes up the shadow government that owns the world. But I have done so for a reason. You need to understand that the dynamics of our current government, political discourse, and social narrative are all constructs. They are designed by people who have no fear of the government and actually do think in terms of world dominance and control. Bernie Sanders is not among the people on that list. Our government has three branches. They are all now dwarfed by the fourth branch of government that has been created by the central planning progressives, who operate at the elite's behest (just as long as they remain useful tools). Our political discourse allows progressives to guilt-trip reasonable people so that we spend our country into oblivion.

Meanwhile, the main discourse among the people divides us on class, race, and sex, so that we are hopeless in uniting against them. We have been indoctrinated through our education to believe the experts and to trust journalistic sources. All the while, the elite are paying both to spout their talking points. There is an epic illusion of choice in our daily decisions, and the illusion that a variety of voices all agree on what is reality and what is conspiracy. In the end, it is an amazingly small group of people that have so infiltrated every corner of the global economy that when they decide to put their finger on the scale of any conversation, the world moves.

The stock market is the ultimate signpost of the global economy. By the stock market, of course, I mean the NYSE. America is the country where these very wealthy people became even wealthier beyond their imaginings, took over the USD and made it the global reserve currency, and ballooned the American economy into the global economy, of which they own a great portion. The rest they don't own is for sale in their casino—I mean, a totally legitimate stock market where real (and definitely not speculative) values and shares are traded in earnest and honesty for the betterment of the stockholder, mankind, and the world. Mind you, everything is for sale, financed through their financial institutions and banks.

The data that I compiled for the previous chapter's summary is not readily available on the internet. It took several days to go to each company's profile on CNN Business and find the dollar value of both the corporation itself and then what the values of the shares were for Vanguard, Black Rock, and State Street. These are three private shareholder institutions, meaning that the owners (and number of owners) are hidden. Every corporation on the stock market is publicly traded, and therefore they have to disclaim the insider ownership as well as the institutional ownership of the company (what the founders and c-suite own in shares versus what the retirement funds, hedge funds, and private equity firms own in shares). But these three funds are immune from disclosure because they are not publicly traded companies. These three private funds are major stakeholders in every single company in the S&P 500. In the vast majority of cases, they are the number one-, two-, and three-ranked companies by percent ownership. Vanguard itself is the largest stakeholder (the company with the highest percentage of ownership) of 456 of the 500 companies currently in the S&P 500.

Total dollar value of Vanguard's S&P 500 shares: **$3.3 trillion**

Total dollar value of Black Rock's S&P 500 shares: **$1.8 trillion**

Total dollar value of State Street's S&P 500 shares: **$1.7 trillion**

Total of the Big 3: $6.9 trillion

For context, Apple is the largest company on the S&P 500, estimated at a value of $2.7 trillion dollars. The combined holdings for these three is larger than Microsoft, Alphabet (Google's parent company), and Amazon combined. And this is just the money that these people are willing to gamble in their own casino! They aren't bringing their life's savings to the slots. The other 'competitors' to these big three are public hedge funds like Berkshire Hathaway, T. Rowe

Price, Fidelity, and Northern Trust. These companies are taking the combined millions of dollars from private investors and investing it in the stock market. These are very decentralized as compared to the ownership of the big three, and sadly, when you compare the percent ownership of the big three as compared to the percent ownership of these other institutional investors ... it's pretty even. The remaining shares in each of these companies is owned by mutual funds. This is your retirement money.

At this point, if you are clued into your retirement or investment portfolio, you might be thinking to yourself that the big three's names sound familiar. You might even think you have stock in them. This is only partially true. Vanguard runs many mutual funds which are public offerings, as well as Black Rock. They are franchising their brand, but these are moneys paid into a fund to be managed like any other hedge fund or mutual fund. These moneys would ostensibly be public and are not accounted for in the figures above; those figures are just what are in their private holdings. The hedge funds and mutual funds are just following trends and advice, and trying to keep up with market forces and get a return on investment that is higher than the payouts that they owe retirees and investors. Even though Vanguard, Black Rock, and State Street privately own about twenty percent of the total shares traded on the S&P 500 companies, they are the only ones who are even close to that level of institutional control.

It is important to understand the level of wealth we are talking about. How much of your paycheck goes into your retirement? Maybe nothing, and you are counting on Social Security (please don't, by the way; that money is not going to be there for anyone under the age of forty). Either way, if you are north of the median income and able to put some money away for retirement, you're putting at most five to ten percent, right? The nearly seven trillion dollars held by the big three is most likely proportionate in what they have to leverage. Remember, this is about percent control for the T.O.D.s. They are not watching the stock price, nor do they care about the value of their dollars. When you have trillions of dollars, you don't care if their value is cut in half overnight, you couldn't spend them in your lifetime anyway!

The maintenance of these stocks is also for domination and control. These holdings grease the stock market's wheels and provide a sense of stability to a market filled with speculative value. It is also for the purpose of having leverage over corporations and boards. For example, if Vanguard wanted something from any one of the S&P 500, it would be very easy to get. They would only need to threaten to sell half their position in the company. That would put their company into a spiral, causing all the smaller players to sell their position out of investor pressure and fear. Then Vanguard could go right back and buy all those shares it sold for half price. But the damage would be done; the c-suite of that corporation would be fired for mismanagement, and maybe some board members too. And, the insider position of the corporate owners would be diminished because their stocks are now worth the new diminutive price. It would take years for them to recover and get back to the pre-dip value. We are talking about people with the ability to blackmail and coerce millionaires and billionaires who run and own the largest corporations in the world; either because they could threaten their executive job, tank their stock, and bankrupt the company, and if that didn't work, they could just simply call their loans.

The national debt and the stock market are both issues that affect every American, along with inflation induced by terrible monetary policy. But it's all part of the plan—a plan crafted by people who are not in the one percent but in the 0.000001 percent. And sadly, their plan is to control the global economy to the point that not even countries can compete with their power, and then slowly destroy those countries by destroying their financial systems. It is a tiny group of people who control the money supply and underwrite the world through their banks. It is the type of person who opens a casino and slowly starts siphoning off everyone else's wealth into their accounts. They are the type of people who can blackmail world leaders, buy nations, control currencies, and manipulate the global economy. It is the type of people who can infiltrate, manipulate, and control the FBI and CIA and use the shadow agencies and black budgets to develop weapons, spying, and technology systems to increase their power and control.

It makes my blood boil that the American people don't know who killed Kennedy. It is an outrage that Congress calls for the declassification of information on UFOs and that the no-such-name agencies are able to stonewall. I have had to stop watching Congressional hearings with intelligence officials. I cannot tell you how infuriating it is to hear them weasel out of questions by saying they are not going to give up their 'sources and methods.' If they can look our elected officials dead in the eye and tell them that they can pound sand, just who the hell is in charge?! And if they are not accountable to the American people, then just exactly who are they accountable to? The so-called 'intelligence community' is the most imminent threat to our freedom today, and it pains me deeply to say that.

In all honesty, their ability to thwart our elected officials, including declassification orders from the president himself, is proof that, at the end of the day, they are the ones actually wielding the power of the government. The term 'deep state' refers to these power brokers in the government, but they aren't just individual, power-hungry people. They are hand-selected by somebody; otherwise, they wouldn't move in such unison.

There is more to it than just being on the 'inside' and covering up for your own. They are hiding serious information from the American people, at the bidding of people who have a lot to hide, at least for now. The 0.000001 percent don't think like you do; they don't have the problems you face. They don't view the world the way that an average Joe providing for his family views the world. They have a level of control that no world leader in history has ever dreamed of. That level of control is apparent, as long as you have eyes to see. The only way out of this mess is if we all truly wake up and see what they are doing. We can still stop them; we have the power and (at least for now) the mechanisms of power in place to stop them. There will come a time when we won't, and then things will become very bleak. I hope that I can be a part of waking people up from their slumber or slapping people out of their woke stupors. Because it will take all of us; dead weight, misplaced energy, and open opposition will greatly hinder our ability to defeat these people and maintain our national sovereignty. I said before that you are dealing with a tight-knit oligarchy—those that are ideologically aligned in their pursuits for power. And when they decide to put their fingers on the scale to affect the outcome, the world moves. It is easy to see, if only you have the eyes to see it.

There are certain things about our world that point to the fact that there are meta forces driving a simulation forward. In philosophy, there is a principle known as Ockham's Razor. This principle is an essential part of viewing reality and seeing it clearly. Basically, Ockham's Razor is a reflective question that helps to determine the veracity of a solution to a problem. For example, I was once canoeing a river, and I saw an old dead tree. All its branches had fallen off, leaving knobs, so the stump of the tree looked like a knobby pillar that rose up about forty feet in the air. About halfway up, there was an aluminum canoe that was wrapped around the tree like a tin can. It was a confusing sight at first. I wondered how that could have gotten there. After seeing that the ends of the canoe (now touching) were pointing downstream, it seemed most likely that it floated down a highly flooded river and broadsided that tree. The force of the water bent it around the tree so tightly that when the water receded, it was stuck on the tree's old branch knobs just right, and it stayed. Looking up at that canoe, it was a wild thought that the water could ever get that high. You could begin to doubt yourself and think of other ways what you are seeing could have happened. But in the end, the idea that people did it as a prank or that it was a manufactured scene, although possible, seems less likely than a more natural cause.

Ockham's Razor states that if a simpler explanation is just as likely as a complex one, deference should be given to the simpler explanation. The inability to apply Ockham's Razor is the downfall of many conspiracy theories, and the bane of conspiracy theorists who just know that they have finally twisted the red string on the cork board around enough tacks to make everything make sense. This may sound like I am down on conspiracy theorists; believe me, I'm not. We live in an age where more information is more accessible than ever before, so it seems strange that in an age where everything should be out in the open, there are so many questions that we can't ask and information we are not allowed to see. Why, for instance, does the intelligence gathered on the Kennedy assassination remain classified? The simplest answer is that it is ultimately not a decision that a member of the intelligence community is allowed to make. That's not a comforting answer, but it would make much more sense than millions of bureaucrats being able to keep a secret, especially since we know that the intelligence community leaks like a sieve.

I want to juxtapose Ockham's Razor with another concept: a cognitive bias known as the Normalcy Bias. Normalcy bias is a phenomenon that has many aspects and applications, so it is hard to define, like trying to define a cube in 2D. It can be compared to cognitive programming in the mind that creates a 'stasis' or modus operandi that your brain relies upon to define normal. Without normality, the brain is less able to recognize and respond to threats. We have a normalcy bias that the sun will rise in the general direction of the east and set in the west. The seasons give way to each other, and that creates a cycle that will repeat. We develop normalcy bias with our friend group, the methods of receiving information, and all the routines of our day. When something is 'out of the ordinary,' our brain will be able to pick up on it and alert us to the change. The normalcy bias, therefore, can be our best friend, but that also means that there are two ways that it can be our enemy. The first is through hypervigilance; this is one extreme that can create stress and anxiety because everything that we see around us is perceived as a threat. The other extreme is when we are so placated by our surroundings that our normalcy bias does not register any stimuli as un-normal. Obviously, we want to be somewhere in the middle, aware of our surroundings, affecting what we can control, and kissing the rest up to God.

Oftentimes, the conspiracy theorist is accused of being hypervigilant, seeing threats where there are none. Everyone thinks that they are the grounded ones in the middle, seeing the world clearly despite everyone else's confusion. This is not a part of the normalcy bias, but it is another function of the brain's 'stasis.' When polled, the vast majority of people think that they are smarter than average. Meaning that at least some of that majority of people are mistaken about their own intelligence. We can't help it; ours is the only perspective we can really perceive the world through, and we think that our unique perspective is somehow 'righter' than everyone else's. Being a well-informed citizen is part of actually being the person in the middle, seeing the issues for what they are, and making sound judgments. Also, being humble and grounding yourself in reality helps.

Another huge component is trust; if someone you trust says everything is fine, you are far more likely to let that thought be normalized, even when there is nagging suspicion in your own mind. But what can trick the mind even more than trust is when your normalcy bias finds itself face to face with an 'unknown unknown.' Donald Rumsfeld made that particular phrase popular, but it is an unknown thing that you didn't even know to be on the lookout for. If your brain deems something 'out of the realm of possibility,' you can bet that you will never be able to see that thing coming. The sad fact of the matter is that the vast majority of people in America have fallen victim to a normalcy-bias malaise. We can't believe that there are forces outside of the two political parties shaping and driving narratives. We can't believe that the trusted names in the news might actually be lying to us—and that those lies are orchestrated. We can't imagine that the intel community would have loyalties that lie outside of this country or that they would have the audacity to usurp our justice system. We can't believe that some of our fellow Americans want to see America fail. That is because we don't have any historical references, and we have never encountered an entity powerful enough to do these things. We can't believe that our government would ever fail or that the stable systems around us would ever collapse. Out of a sense of self-preservation, protecting a feeling of security or comfort, or out of a lack of imagination, most people refuse to even respond, even as the ground is moving under their feet. Proof that the saying is true: "No eye is more blind than the one that will not see."

These two concepts are an important part of understanding reality and then understanding the next-level strategy of the 0.000001 percent. Under ordinary circumstances, abiding by Ockham's Razor and applying our normalcy biases properly is hard enough. But what happens when you encounter a strategy that has purposely been weaponized against you? What happens when you find yourself in a simulation that is designed to drive you mad and make your perception of reality so clouded that you cannot put either tactic to use? We know that social media companies pay billions for psychological research into making their products more addicting and then apply that to their apps to increase your screen time. We know that marketing, sales, and other specialties all use psychological manipulation to shape customer buying habits or to close the sale. So why is it such a stretch that trillionaires would employ these tactics on a populace through the mechanisms of control that they have established? We are led to believe that the simple solution—that a small oligarchy is trying to take over the world—is a cooky conspiracy theory. Don't you know that there are far too many complex systems and far too many forces that need controlling for that to ever happen? Besides, everyone is saying that it is a crazy concept; every legacy media outlet feigns outrage at the mere mention. Is that because they are all seeing reality for what it is, or is the simpler solution that they are in on it?

You can't get one hundred people to agree on any one thing; in fact, if you find one hundred people with the exact same opinion on a particular subject, you've just found a conspiracy of liars! Is it easier to believe the legacy media are colluding or that millions of employees across a myriad of networks are all in an organic manifestation of ideological lockstep? We are being gaslit every day to believe that the simple solution is an impossibility. In fact, we are told that there isn't even a problem that needs solving. To even think that there is a problem with the world is sexist, racist, or some this-ist or that-ist. You can't even have the conversation! That's right, just go back to sleep and let us get our work done; nothing to see here. Our normalcy bias is weaponized against us; the same people who say there is no problem assure us that they can be trusted and that they are the adults in the room who are seeing the world clearly and moving things forward.

One could argue that the legacy media companies all sound the same because they know that fear sells and use similar techniques to craft stories. You could also argue that they know what stories will play and which ones won't, so that is the cause of the coverage overlap. You could even argue that because they are partisan Democrats, their opinions are skewed or their talking points would sound very similar. But that doesn't explain why when someone rightly criticizes George Soros for his policy positions, they are immediately called out as an anti-Semite by the network talking head. That can't explain how the entire legacy media was silent about the Hunter Biden laptop story. Not one journalist looked into it? That doesn't explain their unanimous and unquestioning reaction to the death of Jeffrey Epstein. To think that not a single member of the legacy media dared to question the radically suspicious circumstances of his death defies all rationality and falls into the realm of the implausible. Unless, of course, the simplest answer is that it is all by design. The people who wish to take over the world without having to go to war have to have a good PR team. Their "team" is just another illusion of choice on our part; it looks like a symphony of different voices from across the spectrum singing the praises of globalism, liberal progressivism, and moral relativism. It is the same voice, the same ventriloquist's hand up every one of their you-know-whats. That's power, my friends. That's the kind of power that would make you think that you have the right to rule the world.

So that brings us back to Bernie Sanders, a politician who screams about the one percent paying their fair share. Is that a true statement, or just another bank of fog purposely placed to shroud the true nature of the empire of lies? designed to obfuscate the master plan that the master planners swear isn't happening. People in the one percent include people who make just over a million dollars a year. It includes the billionaire entrepreneurs, and it doesn't even begin to describe wealth or encompass the class of the T.O.D.s that hold way more than ninety-nine percent of the wealth that the one percent hold. It's the 0.000001 percent that controls the strings of power. I am once again asking for your support; the narrative that the one percent ought to pay their fair share is an illusion. It is an old talking point that makes you think the CEO of the company you work for is to blame for the ills of the world. He might make millions a year, even a billion with stock options, and be a highly driven, selfish, and greedy person. But even he is a pawn in the T.O.D.'s game. He is a useful pawn, but a pauper in comparison to the people who own the majority stock position of the company, place the board, and also own the bank that finances the corporation that the CEO leads. Not to mention they control the dollar that the company is traded on and have outsized influence over monetary policy and the government that regulates them.

The true wealth of these people and their exact identities is hidden for a reason; if you saw it plainly, even your dulled American normalcy bias would be going off like a five-alarm fire. That is why they hide behind their foundations and sell their ideas as philanthropies. That is why the WEF was formed: to serve as a seemingly benevolent force that has, since its inception, inserted itself into the conversation of global politics. That is why their stockholdings are hidden behind private companies. That is why their banks hide behind the name "Federal Reserve." It is an empire of lies made to shield their plans from activating your normalcy bias. It is an empire of lies that is built to hide the simple explanation and to obfuscate the conspiracy that is happening in plain sight. And if we do nothing, we will look up one bright, sunny day in 2030 and realize that there is nothing left to be done. Let's not wait until then to know our enemy and begin to fight, shall we? Because it will give me no solace to hear you say, 'golly gee, you were right!' when we find ourselves cellmates in the gulag. The gulag that, as of yesterday, the news assured you didn't exist, built by a conspiracy that you were assured, was outside the realm of possibility.

CHAPTER 4

The New World Order & How We Got Here

In his book *The Republic*, Plato posits an allegory to better articulate his theory of forms. It is called the Cave Allegory, and I am sure that you have heard of it. Plato often wrote in dialogue form, where it looks like a transcript of two or more people talking, usually one character who was a wise philosopher with something to teach and others willing to learn. In this particular dialogue, the character of the wise philosopher was cast as Plato's beloved teacher, Socrates. Plato hated democracy because he saw the democratic senate of Greece vote to put Socrates to death after he insulted their degraded consciences. If an honest man with a clear conscience found himself at odds with our modern American Congress, I am afraid they would do the same. Socrates taught Plato, and Plato taught Aristotle, the three titans of Western philosophy. As far as we know, Socrates never wrote anything down, but both Plato and Aristotle gave honor to Socrates, cut down by brutish men, in their writings. In the Cave Allegory, Plato sets the scene whereby Socrates is giving Glaukon (the interlocutor) a scenario to ponder. He describes prisoners deep in a cave; they are bound up in such a way that they cannot move their heads right or left. They are staring at the back wall of the cave, and behind them is fire that illuminates the wall that their eyes are proverbially glued to. They have been this way their entire lives; all they know is the cave and this 'worldview' if you will. Like puppeteers, the guards hold up figurines and sculptures and dance them in front of the fire, and the prisoners see their shadows on the wall. They hear the noises of the guards and attribute the noises to the shadows they see and perceive as reality itself. Bleak existence, no? But they name the shadow figures and play games such as guessing which shape will appear next. There is a prize structure and honors among the prisoners who can win these games.

After the setup, Socrates offers the following what if? What if one of the prisoners was set free from his bondage? He would turn and see the blazing fire, and it would pain his eyes, but the illusion that he was under would be radically upended. He would see that the shadow was a projection of a real object. He would not yet know that this figurine was just a representation itself. Plato recognizes that the shock may well be so intense that for the prisoner to stay in this limited reality, he might have to be forced; otherwise, he might willingly return to the 'comfort' of his bondage, the shadow world, and the hierarchy and accolades he might win there.

But if he were forced to 'go on' and make the climb out of the cave, he would see the natural light of the sun, and surely it would be a painful experience. But then, after his eyes finally adjusted to the blinding light of the natural sun, his reality would be upended again. The figurine of the horse will have a far different context once he sees a living, breathing horse. So, the prisoner goes from complete bondage in a forced, narrow worldview to all of reality being his worldview. He sees the whole scene and learns how to live a new, expanded, fuller version of life he could not imagine as a prisoner in the cave.

This is when another what-if is posed. What if this person thought back to his former life and his old companions in the cave? Most likely, out of gratitude, he would have great pity for his former comrades, setting off at once to set them free. On the way, he would contemplate his former life. But would he care about the honor and accolades of the games he once played or the prestige he could hold in that court? Just as when he left the cave and experienced blindness from the light, a similar blindness would occur as he descended into the darkness he was no longer used to. When he reached the prisoners, they would welcome him back to their games. As he told them of his adventures, he tried to describe that the shadows are actually many degrees separated from reality. But would the prisoners accept what they heard? They would demand he look at the shadows and tell them what they were, but it would be too dark for him to see clearly, and he would be too far removed from the old names to be able to recall them. Would they not then openly mock and deride him? Thinking that he lost his mind on his adventures, they would dismiss any of his claims out of hand. Eventually, they might even come to the conclusion that killing him would be better, so as to keep the order of their reality together and not have it challenged. Ultimately, it would prove futile to overcome their normalcy bias and convince them that there is a world beyond the simulation that they are being forced into defining as reality itself.

There is so much depth to Plato's Cave Allegory and so many themes and allusions that can be broken down. The perception of reality and the power of discovery to change one's worldview are powerful themes. Another is the natural disconnect that occurs when you come out of an old environment and into a higher and better version of yourself; you feel like a foreigner to your once native space. Another is the power of group think and how a normalcy bias can be used to delude people into claiming moral superiority within the context of their own ignorance and echo chamber. But this allegory offers a particular 'what if' for our time—a pressing question that we must answer in our current day and age. Someone put those poor bastards in the cave and chained them down in front of the "reality" that the imprisoner wanted the prisoner to see. In order for the entire allegory to work, someone had to orchestrate the entire plan. Someone had to invent such an experiment for their own nefarious purposes and think so little of their fellow man that they would not think twice about the misery inflicted upon their prisoners. Who put them in the cave?

It is an apt question for our time given that we are currently being driven into a cave of our own. Some of us are more willing than others, but through our desire for modern convenience and technology, through our apathy or slow acceptance of globalism, and for doing nothing in the face of the progressive movement slowly eroding our country, we are all being herded into the cave. And remember, the allegory does not start by saying the man thought better of his condition and escaped. The first turn of the allegory is that, almost as a cruel joke, they let the prisoner go. He was not able to undo what had been done to him of his own accord, and that is the sad truth of slavery. It takes an act of God over the course of centuries and no shortage of miracles to ever reverse such a thing. And despite his freedom, despite what he saw, he was unable to convince his former comrades that the shadows on the wall were only the start of the journey of what is actually real.

We do not have to suffer through a life of global takeover and the implementation of a new world order. Nor do we have to recline our children to becoming the first generation of prisoners born in the cave, bound their whole lives into a simulation. How we are being driven into the cave is a complex story—a multi-faceted war being waged on multiple fronts. Part I of this book focuses on the economy because it was in economics that the shadow realm, the empire of lies, was born. The coalescing of the economy into the hands of an elite few started with the clean slate of the American capitalist economy. It moved from there to crony corporatism as competitors were 'diversified' into a shrinking group of expanding corporations. Once the balance was tipped through lobbying and cozying up to the government, we entered the age of Voluntary Socialism. This accelerated the coalescence of power until there was an economic oligopoly, reigning over what would become their global economy. The Marxists that they allied with in government took the Faustian bargain and took control of the levers of government power. They did so unknowingly to their peril; the global economy would become the means by which the T.O.D.s would usurp all countries, communist or otherwise, and form a one-world government. The communists would become the local and regional authorities if they submitted their allegiance, and the centrally planned "rule by the expert class," would begin.

The global political and economic response to the 2020 pandemic resulted in the largest wealth transfer in human history. This was another of the designed "lesser resets." Notice I didn't say the disease caused it, nor did I say any one person's personal response. Put all your ire and madness aside for a second to make sure you understand. The perfectly choreographed response from hundreds of nations around the globe that practically worshipped the advice coming out of the World Health Organization caused the conditions by which we lived in tyranny while the T.O.D.s transferred all our wealth away from us. The ensuing terrible policy positions that could not be justified by our Constitution or form of government resulted in a level of tyranny never before implemented by American governance. And it became a great dry run for a 'global response' and how the world could be run by 'the experts.'

Thus, it gave the communists a strong supply of their drug of choice: political power. But it was ultimately a huge leap forward in the game of control for the T.O.D.s. In the post-pandemic world, we have shifted in their plan from oligopoly into the next phase: global economy. Now, they are telegraphing when they anticipate the move to their final phase (one world government). The WEF has made some "predictions" they think will likely "come to pass" by 2030. This is made more ominous by their constant call for a "Great Reset." The first of these predictions is that you will own nothing. That claim would naturally not get rid of ownership per se–just your right to own anything. They even produced a high-quality promo video for the Great Reset of 2030; you should check it out sometime while you can still find it on the internet. We will explore these eight promises—I mean predictions—in the next chapter. For now, I want to focus on the economic front, how we got to where we are, and then take an honest look into the cave that they so desperately want us to walk into without ever putting up a fight.

FROM CAPITALISM TO VOLUNTARY SOCIALISM

Why would actors in the free market choose to be regulated by the government? Doesn't big business hate government interference? That is an old dead Republican talking point from the 1990s, when corporate CEOs and the Wall Street fat cats were allowed to contribute to Republican campaigns (unlike now, where they exclusively fund Democrats), and they could even be registered Republicans and keep their job. Now that the elite have economic control and their political cronies have political control, they have gladly kicked the Republicans to the curb. The Republicans used to be referred to as the 'country club' party, the party of the rich. There is currently a major realignment occurring in politics due to the Democrats now being the party in bed with big business and big tech. Anyway, the platitude is dumb on its face because it does not comport with reality. It is as equally disingenuous as the Democrats' call to vilify Republicans for daring to cut regulations.

The truth is, mega corporations can do what they want behind their billion-dollar wall of lawyers and lobbyists. They are not accountable to their customers or the government. Hell, pharmaceutical companies are exempt from liability if their product doesn't work—or even injures someone. I'm not going to argue that point with people who think they are safe and effective. But the vaccine mandates are a prime example of how we have been programmed to accept the terms of the elite's voluntary socialism. Long before the term COVID became a household name, pharmaceutical companies have been taking billions in grants from the government for 'research and development.' This means our tax dollars were funding their research, as long as they researched in the general area outlined by the grant. So, in order to develop drugs and vaccines, they were being subsidized by the federal government. When the lockdowns came around, they were given even more money by 'project warp speed.' Then, when an experimental vaccine was created, they were allowed to sell it for profit—even back to the federal government that underwrote its development. Then, the progressives screamed, and the media touted their narrative that it was imperative that everyone must take it. You were a granny killer if you did not consent. The government would even foot the bill, and the insurance companies would sort it out on the backend. Money was no issue! You just had to comply. But this is not even the most sinister part of this story. These same pharma companies lobbied the government to give them immunity from any side effects or harm that the experimental drug might inflict on the American people. And they got it! No one who received a vaccine and experienced myocarditis or any other ailment had any recourse; they could not hold Big Pharma accountable in any way. That is the definition of socialism, my friend: that the government and the corporations walk hand-in-hand every step of the way.

Big Pharma is always a very contentious subject because everyone generally agrees that the cronyism in the industry is problematic. At the same time, the same people have extremely strong opinions about how important and essential their products are. It is a cognitive disconnect that most people fail to realize. If people were to give you their honest opinion about the pharmaceutical industry, I bet the vast majority of people would say it is corrupt, too tied to the government, and that they would like to see it reformed. Also, in the same breath, they might vehemently defend vaccines as a prerequisite to health itself! Fascinating that dirty old greedy men who run one of the most corrupt industries in the world would also be beyond reproach concerning the product that they are pumping out. I just look at the nature of the beast and the revolving doors of corruption between Big Pharma and the government. People go from "government regulator" to the C-suite of these companies, and then back again by the time a president has served his first term.

The U.S. government holds vaccine patents—and that doesn't create a conflict of interest when they decide vaccine regimens and frequency? Or—like during COVID—they try to mandate them? It is the most lobbied industry on Capitol Hill. The bottom-line number for the pharma industry is that the more drugs they sell, the more money they make. If they need more sick people to make more money, what is going to drive their decision-making process? And these are the people who, when it comes to the product they are pumping out, get the mark of sainthood and the halo of unquestioning righteousness? Something tells me that if you can be mad at an industry's corruption and simultaneously be absolutely unquestioning of their product, maybe you are the one who is not seeing things clearly.

One thing is clear: no matter how mad, exasperated, or disappointed you are with my thoughts about modern healthcare, you cannot deny that the pharmaceutical industry is a prime example of a post-capitalist economic apparatus, one that the national socialists of Germany would have been proud of. But it does not stand alone as a sole example. Mark Zuckerberg begs the government to regulate Meta and all its tentacles. So do all of the other major tech platforms. If the government decides on a regulation, then all they have to do is tailor their algorithm to it and ensure that there is no mechanism by which competitors can rival them. Then they employ their army of lawyers and lobbyists to poke around the edges, making it more profitable, easier to cheat, and easier to obtain and trade the real tech gold: information. China obliges their begging; they provide the regulation, and these companies are only too willing to bend the knee. They hide information; they keep vital information from the outside world away from the Chinese people. They help the Chinese government maintain their social credit score system. To a slightly lesser degree, they do that here in the United States as well, mostly at the behest of the intelligence agencies. We are coming to a very scary time to live in a world where private companies own the public square and the dissemination of information.

Companies that are worth trillions of dollars are more powerful than most governments. The government contracts these companies have make it hard to tell where the government ends and the private company begins. And that is where we are: the voluntary socialism machine that no one can compete with, divide, or usurp—not even Congress, the President, or the Supreme Court. The reality is that the empire of lies views both the government mechanism and the tech platform as parts of their overall global mechanism and can't wait to get their hands on it and see just how much control they can wield.

Our political discourse has not caught up to this change of the guard. Democrats, and ironically, the most collectively minded ones, rail against this voluntary socialism, claiming that it is the evils of capitalism! Bernie Sanders thinks that these giant "cohpohrayshuns" are the problem; I tend to agree with him. I just disagree fundamentally with his "solution" to completely collectivize our country. One, because communism is evil and contrarian to my worldview, but also practically, it won't do a damn bit of good reigning in the T.O.D.s that control them anyway. Meanwhile, Republicans are glitching out on old talking points about Google being a private company and 'how dare we intervene in their daily business.' The worst is when I see Republican pundits talk to collectivists, and in their attempt to unabashedly be capitalists, they end up defending these awful mega-corps and their abuses of power. Newsflash: Crony corporatism is not capitalism. America in 1880 had much more of a capitalist economy; we don't have a capitalist economy anymore. Sure, you can start a business, get access to legal assistance, and do many other things that many non-Americans don't have access to. But you don't have the privilege of ever competing with the T.O.D.s; that has been completely baked out of the equation. And if we do not have equal opportunity in the economy, then we aren't living in a capitalist society.

The collectivists know what time it is, in the sense they can use the beginnings of voluntary socialism to create the allusion that our 'capitalist' economy needs reform. They are in it to win it, so even though they know the system currently in place is just 'socialism lite,' they will still sell it as the evils of capitalism. It's not hypocrisy; it is the strategy of relativism at work; the goal is to have their way; it is not to be honest, have integrity, and adhere to moral standards. Both the Democratic and Republican establishments are too corrupted by the campaign funds they receive to ever turn their backs on their donors. The new movement in the Republican Party of populism and America first seems to be the greatest threat to the T.O.D.s, based on how their PR firms—I mean the legacy media—portray them with such vitriolic bloviation. I hope that the working-class Democrats, the Conservative Republicans, and social moderates can form a coalition around making sure that we break the back of voluntary socialism. In conclusion, I want to address the platitude I started with: 'why would corporations want to be regulated by the government?' Well, if they were independent businesses that weren't already monopolies in their industry, they most certainly wouldn't. But that isn't the case, is it?

In every single industry, in every single field of production and output, there are one to two giant corporations that control the industry, pricing, flow of goods, etc. The rest of the industry is populated by comparatively tiny businesses that operate on the fringes, like in rural areas, not worth the box store's time. The idea that the local rural hardware store is a 'competitor' to Lowe's or Home Depot is a laughable proposition, and you know it. These giant corporations can lobby to get what they need to make sure that there is never an inter-industry power struggle. It's like high school drama; the popular guy gets the popular girl. Why? Because she's hot and he's captain of the football team. That is the extent of their common interest. Yeah, the popular guy is tied down now, but with the prize of the school! It only drives both of their cool points up. Dude Bro accepts the terms that hot stuff is dishing out because he locks down the hot stuff that every other dude bro is dreaming about. High school romance based on popularity and voluntary socialism have one inevitable thing in common: they are destined to fail, and things don't end pretty. But for now, being the only game in town for the government means these corporations get all of the government contracts; they lobby the government to make their position stronger and inhibit the chances of being usurped by the competition. At least for now, they have become too big to fail; too tied into the government itself to be separated without both collapsing. Eventually, the government that thinks that they have control will realize that they are held hostage and that they are in way too deep. And the exit strategy isn't going to be negotiated at the CEO level but much, much higher. Again, that is not the threat but the promise of the WEF: that they will be able to rescue us from the crisis they created in the first place.

FROM VOLUNTARY SOCIALISM TO OLIGOPOLY

Voluntary socialism really began to take off in the 1970s, reached its height in the economic boom of the 1990s, and culminated sometime in the late 2000s. In that time, there was the .com crash and the housing crisis. Just collateral damage along the way. This was also the hollowing out of American industry and the beginning of the T.O.D.s globalizing their holdings. In order to have voluntary socialists, they are de facto oligarchs to the political powers that be. In this sense, we have always had oligarchs in this country. But what is different now is that this has become a smaller, far more elite group. Naturally, as that group gets smaller, they become more isolated from the world. In doing so, their world views come to align by virtue of shared outlook and experience. America's echo chamber is awash with 330 million voices that are in various stages of people who can't pay bills, have debt and/or legal troubles, struggle to keep their families together, and many feel trapped in their economic and social conditions. The echo chamber of the middle class resounds with tens of millions of voices that have what we like to call "first-world problems." The wealthy in the top one percent have their own cacophony of three million voices in their echo chamber, but perhaps they are talking about retirement, their scholarship fund, or their family trust.

As you come up the ladder of echo chambers and into the top 0.01 percent, the echo chamber of only a few hundred thousand becomes more like the same thoughts through different lenses: business success, wealth creation, etc. Now think about what the echo chamber of the 0.0000001 percent sounds like—the Rockefellers, the Warburgs, and their twenty or thirty closest friends sound like. I bet it sounds far more like a choir than anything else. People who want for nothing, who actually own the mechanisms of the global economy, and who look at every human problem in terms of numbers and utilitarianism. Sometimes that view rebounds to the 'good of man,' but you can be assured that it will always be good for their bottom line. That isn't a conspiracy; that is just a fact of circumstance.

If you don't believe me, listen to Yuval Harari speak about the latest science and advancements that the WEF is working on. He is one of the intellectual leaders of the WEF, so his net wealth is beside the point. Like Klaus, he is there to legitimize the intellectual veracity of his handler's ideas. Listen to him speak about gene manipulation, uploading our brains into the cloud, and how we can just 'twist the knobs' of the human condition into whatever reality we want. He is talking about people, but as though they were livestock. Hell, not even livestock; like insects we experiment on for which we have no empathy. The economic game of the T.O.D.s continues, just as it has for over a century. But there has been a fundamental shift in the categorization of the T.O.D.s. It has become a smaller and even more elite group. Fewer people with a bigger piece of the pie means fewer voices. When Forbes releases its top one hundred richest people list, you notice names like Elon Musk, Warren Buffet, Bill Gates, and Jeff Bezos usually top the list. They are usually way richer than the bottom half, which is mostly Hollywood celebrities and music artists.

Now, if you depart from the narrative in Hollywood, you get cancelled. If you depart from the narrative in the corporate world, you find yourself out of a job. And even among the ten richest people on the Forbes list, really only Elon Musk is a contrarian, and even he considers himself on the left. If that group of people is this ideologically aligned, imagine how truly aligned the T.O.D.s are.

You don't have to take my word for it; we have proof. They are so aligned, they have formed a political action committee with promises, a coherent agenda, and a political plan. The WEF is the PAC of the people who would not dignify Forbes by being on their list. In fact, they must hide their net wealth for fear of startling the peasants (a category that, in their minds, includes you, me, and Oprah, just so you know). Once the T.O.D.s gained control of the corporate scheme of diversification and voluntary socialism, the fix was in and the game was set. At this point, they just had to operate wisely, use their secret weapons (their banks) shrewdly, and slowly diversify the corporations into globo-corps. Once the vast majority of industries had aligned behind one or two corporations, the lobbying could really begin to be honed toward ideological ends rather than business interests.

When you don't have to consult the market (because you own it), you don't have to act in the best interest of the company. Building out an oligarchy was easy; the tycoons of industry bought up all their competitors in the name of the bottom line and increasing stockholder position. Meanwhile, it was their stockholder position that was also getting stronger! After an oligarchy was established, it was time to make it permanent. There had to be a thinning of the herd in the American oligarchy, and that is what happened through the Great Depression, getting off of the gold standard, and moving to a debt-based economy. Each time, the T.O.D.s could buy up their less wealthy competitors, diversify those holdings into their own corporations, or just gain an outsized stock position in their competitors' businesses. Whoever owns Vanguard holds exponentially more power than someone like Elon Musk. I am sure that the owner of Vanguard gets along great with the owners of State Street and Blackrock. I am sure that they see the world in the same way. It is no conspiracy to say that these people are obviously like-minded; they are doing like-minded things in a space that no one else can operate in or compete with. Common sense would tell you that their worldviews are similar. The fact that they founded the WEF tells you that they plan to do something about it.

FROM OLIGOPOLY TO GLOBAL ECONOMY

This transitory stage is the simplest one and one that was a natural progression of establishing the oligopoly in the first place. When the American economy was converted from a production and manufacturing economy, we were promised that it would become a 'white-collar' economy. We were told that we would share in the wealth and riches of the expatriation of our economy. The corporate landscape changed in two ways. It became far more centralized as more and more corporations merged or were acquired, forming giant multi-national conglomerate globo-corps. While this was happening, they were simultaneously becoming decentralized in the political context by spreading their tentacles throughout the world. As the c-suites became smaller and more centralized, they became powerful entities unto themselves that, outside of paying taxes, were really not beholden to any one country. Their allegiance was to none other than the almighty dollar. The laws of governments and their regulations were just part of doing business—the regional rules of the road. Do you have any idea how few corporations are behind the thousands of brand names you interact with every day (who were all once independent, American companies; who made their things here with American labor)? When you walk into the grocery store, you have multiple brands to choose from for the exact same product. There is great variety in our stores, and I am not knocking that; the more, the merrier! But did you know that all of that variety, all of that illusion of choice, is delivered to that store by only ten companies? Nestle, Coca-Cola, PepsiCo, Kellogg, General Mills, Unilever, Danone, Mars, Mondelez, and Associated British Foods. These ten companies have complete hegemonic control over the food industry.

Industrialized farming has been built to deliver patented crops to these companies that have been modified to be easier to harvest, not modified to be a healthier or higher-producing version of themselves. They account for thousands of brands and the vast majority of offerings in every grocery store. All their offerings are highly processed, high in sugar, sodium, fat, dyes, preservatives, and the cheapest possible filler ingredients. But it sure is cheap. And it lasts longer on the shelves, and it's good for business. Don't you dare say that they are in any way responsible for the obesity epidemic in our country! And certainly don't point to the fact that the poorest Americans, who are forced to eat the cheapest offerings of these unhealthy foods, are oftentimes the most impacted.

It's not just grocery store food; the Darden Group is the corporation behind the vast majority of America's chain restaurants. From Olive Gargen to Eddie V's, almost every national chain restaurant is owned by just one company. It is like this in every single American industry, most notably in the media industrial complex. Six companies—GE, Newscorp, Disney, Viacom, Time Warner, and CBS—control an unbelievable ninety percent of what we read, watch, or listen to. That's right: thousands of channels, multiple networks, millions of streaming options, websites, print media, magazines, periodicals, newspapers, all controlled by six companies. It's no wonder they all sound the same and point in the same direction. The sad reality is that these globo-corps keep the brand names from a bygone era for the sake of customer nostalgia and for the sake of lulling us to sleep with the illusion of choice. We live in a global economy where you cannot function as a normal member of society without being beholden to an ever-shrinking group of elites that control more than you realize.

During the great expatriation and the promise of an economic "white-collar" future for America, the greatest generation and the early boomers were promised that if they sent their kids to college, they'd all come to be their own little titans of industry who could make more wealth than even their parents. I don't blame them for buying into the model or wishing better for their children. I just wish that the golden ticket that was sold to America right before its economic raping had actually been more than fool's gold and salt in the wound. What was worse is that another economic event happened at the same time that would only accelerate our economic woes and set up a path to government spending that would ultimately drive us to complete economic ruin.

Getting off of the gold standard (or any semblance that our money was tied to something of value) in 1971 officially established the U.S. dollar as a debt-based currency. It was going to be driven by market forces instead of being backed by any real, tangible asset.

Just like the stock market before it, the USD would go the way of the speculators. What would this mean for the average American? It would mean that, for the first time in American history, the rate of inflation could actually make saving money a money-loss venture. Some smart ass is going to read this and say, 'Nuh-uh! The bubble of 1896' or some other nonsense to 'disprove' what I am saying. They can stuff it. Go to the website WTFHappenedin1971.com and look through the immense amount of collected data. In every single metric, we are doing worse economically than people fifty years ago. We make less money despite our productivity rising drastically. The vast majority of households have two working parents just to make close to the same as what one working parent brought home in the 1960s (adjusted for inflation, mind you).

Income inequality is at an all-time high, including data from the roaring twenties. In 1971, a new starter home cost $25K; imagine that! But the worst thing that happened to us in 1971 was inflation. Inflation is particularly high right now, but it is up over 2,326.58 percent since 1971. When you Google search this, they talk about the 'buying power' of the dollar and how it has increased with inflation. This is purposefully misleading. Nothing changes the fact that average rent in 1971 was $150/month. As of October 2023, it was $2,046, according to Zillow.com. What the hell happened? I am pointing to simple figures that you and I would relate to for a reason. This increase in money supply and economic demand is a simple equation of "pay to play." We pay more for rent; everything is financed, which drives all prices up; and in a debt-based economy, there is no 'getting ahead' for most people. There is certainly no mechanism for the 'have nots' to 'catch up' to the 'haves.' This was designed to wash any value that individual persons were to gain in the economy out with the tide of inflation; it is for the purpose of making us perpetually poor. To kill the middle class. Why would an economy do this? I know, in your mind, you're thinking, 'Oh the horror!' But that was how the world operated before America.

Europe could only attempt to emulate our middle class in vain. We were the OGs of creating a middle class. But that is convenient for creating a strong country with strong people who can't be F'ed with. Unfortunately, the T.O.D.s intend to re-imagine the world in their image, and that requires that they set the table in such a way that when they F around, they can't be held accountable when it's time to find out. We, as Americans, are being destroyed because they can't win as long as we can't be F'ed with. I don't care which side of the political aisle you're on. You better wake up, or the aisle won't be yours anymore to debate or cross. If you don't wake up and realize that the progressive movement exists to destroy our country and put us in a position where we only have the WEF to grovel to, then that is exactly what will happen. By their estimation, the agrarian society of the Middle Ages worked just fine for the kings and queens of antiquity. They seemed to rule with an iron fist and have much more control over their subjects than Western democracies do today. Your well-being, your way of life, and your prosperity are not being baked into their equations for how they will rule once they take control. They want your retirement to be destroyed. The further and more desperate your hands are as they reach out to their 'charity,' the more control they have. This is the age of the global economy.

Think about it. If you were going to try and survive without the banking system, big tech, or purchasing anything from S&P 500 companies, you wouldn't even be Amish! You'd be reduced to the life of a caveman, living in some dugout somewhere, hoping your potato crop would get you through the winter. Just think about how you would operate if you didn't have a bank. We have become beholden to the global systems around us! Not a single aspect of our lives can be done apart from it, including having our personal conversations; you know that Siri or Alexa will always be listening in.

Whether you like it or not, we have arrived at the age of the global economy, and we are now personally beholden and over our skis in this game. With the advent of virtual reality and AI, we are only more susceptible to being completely captured by it. There is no mechanism to 'rise up and challenge' the system that has been created because the capitalist economy and the free-market place of ideas no longer exist. We are the insurgents; we are the guerilla fighters on the fringe of the realm that now must fight the empire of lies to win our freedom back. It is time to, as the youth say, "recognize what time it is." It is time to realize that we are in the jaws of defeat, in the last stage of their game: the transition where their global economy becomes the means by which they rule us all with a one-world government, establishing a new world order.

FROM GLOBAL ECONOMY TO ONE WORLD GOVERNMENT

When someone begins to speak about a 'one world government' or a 'new world order,' most people respond with an eye roll, dismissing that person out of hand as a conspiracy theorist. That is because most people don't possess the imagination to put themselves in the shoes of the people who are in the process of creating one. Although all of us have dreamed at one point of being president or king of the

1971 COST OF LIVING

LIVING

New House	$25,200.00
Average Income	$10,622.00 per year
New Car	$3,560.00
Average Rent	$150.00 per month
Tuition to Harvard University	$2,600.00 per year
Movie Ticket	$1.50 each
Gasoline	40¢ per gallon
United States Postage Stamp	8¢ each

FOOD

Granulated Sugar	62¢ for 5 pounds
Vitamin D Milk	$1.17 per gallon
Ground Coffee	98¢ per pound
Bacon	80¢ per pound
Eggs	45¢ per dozen
Fresh Ground Hamburger	62¢ per pound
Fresh Baked Bread	25¢ per loaf

SeekPublishing Remember When 1971

Infographic compliments of WTFHappenedin1971.com

world, it is in terms of narrow issues and hypothetical 'what would you do?' scenarios. Most people like to put that proverbial robe on and put themselves in that mindset for a moment, but they would be terrified to wear the crown full-time. If you are scoffing at the idea that people are out there with enough hubris and sense of privilege to think they ought to rule the world, well, I can't help you there.

There are countless historical examples of truly depraved yet genius psychos who had illusions of grandeur that drove them to unimaginable depths. The fact that you really can't empathize with them or that it feels very off-putting when you put yourself in their shoes means that you are normal—and in this case, that is a good thing. When raccoons feel trapped or afraid, especially babies, they will cover their own eyes in an attempt to disappear from your view. I walked into my shed one day to find a full-grown male raccoon hanging from one of the rafters. After looking me dead in the eyes and seeing I was blocking the only way out, he decided 'stealth mode' was the best course of action. So, he ducked his head under the rafter so his head was hidden behind it; his entire body was still in view. I got a really good laugh at that. Most people are not aware of the truth behind the Fed, the stock holdings of VG, BR, and SS, or that just a handful of corporations own all of American industry. When I talk to them, I usually get the raccoon reaction—the slow nod with a blank stare—and then they turn their face away from you just as soon as humanly possible.

It does not offend me anymore; what I am asking them (and you) to see is an ugly and painful truth. What most people want to do is return to the cave and watch the old, comfortable shapes dance across the wall. The move to a global economy has been happening because it has been more comfortable for us to look away. GDP ticked up a point this year; I got my bonus because of the new acquisition; I have enough in my retirement account to retire without moving in with my kids; or I sold my business because globo-corp gave me an offer I couldn't refuse. Politically, we've said it is easier to print the money and take out loans than be fiscally responsible, the social programs we can't afford must increase because it gives Democrats the 'moral high ground,' it is more politically expedient to placate the radical left than stand up to their destructive policies. As a country and as an American people, we have been saying 'that's not my problem, and besides, that's a tomorrow problem anyway' for way too long. In the meantime, there has been a group of people who have been doing something in the vacuum created by a liberal culture morphing into a morally vacuous one. They are now poised to make their long-anticipated vision come true. They are so confident, they've even set the date.

In the previous chapter, I mentioned a conversation between a friend and myself about the Federal Reserve and whether or not they had the capability (regardless of whether or not they had the stones) to take over the federal government. I thought they had the ability (although it would be an ugly engagement) in 2012. Our national debt, the inflation rate, and the stock market have all radically changed since then. Not to mention that it has changed overall in their favor and strengthened the position of the T.O.D.s. The question we have to be asking ourselves now is: what percent ownership, what level of consolidation, and what level of control do they need to consider their takeover a foregone conclusion? That is what we are flirting with now, at a time when social and political tensions have never been higher in this country. We are one crisis, manufactured or otherwise, from an economic and societal collapse that could permanently destroy our country. Of course, when the global takeover happens, things will go somewhat back to normal.

When things are reset, we will have a functioning government making policy decisions on a semi-local level. They will be run by a regional parliament or some delegative body, and they will all have delegates in the global delegation. But these delegates would be party members, and there would be only one party. Your delegates will look like you, talk like you, and be a convincing local yokel. But they will have been vetted through something like a social credit score. They will walk the walk and talk the talk, or they won't be a member of the party. It will be their job to communicate the globalists' policies to the plebians in simple language so we can all understand. It will be their job to name the figures that dance on the cave wall in front of our eyes.

The people of the United Kingdom think that they are free. They generally get to do what they want and handle their local politics the way that they want. But built into their constitutional documents is an escape clause for the king. Basically, they are free so long as the authority says they are free. So, the people have a right to 'step out of line,' so to speak, and express their constitutional right to protest the government. But if the government deems that a "bad look," then they just freeze their sovereign rights and bank accounts. The Canadian trucker rally showed just how top-down the United Kingdom can unilaterally act against its people (when it so chooses). And thus, it will be with the new world order. There will be an unnamed expert class that informs the world delegation, and as long as everyone toes the line, all will be well.

They will create the illusion that there is freedom and autonomy throughout the land. But when they want to implement ESG policies for businesses, they will do so. When they issue their climate edicts, we will obey. And when they tell us to live in the pod and eat the bugs, we will have no choice. If one of the districts revolts, it will be immediate top-down enforcement, and the local delegates will employ the local branch of the global police force to make sure that the global experts' whims and caprice prevail (I bet they call their police force 'global peace keepers'). They will cut off the electric and water supply, the food supply, and every other industry because they control it all. They will probably still call our districts by our state names and our regional districts America, and our children will tell

American stories of freedom and greatness to their kids and how not much has changed.

When you live in a world where the party has complete control, especially over the flow of information, it will be very much like Orwell's *1984*: "Every record has been destroyed or falsified, every book rewritten, every picture has been repainted, every statue and street building has been renamed, every date has been altered. And the process is continuing day by day and minute by minute. History has stopped. Nothing exists except an endless present in which the Party is always right."[4] The Soviets only dreamed of the level of hegemonic control that today's T.O.D.s have over the global media, global economy, and global culture. And now, in the age of the technology revolution, we might not know the extent of their control or the power they can truly wield: 2030 looms on the horizon—the date that they have set with their political action committee. What do they know that we don't?

CHAPTER 5

Their Ultimate End: The Great Reset

As promised, in this chapter we will explore the WEF's eight predictions for the world by 2030. These come directly from a highly produced promotional video that was displayed on the WEF website. It can be found at the URL: http://wef.ch/2gmBN7M. As it has been trolled more and more, it is becoming harder and harder to find. In the video, the following bold predictions are made. Let's look at the list, and then take each one in turn:

- You will own nothing and be happy; whatever you want you'll rent and it'll be delivered by drone.
- The U.S. won't be the world's leading superpower; a handful of countries will dominate.
- You won't die waiting for an organ donor; we won't transplant organs, we'll print new ones instead.
- You'll eat much less meat; an occasional treat, not a staple (for the good of the environment and our health).

- A billion people will be displaced by climate change; we'll have to do a better job at welcoming and integrating refugees.
- Polluters will have to pay to emit carbon dioxide; there will be a global price on carbon (this will help make fossil fuels history).
- You could be preparing to go to Mars; scientists will have worked out how to keep you healthy in space (the start of a journey to find alien life?).
- Western values will have been tested to the breaking point; checks and balances that underpin our democracies must not be forgotten." [5]

YOU WILL OWN NOTHING

But don't worry, you'll be happy about it! This has got to show you the sheer audacity that these people have. They clearly did not field test this before going straight to production. This is the clearest evidence they truly believe, percentage point by percentage point, they will one day own everything. Remember, the communist-sounding statement "you will own nothing"[6] does not mean that private property is abolished. It just means your right to private property will be abolished. They fully intend to own everything and rent it to you. You're supposed to be thankful for the experience and for the fact that a drone dropped it on your doorstep (at least you didn't have to get on your electric moped and drive down to the widget factory to pick it up directly). I don't even think that Joseph Stalin, at the height of his power, would have had the audacity to say the quiet part so loudly.

This is a prediction, mind you, something that they 'think' might happen by the year 2030. Can you imagine the world changing that drastically in less than a decade? Well, obviously, they can. Think for a second: what paradigms would have to change in order for the West to accept this new way of life? Americans have never known a world in which private property wasn't a thing. By 2030, the country will have had a 250-year history of private ownership. But despite all of that, the collective 'we' of the world will no longer have the right to own the fruits of our labors? Perhaps that means in order for this prediction to come true, it will require the death of every red-blooded American who opposes their takeover. That is one giant red, white, and blue omelet, but I guess it still fits on the plate of world domination.

Serge Monast was a Canadian writer who published a book called Project Blue Beam in 1994. In his book, Serge laid out a pretty clear vision of how a one world government was to be formed. Although it probably sounded absolutely insane to readers in the early nineties, those of us living through the UAP (unidentified aerial phenomenon) hearings on Capitol Hill might be willing to give his work a second glance. Project Blue Beam claims NASA would deploy a technology that would simulate the apocalypse, or the Second Coming of Christ. It would be giant space lasers, holographic simulations in the sky, or something similar. With assistance from the United Nations, they would set up a new world order that centered around a new religion, of which Serge believed the Antichrist would be the head. Then simulated earthquakes and other phenomena would 'reveal' new fossil and historical records that would upend our previous understanding of mankind and our role in the universe. After that, telepathic technology would be deployed for complete mind control of the population. From there, the orchestrators of the conspiracy will have made over the world in their image and controlled the world through their theocracy. It is a fascinating take on how someone would attempt to upend the world order and establish a new one.

We have seen echoes of Serge's predictions in the past few years—phenomena like UAPs being caught on camera by military pilots, intelligence operatives being stricken with 'Havana syndrome,' and other things bordering between science fiction and the fringe. Although I think that Serge is right about many things, the one thing that I know he is absolutely right about is the scale of imagination it is going to take to change all of the global paradigms at once. It is going to dwarf their previous experiments, like the crisis surrounding COVID, manufactured wars, etc. This is one of the issues that will take preparation. We will have to be ready to sort fact from fiction, not if but when it comes. Because, remember, by 2030, you will own nothing. Maybe it's a prediction. Maybe it's a threat. One thing is for certain: for that to come to pass by 2030, it will take a violent upheaval of our way of life to make it so.

THE U.S. WILL NO LONGER BE THE WORLD'S LEADING SUPERPOWER

If you are an American, when you see this as a leading prediction from any political, social, or cultural source, be it foreign or domestic, how does that make you feel? If you feel threatened, you're normal; if you don't feel threatened, it's either time to recognize what time it is or to declare yourself in the camp of our declared enemy. Again, did they focus group any of these points? I think they just want to piss us off. We are the only country on the list that is called out, by the way. This is very telling, proving the fact that America is the crown jewel of the West. It is the lynchpin that must fall. The whole of Europe could turn to globalism, but the globalists won't truly win unless they drag America down too. Notice as well what they pose as an alternative: a handful of countries will dominate. Once again, America is not necessarily included or primary in that statement. Most of the countries in the European Union are in great financial shape. They don't carry huge deficits like the United States does. Part of the reason they don't go into debt is because they don't pay for their share of NATO defense spending; they let the U.S. put that on the credit card every year. They are very invested in the green initiatives and the global initiatives, but the truth is, they don't foot the bill; we do.

A huge part of the reason that we as a nation are in massive debt is because we fund globalist research and philanthropic endeavors throughout the world. We are the almost exclusive funders of NATO and its many proxy wars. The European Union does not support nearly the regulatory and bureaucratic bodies that our federal government supports. There is a lot of other careless domestic spending too; don't get me wrong. But it seems like whenever a nation needs support or financial relief, it is the U.S. paying the outsized share. It is certainly the expectation of the cowering liberal regimes of Europe that when a nation must defend itself, we, the United States, must go to their aid. When the globalists pull at the world's heartstrings, why is it that we are expected to step up and foot the bill? If an advancing Russia is a threat to anyone, it's a hapless and defenseless Europe! Perhaps it is because the collapse of America at the expense of their globalist endeavors is part of the plan.

When you look at the other Western nations and how stable they are, it should give you pause. Their politicians are just as radically left-leaning and progressive as our American politicians on the left. They deal with the same climate protesters and the same leftist activism. Hell, they are even dealing with their own immigrant and assimilation crises as well. So why is it that we are footing the globalist agenda in America and the rest of the West can't be bothered to spend? The U.S. national debt is the greatest threat to the survival of our nation. We have a mountain of debt that will already take half a century to pay back (and that is if we were going to get aggressive about the payments that we aren't currently making).

If the banks behind the Fed were to call those loans and force the Fed to pay up or foreclose, we would be in a position to negotiate land, treasure, assets, and the rest for settlement. I think that this has been their plan all along: to create such a desperate situation for the American people that they would abandon their freedoms for security. A level of economic collapse has to be in place for Americans to willingly trade their worthless dollars for Rockefeller bucks, or whatever the global digital currency is going to be called. They will have to create such anarchy that the American people will accept their globalist, collectivist model and assent to their progressive political delegates.

Take note of the "lesser resets" that are occurring and will occur in the coming decade. The rioting and COVID are just dry runs, trials to see how far they can push. Once America is subdued, it will be like the other European nations, waiting to take their orders. By 2030, I believe that these people plan to have incorporated many countries into the European Union, including what has become of the U.S. There will be certain countries chosen to be in their 'small handful' that will dominate; this will be based off of historic peace and other terms that will justify their selections. But ultimately, it will be to make good ol' neutral Switzerland the de facto new international capital of the League of Nations (or whatever they decide to call it). As a known safe haven for banking, it will become the home of the banking system, and even local banks will all become subsidiaries of the T.O.D.'s banks; there will just be one 'Bank Corp' from which all money flows via absolutely controlled digital currency.

Davos, where the WEF meets in person every year, will be the ruling seat of the 'experts' who will allow you to function semi-autonomously within your particular realm but be able to swiftly crush any dissenters with top-down power. They will have the ability to slowly choke out any countries that refuse to join their league of nations. None of this is possible as long as America stands. That, my friends, is why they so hope that this 'prediction' comes true. It is the hinge upon which the rest of their plan stands.

So, how do you feel about foreign adversaries telling America that we will no longer be in charge? The fact that we won't be a superpower does not mean that a vacuum will stand in our place. What they are really saying is that they predict they will usurp America as a superpower. So, the logic is simple: the argument that being an 'ignorant supporter' of the WEF and their 'global benevolence' is swiftly dissipating before our eyes. It will soon be the case that if you are an American who supports the WEF, there will only be one Constitutional designation for you: traitor. It's time that we at least start adopting this sentiment, even if we don't start prosecuting right away (the guilty mind you, not the poor people who fell victim to their crimes).

WE WILL PRINT NEW ORGANS

I don't suppose this one is too disagreeable on its face. But again, it does show these people's hubris in thinking they can manipulate the human body and mind as though it is a machine and not a magnificent creation of God. But they don't believe in God; they believe in a more Nietzschean mode of thinking. They believe themselves to be the Übermensch, who will make themselves gods over all reality and rule it in their image. The idea that 'health' is equivalent to the body being in 'stasis' is a fundamental error that modern medicine has been struggling with ever since we decided that synthetic drugs are the solution to every problem. Doctors are almost viewed as mechanics of the machine of the human body; they only need to monitor the gauges to see what is wrong and twist this knob and that to keep the engine in 'stasis.' And if the body gets out of whack due to the fuel you're putting in or the fact that it's being overstressed, you just put some lubricant through it in the form of pills. Taking anti-depressants doesn't cure depression; taking anti-anxiety meds doesn't cure the underlying cause of the anxiety. Taking blood pressure medication doesn't fix the body—and the reason you have high blood pressure. Obesity is not cured by surgery to make your body worse at digesting food.

As long as the body is just a biological meat sac, then all these cures are valid. But many of us had medical conditions that had to be cured by actually healing the body. We had to take our health into our own hands. I am ultimately thankful because I learned the importance of guarding my nutrition, not becoming reliant on crutches and temporary fixes, and reaching a level of healing and flourishing instead of the stasis of survival. To do so, you have to have awe of the human body and the fact that it is one system, not a series of easily divisible systems that can be manipulated purely by specialists with drugs. You cannot centrally plan your healthcare as though your body is a carbon copy machine, nor can you rely on the central planning model of healthcare to give you optimum health. But the WEF thinks they know better about what is good for your health, your wealth, and your way of life. They think they can not only create a healthcare assembly line, but that we will one day separate our consciences completely from our bodies. They call this movement transhumanism. And anyone who wants to divorce the human body from what it means to be human is truly a psycho, whose worldview can only lead to death, misery, and destruction.

The T.O.D.s of the WEF are so divorced from reality that they wholeheartedly adopt transhumanism not only as good but as the next necessary part of human evolution. They hope to upload their brains to the cloud and thus live forever. But separating the essence of consciousness from the human body and the human experience creates a position so foreign, so distant from reality itself, that you almost get back to the point where the T.O.D.s started viewing humanity in the first place. And so here we are, talking about 3-D printed organs, as though it is the most natural and inevitable conclusion we could come to.

YOU WILL EAT LESS MEAT

This is yet one more prediction that they obviously didn't field test. I really do think they put three of the most off-putting ones at the top of their list just to stab us (Americans in particular) in the eye. But then again, they are freaking psychos, so I guess in a backwards way, this all makes sense. Right off the bat, they have told me I will no longer be able to own the fruits of my labors, that they will subjugate me by destroying my country, and now I won't have the choice to eat what I want either. I'm sure people will line up by the throngs for that plan! Many other cultures around the world eat insects for protein; I don't judge or begrudge them. But no first-world country eats bugs as a protein staple. As soon as someone has an alternative choice, they take the meat. In the medieval period, it was a sign of wealth if you could eat meat for every meal of the day. Poor people ate mostly bread and potatoes or whatever else they could scrounge to survive and would save up enough money to buy meat on holidays (or would be granted a feast by the state, which sounds worse somehow). Perhaps it is a signpost for things to come; they are letting us know that we will be such starving wretches under the NWO that we will be happy to eat ze bugs.

Part of the reason is humiliation. I guarantee they don't intend to eat bugs as a regular staple and only have meat as part of an "occasional treat." [7] Another part of it is foisting a culture's taboos on itself; podcaster and author Michael Knowles points this out. If you can make people go against their culture's taboos, you can unseat them from their own culture, identity, and sense of being. That is certainly what the next prediction is about when it comes to culture, assimilation, and breaking down homogenous societies, but we'll get to that in a minute. The main reason they give for not eating meat is "for the good of the environment and our health." [8] The articles about cow farts and farm-produced methane make me crack up every time I see them. If animal farts cause climate crises, then how did the dinosaurs' farts not make our atmosphere look like the atmosphere of Venus? I digress. This is such a contrived position, coming mostly from animal rights activists who are wanting to reduce meat consumption for other reasons. The same people would argue against the consumption of meat on nutritional grounds, but this is a very hard argument to make. It is an argument you can kind of justify in a first-world country with multiple protein alternatives to meat. But just like the bugs, the protein powder gets left by the wayside in the wake of the alternative of meat. The WEF's argument is not the vegan's argument; theirs is not a principled argument but an argument of control and central planning. Coming from, mind you, people who have had seven-course meals their entire lives. All organic, all prepared fresh. They've never been in a grocery store, and if they ate the food in there, they would be just as sick and miserable as the rest of us. This type of demand is obviously a 'rules for thee, but not for me' scenario from people who do not plan to live by the central planning that they deem fit for you and me—the hoi polloi.

A BILLION CLIMATE REFUGEES

Although the framing of this one is around climate change, I believe that they have overplayed their hand with the multiple immigrant crises throughout Europe—all of which are dwarfed by the crisis on our southern border. No North African or Middle Easterner who marched on the European countries by the millions has done so because they were 'displaced by climate change.' The attempt to marry the two is a disingenuous argument. Many people from outside of the West grow up in dictatorships and so-called 'communist governments' (which don't exist, by the way, but we'll get to that later). The freedoms and democratic processes of the West are foreign to them.

Displacing them into cultures foreign from their own is a clever design (which, on its head, would seem counterintuitive to their flourishing after relocation). This one is about guilt-tripping the West, and Americans specifically, for having the gall to reject foreign nationals living in their country. Foreigners who, by virtue of their occupation, ultimately shape the character of the American people, our political discourse, and the subsequent social policy that will come from it.

It is also designed to hold American conservatives' Christian values against them and weaponize the Gospel into a false gospel of endless niceness and tolerance. "No person is illegal" is the worst of the slogans. When a white, fellow citizen, and deranged maniac comes to stab the person holding that sign, I bet their sentiments change. The entire purpose of the waves and waves of people invading the West, and America more specifically, is for destabilization. Destabilization by people who do not share our values of sovereignty, freedom, and personal autonomy. God love the poor people who think they are going to have a better life in America under the globalist regime; it's not their fault. I don't think that the individuals coming here are to blame; it is indeed an invasion of a strange kind. But if economic conditions have been poor for a century in their country, and at any time the young men of those countries could have packed it in and left, why have they waited until now to do so—en masse? Why is there just now a border crisis of biblical proportions on our southern border? You can call me a conspiracy theorist if you'd like; I think I am just seeing the obvious.

Obama would have had a much easier time opening the border; he could have just called his opponents racist like he always did. The mass movement of people of the magnitude that we have seen in the past few years does not and cannot happen organically. It requires mass campaigning, advertising, and, most importantly, the infrastructure of transportation and the logistical support required to move millions of people and keep them hydrated, warm, and fed. The scale can really only be compared to a military operation, and those things don't happen by accident. If conditions are so poor in their country of origin, then there aren't the economic and logistical resources to be had to prepare them for the thousand-mile trek to America. So, who is providing those resources? I doubt you get a complimentary starter pack when you pay the cartels thousands of dollars for so-called "safe passage." If people are so impoverished that they can't be asked to stay another day in the poor working conditions of their country, who is supplying the multi-thousand-dollar cartel fees? It doesn't add up unless there are forces at play providing massive outside help.

People who grow up under despotic regimes and without personal freedoms tend to be much more obedient to the regime in power, rely upon it for guidance, and seek out the methodology of compliance. Once again, it is not their fault; it's how you survive something like the Soviet black Marias. Yeonmi Park, who defected from North Korea, speaks about how, when she first came to America, she had to train her brain to think functionally through her day and her decisions. The rational, self-autonomous decision-making part of the brain had been turned off as a means for survival under the Kim regime. The idea of self-directing your life and even personal moral responsibility is deeply diminished in people who live under totalitarianism, which is based on atheistic moral relativism. That is not my opinion; it is simply a fact. The current religious demographics of East and West Germans will attest to this fact. When you mix millions of those people into Western democracies in high enough concentrations that they can create 'micro-cultures' that do not have to assimilate into the broader culture they are now in, you have created a situation where the invaded country has to 'meet in the middle' on the invader's socio-political demands. We now have to listen to two raging anti-Semites in Congress make excuses for Islamic terrorism because of this strategy.

It is the same tactic that progressives have used in politics here in America. Ostensibly, there is a right and a left political party in this country, yet over the past sixty years, the country has slowly shifted on the spectrum to the left. This same tactic is meant to destabilize the arguments for a constitutional republic and personal freedom in the birthplace of a constitutional republic and personal freedom. Once the economy is destabilized to the point of chaos, there will be millions of "loyal subjects," who are nothing more than citizen interlopers, there to beg the WEF to step in and make their situation better. It is said that only three percent of the American population actually took up arms in the Revolutionary War. Imagine how the outcome of the war might have been different if the British crown had shipped in millions of, say, Indian migrants from their colony a world away. Promising them, of course, care and support via the crown. Would the three percent have been able to stave off the British and their migrant class? Who is to say? We, on the other hand, will have to answer that question soon, for just such a conflict is being brought to our doorstep.

POLLUTERS WILL PAY

I think it should be a matter of international law that fossil fuel use should be banned for everyone who protests the use of fossil fuels. If they are truly on the moral high ground, they would get off the evil dirty fossil fuel grid, walk everywhere, and only consume food and goods that are made without leaving behind the 'carbon footprint.' But, of course, they will not; it's all a complete and total sham. These activists are going to fly to their stunts, get in the rental car and drive, stay in a hotel, get their Starbucks in a plastic cup, and roll into their stunt at the crack of noon. Just to block a roadway, back up traffic, and cause even more pollution! It is so disgusting, and it is cultish. The vast majority of people do see this clearly; we want to advocate for a cleaner planet and better renewable systems. That is quite different from the sadistic person who wants to end fossil fuels today. That is the ultimate "you have to crack a few eggs to make an omelet" position. If those people got their way, billions would die in the next calendar year due to starvation, heat, and cold (which would kill most). It would affect developing countries the most. But they couldn't stop fossil fuels throughout the world; ultimately, they are just asking America to put itself back two hundred years and be in a position to be overcome by its enemies.

Therein lies the central position of the WEF. This hysteria set around the climate crisis is itself the existential threat to humanity. But damn, is it good for business! Those T.O.D.s are heavily invested in renewables and have convinced most Western governments to further subsidize them. By now, it should be obvious as to why. If they could control production and the grid, they could starve out anyone who opposed them, and they would not have to share that power with the dominant forces in energy that are responsible for powering the world. All that aside, one crucial question remains: who are the 'polluters' going to have to pay? Is there a jar somewhere that the WEF throws a dollar in every time they jet set around the world? If the climate was truly in crisis, would over a hundred dignitaries from around the world fly into Davos every year for the summit? A Zoom call would work just as well. But then the after-hours orgies might get really weird … And besides that, you wouldn't want all the Davos hookers to be out of a job, would you?

GOING TO MARS

Apart from the organ printing one, I suppose this was the most inspirational and innocent one. I find this one particularly funny because 'colonizing Mars' might just become their euphemistic expression for where the political dissidents have disappeared to. I don't find this one inherently repulsive; it's just foolish. Again, they are relying on the crutch of scientific advancement here—the idea that science would make a path to keeping people healthy in space. Then the 'what-if?' of maybe finding alien life. NASA has calculated on the Mars mission that it would take seven months for a shuttle to get there. Even then, it will be a lot like the moon: barren, mostly dust and rock, and radiation exposure due to the lack of electromagnetism. It's a cool concept. But I think ultimately, they are making a prediction that NASA or someone will have the technology and ability to go to Mars, and framing it in the 'you may be getting ready to go' is just wishful thinking that they could colonize it. Why not own Mars too?

However, as part of their 2030 plan, I think that Serge Monast was onto something. If alien contact were made, it would be a world-altering event. But if the illusion of alien contact were made, it would be the most convenient for the powers that be.

First of all, because the WEF is a global network that pulls so many strings of power, their goal of world dominance is an 'alien' concept in the fact that we have never seen anything like this before. The literal act of aliens taking over the planet and the WEF taking over the planet would be, in essence, the same mechanism. But the simulation of it being aliens would create an atmosphere of the world coming together to fight an existential threat and break down every former political paradigm. It would upend many different religious ideologies and certainly many socio-cultural ideologies. It would be a catalyst for rethinking everything we know about the world and our place in it. Instead of actual contact, the illusion grants the WEF the power to control the narrative of how the world could be made new. I am not making any predictions of my own, but I think that we are deluding ourselves if we think that they wouldn't try to orchestrate the appearance and use it to their own devices. Be careful of what we see in the coming years about UAPs and aliens. AI and many other technologies that were once science fiction are blurring the lines between our ability to see fact from fiction, even when it is right before our eyes. We could easily find ourselves in a maelstrom of voices, sounds, sentiments, fears, and thoughts, all spiraling out of control—and all on purpose.

WESTERN VALUES AT A BREAKING POINT

This last one, I think, is the darkest and most veiled threat; they are wanting to split the baby here and keep the liberal stuff and throw out the Christian stuff. They want to pretend to have moral high ground and embody the values of the West, when in reality they are just trying to preserve their liberal values despite—and to spite—Western values. Western values are Christian values, plain and simple. The T.O.D.s values are based on liberalism and relativism and are therefore opposed to Christian values. They want to say that the liberalism part is the 'enlightened' part, and that's the part that brought about everything beautiful and wonderful about the West. Culminating in their vision of 'democratic socialism,' which hasn't been implemented yet, has never existed, can't exist, but they just know it's oh so good. What they want to say is that populism, conservatism, patriotism, and nationalism are all evil, terrible, no-good things that caused all the brutality of the West. These aren't the real Western values that we ought to defend, like globalism, liberalism, and democratic socialism. These are the real Western values, and as long as we are pretending our Christian roots ought to be defended, we are defending a bad premise and deserve to be broken off from polite society. In relativistic fashion, it is the same tactic that The Party uses in Orwell's 1984. Oceania had always been at war with Eurasia, didn't you know? The WEF and their political machine will tell a similar story about the 'pre-Reset' age. The evil people ruled our society in the time before history; they had oppressed and destroyed you, see? They were terrible, no-good people who worshipped a sky fairy, had a draconian legal system, and did not provide for humanity the way that we do now. You're safe now! You're cared for now in the post-reset age. You have the metaverse, a pod, and a locust hot pocket! Who would ever want to leave? Religion will be gone; the party's orthodoxy will become both political science and theological doctrine. Every record will be falsified, and every telling of history will be altered to tell a tale of the evils of the things that made Western civilization the greatest bastion of human flourishing that the world has ever known. But, you see, it will all be okay. The winners write the history books; and now the rightful winners will finally be able to get the retelling right.

IN CONCLUSION

We are going to go into these topics much more in Part II, which will focus on the political aspect of each of these predictions. For now, I want to focus on the head of the snake, what is intended by the WEF, and just how they might try to put their finger on the scales to make their 'predictions' into 'foregone conclusions.' If you are a futurist and an optimist, you will think that the overall tenor of these predictions is good. But don't be fooled; these aren't futuristic predictions of the triumph of man over the universe; they are just the triumph of certain men over the rest of us. They are the promises of cynics who believe it is their right to make these predictions a reality and then rule over the outcome. It is the pre-loading of expectations for a NWO. Great change is coming, and many things that once were will be no more. And still, many things that never were will come to pass. For instance ...

You can no longer be trusted to own anything—not even your home, your production, your creativity, or the fruit of your labor. You will not be devoted to family and community but to the central planning office, which will own everything. Countries that once led the world will be reduced to members of a league of nations whose purpose is to serve the central planning office. Instead of building national identity and culture, the regional delegations are to promote global collective unity. No country or people will ever be able to challenge the central regime, and they will pay dearly for going against the prevailing orthodoxy of the party. If you play nicely, and follow the central party's rules, you will be eligible for the centrally planned food and healthcare programs. When these programs inevitably fail your health and well-being, you will be further reliant on the party's good graces to save you from their failed system. If your social credit score is worthy enough, they will allow their technology to be used to replace your failing body parts. The centrally planned food system will be focused on efficiency, of course, and it is much cheaper and easier to feed you insects than employing traditional farming methods. As such, you will eat almost exclusively highly processed, homogenous foods with "protein alternatives" in them. You will not be allowed to own animals, farm for yourself, or provide yourself with alternatives. You will eat ze bugs for the good of your health, meaning if you want to remain in the good graces of the party, maintain an appropriate social credit score, and not be sent off to "colonize Mars." If you remain in the good graces of the party, they will allow you to have a semblance of societal normalcy.

However, if you ever become a cohesive enough unit to stand united, your community will be inundated by throngs of people from the other side of the globe, or you will be shipped off to some far-flung place to cause the same upheaval. You will use the energy that the party provides, no matter how unreliable it is or how little you are provided with. There will be a price to pay for your disobedience, or if you have the audacity to use alternatives. Lastly, the party will be deploying double speak to ensure that they are the heroes upholding "Western values." By which they mean liberalism and moral relativism—the values that usurped Western values. But you will be sent off to "colonize Mars" for pointing this out. History will be rewritten so that party orthodoxy has always been the source of success, truth, beauty, and goodness in the civilized world, and every bad thing will be attributed to the evil Christians, Greek philosophers, and the canon of classic Western literature who have always been the interlopers seeking to undermine peace, prosperity, and human flourishing. Only approved texts will be read, only approved speech will be spoken, and only approved social norms will be practiced. This will be the position of the party, and you will hold no opposing position unless you want to end up in a shallow grave—I mean—becoming a space explorer. By order of the Experts™ of Central Planning, this edict shall be enforced by the League of Nations this day, the first day of the month of Morgan, in the year of our Marx 1. This decree shall be read aloud by the regional delegates, and the international peacekeeping force shall hereby enforce it for the good of society and the prosperity of the people. Hear ye, hear ye!

PART II

POLITICS IS DOWNSTREAM OF CULTURE. . .

(YOU KNOW, EXCEPT WHEN IT'S NOT)

CHAPTER 6

The Soul of America

"Politics is downstream of culture" is a quote often attributed to Andrew Breitbart. It is true in so many ways, but it is not a truism. That is to say, it is not always true that every aspect of political action and discourse is always downstream of culture. I believe that it is true in the sense that the progressives have gone on their slow, century-long march through the institutions, and now that they have control of the culture, we are sliding left as a result. But I think it is also true in the sense that highly cultured, reverent, and God-fearing men created an early colonial American culture that produced the greatest government ever to exist in the history of the world. We all know America is a terrible, awful, and rotten place. It's the worst government in the world! Except for all of the others, of course. There is something uniquely special about America that it does not have in common with any other nation. Of even the great powers of Europe, they were all monarchies that were founded on a family name. Regions, geographies, and peoples have all made distinct nations. But no nation before America ever founded itself as a nation subservient to, and in allegiance with, God's law. Which means that to be a good American, you must do the same.

Many, many world leaders of antiquity called upon the name of God, took patron saints for their countries, and bore the name Christian. But America is the only country in the world to have enshrined God's omnipotence in their charter. Sorry if that makes your head explode or if you're too cool for religion. If you do not believe that you were created by a Creator, you cannot hold life, liberty, and the pursuit of happiness as 'self-evident' truths. They are only self-evident in the dignity of man, which exists because we are created in the image and likeness of GOD. This is not to say that you can't be an American atheist, because we certainly have our fair share of those. It does mean, however, that the American framework only works in a certain context that necessitates that there is a God, and the president ain't him. There are many things that make America unique, but this one principle stands alone as the most important one for our time. Because the soul of America is being forced into an ideological war with the global communist movement, which is now here in America in full force and striving to completely take over the government.

In 1979, Pope John Paul II was given permission by the U.S.S.R. to return to his native land of Poland to see his people. Poland fell on the eastern side of the Iron Curtain, and they lived under the tutelage of Russia's communism. So many Poles flocked to see JPII that Masses and gatherings all had to be held outdoors; there was not a church in Poland that could fit the crowds. During one such open-air Mass, the people of Poland began chanting a simple slogan. "We want God! We want God!" It exposed the situation in Poland and, indeed, the entire Communist regime for the Godless, debased tyrants that they were. As we wrestle through this postmodern-liberal, neo-progressive moment today, we as a nation will have to again find a longing for the God whom our Founders so trusted in. Without that, the American experiment will collapse; the government may survive—the names, titles, dignitary positions, and the rest of it. But if we abandon God, we will have turned our backs so fundamentally on the country's formation that we could not, in good conscience, pretend that the old and the new are one and the same.

The Declaration of Independence is our founding charter. There is one main philosophical argument that flows throughout the document, and it is the one and only basic American promise. The Declaration did not promise that America would create a perfect government, or even a government at all, for that matter. Nor did the Declaration promise Americans prosperity, opportunity, or even guarantee us our rights. The Declaration of Independence tells us that to be good Americans, we must believe in a singular God who is the source and summit of all things. We must believe that this same God endows us with our dignity, our rights, and our reason, and no power on Earth can claim the right to usurp those divine gifts.

The bold claim of America is that the sons of God who live by his law are free men who deserve every right and privilege that comes with this sonship; that men are free and deserve to live in that freedom that only God and his law can give. And a government that dares to usurp the God-given rights of man deserves to be justly rebelled against and, if possible, overthrown. This principle applies to all earthly powers, including the government that America formed in 1789. The promise of America is that we are free men, and we will do the hard, humble task of establishing that freedom in our lands. This is the ultimate duty that this promise requires: that allegiance to God and his law come first. God first, so that our family and the formation of future Americans will naturally flow second. All of this, so that an America worthy of her name and God's Providence will never be erased from the face of the earth. God, family, country. Where have I heard that before?

"Of more worth is one honest man to society, and in the sight of God, than all the crowned ruffians that ever lived."[8]

—Thomas Paine, from *Common Sense*

THE BRIEF DEFENSE OF AMERICA'S PROMISE:

There is a singular force behind the universe, that is the Creator of all things visible and invisible; as such this Creator is the supreme authority of the universe, higher than any ruler or principality. This Creator has a unique relatability to each one of us, because we are created in its image. As such, we are capable of seeing this force's intelligibility in the world it created, and most importantly, in ourselves. We are endowed by this Creator with unalienable rights, among those life, liberty, and the pursuit of happiness. This Creator, not the powers of men, is the source of both our reason and our rights, which cannot be usurped by governments instituted among men.

In response to these gifts endowed by The Creator, we owe this supreme authority our allegiance, and our sacred honor above all earthly rulers and principalities. This Creator is the just judge of us all, and by his justice should we, in turn, rule. That is, when governments are instituted among men, they must be:

1. Instituted by the powers of reason endowed to us by The Creator, and
2. Our reason must always be directed toward preserving the rights and dignity with which we are endowed.

The only legitimate government instituted among men is one that accords to this Natural Law, a law that flows from our human reason serving the just end of protecting the human rights with which we are endowed. It is only by this means that we preserve the right ordered dignity, which humans are owed by their fellow man; a dignity given by virtue of their divine inheritance. This is the proper ordering of man while on Earth, a disposition which must precede all other human relationships.

This right-ordered relationship with the Creator, and embracing the moral demands therein, is the preeminent disposition from which human relationships and agreements must proceed. It is out of this lens that the Founders saw the world, and as such, this is the lens by which anyone hoping to understand the American system must also look. Failing to do so will create not just errors in our form of government but also errors in our view of human dignity, the nature of our rights and their source, and the erosion of the intellectual and spiritual character of our entire society. If this decline is given long enough, the nation will become corrupt and cease to know the favor and Providence of the Creator. What is left ruling over this nation will be nothing more than a corrupt government worthy of being justly overthrown itself.

THE LONGER DEFENSE OF AMERICA'S PROMISE:

This first principle, that God endows us with rights, is the foundational principle upon which our government was founded. Without this principle, the entire American form of government breaks down. If there is no God, there is no human dignity. Without God, all moral arguments fall apart or are at best a social construct no more authoritative than your opinion on which sandwich is superior. It is an amazing indictment of where we are as a country that this statement is controversial. Not even Thomas Paine, the man the moderns love to hold up as the Founding atheist, would have argued against this position. In his most famous work, *Common Sense*, Paine quotes Scripture many times. He invokes the name of God over ten times. His problem with invoking God did not come from disbelief; his main problem centered around the fact that we could not rest on our laurels when it came to God's omnipotence and the rights with which we are endowed. He saw that there was more to the equation and that these rights needed to be enshrined in human institutions if they were to prevail.

Common Sense was a radical work in its time and remains a controversial work today. It was written for a Christian audience, written by a philosopher, and it laid out a political vision for a right-ordered government. Paine was a staunch anti-monarchist; he cited the abuses the Americans were experiencing at the hands of the British King as nothing more than the rational and inevitable outcome of this form of government. He was also not naïve; he did not try to make the case that man can live in peaceful anarchy, perfectly binding himself to the laws of nature and nature's God. Governments must be instituted among men; so, the real question for Paine was: what does a right-ordered, just, and lasting form of government look like? In perhaps one of the most well-known verses of Common Sense, Paine makes the following case:

> *"But where, say some, is the King of America? I'll tell you, friend, he reigns above, and doth not make havoc of mankind like the Royal Brute of Great Britain. Yet that we may not appear to be defective even*

> *in earthly honors, let a day be solemnly set apart for proclaiming the charter; let it be brought forth placed on the divine law, the word of God. Let a crown be placed thereon, by which the world may know, that so far as we approve of monarchy, that in America THE LAW IS KING. For as in absolute governments the King is law, so in free countries the law ought to be King; and there ought to be no other. But lest any ill use should afterwards arise, let the crown at the conclusion of the ceremony be demolished, and scattered among the people whose right it is."*[9]

Methinks the atheist doth protest too much. What Paine articulates is clear: the King of America is almighty God. America should be a nation not of men but of laws, and those laws must derive from the source of justice; namely, America's laws would derive from God's law. This passage is an elegant one that articulates a vision of founding a government in a hierarchy of ideas. That a Constitution would be the source of our government, and that Constitution's foundation was not mere philosophy or human reason. Rather, this Constitution would derive its power to govern us because the Constitution itself was founded on God's law, and the mind of man must bend to the will of God in his reason, his political philosophy, and his governance. I love the coronation imagery that Paine eloquently speaks of. In his mind's eye, he envisions a royal and solemn celebration, not unlike the ceremony that Moses performs, at God's direction, to make the people of Israel God's chosen people. Paine sees the people founding this government as a sort of chosen people among the nations, crowning their Constitution. Not because their Constitution is a product of man and his triumph over God, but precisely the opposite. The Constitution is crowned because it embodies the law of America's King, who reigns in Heaven. Oh, how I wish that on July Fourth we performed this coronation as a ritual for our country! That in a solemn location the Bible was placed in a position of honor.

As Paine describes, the Constitution is placed upon the Word of God, symbolizing the harmony of the two in creed. Then, as a symbol of our assent to both sets of laws, which should forever remain inseparable, we place the crown of America's King. Perhaps even Paine envisioned a continuation of the ceremony where the Constitution was read aloud to the people, much like Moses read the law aloud to the people in Exodus. In a similar way, the people would all pledge their faithful allegiance. It might end with water from a sacred American source being sprinkled on the people to symbolize the freedom with which we walk by, embracing such a form of government (not unlike the blood of the sacrifice being sprinkled on the Israelites). I don't mean to sound cultish or make false comparisons; I only mean to say that if we take Thomas Paine's words seriously and our laws derive from those of Almighty God, it would be a beautiful ceremony and not sacrilege.

Whether or not Paine had more to elaborate on the subject, the coronation of the Constitution is not the end of the ceremony he envisioned. Ultimately, the crown would be removed. I think that this is beautiful in its own way for many reasons. First, it is because the Constitution is a working document; it is not at leisure to sit upon its throne all day, idly giving edicts and decrees. A nation of laws has things to arbitrate and justice to seek. The second part of this is that the crown is smashed and distributed among the people. The power of God is diffused into all of us; the power of justice and allegiance to God's law is both our right and our responsibility. Because God is America's King and we are his children, we are therefore all princes of both our Father's Heavenly realm and the principalities of ourselves, our families, our communities, and our nation.

We share in the process of making a worthy self, capable of being held as a worthy people, who can in turn make a government worthy of being crowned with the Providence and blessings of God. I can imagine Americans throughout this country making a crown cake on the Fourth of July, crowning their copy of the Constitution, which rests upon their Bible, and then distributing the crown cake to their family and all those in attendance. One final note on my talk of ritual and ceremony. If you are a God-fearing person and you find yourself offended, you have missed the point entirely. If we are God's children, and if we are a free nation because we are a nation of just laws, and if those laws are in accordance with God's law, then we have every right to vaunt our Constitution in this way, and God will certainly not condemn us for it.

An apocryphal story has arisen that Paine denied well-wishers and friends on his deathbed, particularly to keep them from trying to evangelize him in his hour of death. I think that Paine, not unlike Jefferson, struggled with what they perceived to be the more superstitious parts of Christianity. After all, Jefferson took it upon himself to edit the New Testament to make it more palatable to himself. The other religious work that he wrote was "The Philosophy of Jesus of Nazareth." Regardless of their individual religious persuasions, it is clear that both Jefferson and Paine held the existence of God to be a foundational first principle. The fact that this is a deeply controversial topic in modern American politics is proof that we have not been doing such a good job lately of prioritizing God, family, and country.

The progressives have been working very hard to make sure that all three metrics are being both socially and politically attacked. Perhaps an overused quote from John Adams is that "Our Constitution was made only for a moral and religious people. It is wholly inadequate to the government of any other."[10] Overused though it may be, if the modern state of American faith and governance is not proof of Adams' prophecy, I don't know what is.

HOW AMERICA'S KING CAME TO RULE OVER AMERICA

Humans are not inherently inclined toward good, nor are they inherently inclined toward evil. The only thing that can be said definitively about human beings is that they are immensely capable. In their capacity, they are met with the intricacies and messiness of life and the opportunity to act in good ways and in evil ways. You probably didn't disagree with this statement at all, and in your complacent agreement, you assented to a moral authority that reigns over human beings. And you also passively accepted the fact that human life is capable of being 'messy' in a moral and circumstantial sense—something we don't normally attribute to the busy lives of squirrels. We don't talk about the moral culpability of animals or hold murder trials for carnivores. If a mother wolf abandons her cub, she is not judged, while a human infant left in a dumpster to die is a moral outrage (or was once considered so by our forebearers).

The idea that an animal and a human can perform the same act, and yet there is a gravity to the human's actions, is a profound reality of the human condition. A reality that must be dealt with—without the privilege of knowing where this sentiment comes from, why it is intrinsic to the human condition, and why it persistently asserts itself in our reality. Still, with no sense of right or wrong, there is no human relationship, no civility, no society, and no culture. It matters that good is perpetuated in society and evil curtailed. To that end, that is why it matters what your neighbor thinks is right and wrong, and what you collectively choose to teach your children about what is right and what is wrong. There has been a cohesive ethic throughout Western civilization that has advanced social progress in Europe and America, where it has stagnated elsewhere. There is a specific reason why Dallas is different from Baghdad. The populations of both greater metropolitan areas are very similar. So why are there courthouses in one and stoning pits in the other? Why is there equality and justice for all in one and crucified homosexuals in the other? There is a reason that the West enjoys due process, civility, and relative peace more than the rest of the world.

Christianity has dragged Western civilization kicking and screaming into the modern world in which we live. Despite itself, Western civilization's tumultuous relationship with Christianity has transformed it into a more just, more tolerant, and fairer society than most of its international counterparts. The fact that the Christians were willing to fight for philosophic principles like universal human dignity and God as the arbiter of objective justice was fundamental to making Western civilization more egalitarian and more just. Christians fought for the rights of the individual while still recognizing the responsibilities that the individual still owed to society. Striking the right balance between solidarity and subsidiarity is paramount in the conversation about freedom and liberty. Western civilization became the prevailing world culture not because it was special in any way, but because Christianity has permeated it for two millennia. The people of Britain weren't superior humans; but they did create superior institutions that thwarted the baser wills of mankind. What could explain such a phenomenon?

King John did not voluntarily sign the Magna Carta. This is the document that the British point to (and rightly so) as a huge innovation and a giant contribution that Britain gave to the world. And yet, why was it signed? I doubt the oppressed oligarchy had pure benevolence and the dignity of their underlings in mind when they forced King John's hand. Magna Carta (1215) was signed not because a benevolent king from a superior people mysteriously rose above the human fray and thwarted history. It was signed because an oppressive king (the norm of history, the world, and the human condition) was held to account by the Christian principle of basic human dignity. He was forced to assent to the objective cultural norm of Christ as the High King, the Lord of us all, and that even he was subject to Christ in his earthly rule. Christianity forced even the rulers of the Western world to succumb to morality in their governance.

This is not a time to be offended; I realize that many humanist movements have domesticated Western civilization as well. Even if you are a humanist, an agnostic, an atheist, or a downright virulent anti-Christian, the historical record is very clear; I am not making some flippant point and puffing up my own religious beliefs. It also goes without saying that many people have abused the power of Christianity to their own selfish ends, and that corruption continues even today. Western history is fraught with leaders who did what every ruler had done before them: become drunk with power, manipulate their position, and exact their own relative laws and standards on a helpless populace. If there is anything that sets Western civilization apart from the rest of the world, it is the slow march of Christian morality through its ranks.

Author and podcaster Andrew Klavan makes a great analogy of Christianity being like radiation; it permeates and radiates everything that it comes into contact with, so that the thing affected is simultaneously still the same yet radically transformed. The idea that human dignity, subsidiarity and solidarity, liberty, responsibility, and freedom would all be part of the cultural and political process sprang from the marriage of Western society and Christianity. Humanity has made true progress in these philosophies and principles, even though they have been constantly abandoned in every age by every single one of us. In every power dynamic, no matter how big or small, when we choose to serve ourselves at the expense of justice, we abandon these principles for the much easier, and often more lucrative, ways of barbarism. It takes a fortified cultural norm and a politic fortified by morality to have a just society. What we have in America today is not the status quo of human interaction on any scale. As we lose belief in these morals and principles, we will continue to grow further away from those that have created our security and sense of normalcy in our civilized world.

People often attack the defenders of Western civilization. I want to clarify that I am defending Christianity in its correct philosophical beliefs. I am not attempting to defend or judge every saint or charlatan throughout history who adopted the name Christian. Nor does any real Christian deny the atrocities that (self-identified) Christians and Christian institutions have committed over the centuries. But the crime itself proves the rule that Christianity ought to be good, and a bad Christian is a uniquely bad person for his badness (even more so than an equally bad agnostic or atheist). The failure of the sinner cannot exist without the standard set by a religion that recognizes sin; there is no disconnect between an evil man and his evil actions.

Many megachurches and protestant denominations today have gone off the deep end, preaching bad Gospel and bad philosophy; no good Christian would defend them. A distinction between what is being defended must be made; otherwise, we fall into the intellectually weak and philosophically degenerate world of the New Atheists. And while we are on distinctions, let's clarify: I am not defending Western civilization. I will hold and defend its good examples, and I will criticize its bad examples. To point out the superiority of Western institutions is not to compare their perfection to everyone else's imperfections and failures. Nor is it to say that Western civilization triumphed of its own accord. It has succeeded despite itself, even after the murders of Socrates and Jesus. No one expects North Korea to reform its social laws, and why would they? It is only the West that is held in contempt for its failings, because we all accept the premise that Western societies ought to be good, fair, and just. That is why the rest of the world flocks to Western countries, and the people who feign their terror over the West's failings refuse to leave.

Society will always pull toward relativism, and in this way, we can appreciate the total depravity argument of the Calvinists. Now, when it comes to total depravity, Calvin is spot on about twenty-first-century Hollywood. However, I don't know how right he was about the broader population. In our age, we find ourselves particularly far from classical philosophy and very deep in the weeds of relativism. And it shows. Modernity, in its prevailing relativism, has an almost fearful relationship to moral rigor. The shrieking rejection of it as religious lunacy is an indication enough that many modern ideologies fly contrary to those that grounded us in the past.

I digress; let's focus back on the topic at hand. When history doesn't repeat itself, it certainly rhymes, and that is due to the fact that history is the story of people. People are capable of great feats, both good and evil, and the greater the figure, oftentimes, the higher their highs and the lower their lows. Although the tolerance level varies greatly from person to person, all people have their breaking point—the point where they will do something that might sting the moral conscience in order to achieve something they perceive as a greater good. We all hope that, like the martyrs, our breaking point is just beyond death. But we can't be sure what allure might come our way. Those perceived greater goods could be power, money, security, etc., but oftentimes it is not a moral good in and of itself that one compromises their morals over.

If you perceive the world through the lens that people are inherently good, you will inevitably perceive the world wrongly. Conversely, I think you deprive humanity of their ability to direct their own goodness when you perceive people to be inherently evil. Either premise will inevitably leave you unable to judge history, see people for who they are, and hope for a society worth having. If people were inherently good, there would be no wrong in the world. As the famous line from James Madison goes, "If men were angels, no government would be necessary."[11] Since we are clearly not angels (nor are we ruled by them), it would seem that we must believe that people are inherently evil. Although you will be shocked less in life and be disappointed less often if you take this approach, if you follow this premise to its logical conclusions, you will find that no good can come out of the world. Which we also know is untrue.

I think the proper response is to take a measured approach and to recognize that this is not an either-or question. It is a question of formation, circumstance, and action. Then it is a question of how those actions formed the course of history; what do they tell us about the moral ethic of people and the moral fiber of their societies? Humans, not understanding their true nature, tend toward weaker positions. People too often choose safety over freedom, the semblance of peace over the work of reconciliation, and the baser desires of wealth and power over true inner peace and happiness (which can only truly come through discipline and moral rigor).

We certainly know that we would rather live in a good society than a debased one, but our debased attachments often put that good society just out of reach. It takes work to have good things and to make sure that the good things remain vaunted in society. Christianity and Western classical philosophy have been the mechanisms by which the West could course correct its brokenness to where it is today. If we abandon the study of truth, goodness, and moral virtue that leads us to the deepest desires of our hearts, we will be led astray by relativism and the utopian visions that can be conjured under its spell. Form yourself into what is good in order to prepare yourself for the circumstances of life. Even if you sometimes fail, you will still succeed more times than not and move toward an ever-better version of yourself. That has been the simple 'ask' of Christianity over the centuries, which has borne out in Christian societies the progress and peace that we see in the West. More than any other force in the world, Christianity produced American society. The chaos that we see in our political discourse and between our fellow Americans is proof that we are abandoning the moral demands necessary for the American system to function properly.

THE RIGHTS OF THE SONS OF THE KING

The Declaration of Independence tells us that we are "Endowed by our Creator with certain inalienable rights, among these Life, Liberty, and the Pursuit of Happiness."[12] These are the foundational premises upon which we argue for the rights in the Bill of Rights of the Constitution. Whenever you hear a political pundit or a lawyer dismiss the Declaration of Independence out of hand because 'it is not a legal document,' be prepared for an ad hoc argument that is tailored to make whatever convenient and relativistic point that they are trying to make. Legalism, as a practice to reach convenient ends rather than uphold the dignity and integrity of the legal system, has sadly become the status quo. But it is absurd to think that the Bill of Rights can exist in a society that doesn't respect the fundamental rights in the Declaration.

We live in an absurd moment, however, which perfectly illustrates this point. It is no coincidence that half the country, which is secular and led by Godless progressive communists, wants to make the government the arbiter of truth and the grantor of rights. It is simply the logical conclusion of thinking that God's Providence is simply a happy accident and will always remain in a country that has abandoned God and his law.

The great scientist Isaac Newton once penned in a letter that "If I have seen further it is by standing on the shoulders of giants."[13]

Our country is much the same way, but each generation must be a pillar that takes America upward and onward in pursuit of America's promises. We are at an event horizon where we must either add to the pillar or pretend that we can fly away without consequence. If we leave the foundation behind, we will no longer be able to rely on its strength and stability to keep us free. If we leap from the pillar we are on, we will not soar with the eagles in some utopian vision. We will discover just how far we will fall when we abandon God and his law. We will fall into the alternative, which is worldly relativism, where the person with the biggest stick and the loudest mouth wins. There are no inherent rights of man in the tyrant's world because it is easier to dominate you in a world where he grants none to you. We need to understand our rights, where they come from, and what responsibilities are required to keep them.

The promise of America must first be upheld if we are to be worthy of our rights. That promise is to have allegiance to God and his law above all else. If you keep that promise, then you are a son of God. You are the son of the King of America, and being the son of the King has its privileges. Those privileges come with the duty and responsibility to uphold such a kingship. The unique ability of all Americans to be allied with God and therefore all sons of the King is the source of our equality. We, as Americans, have a royal post to create a government worthy of ruling over the King's land. That government should recognize the rights of man as given by God and not usurpable by earthly powers. This government would clearly allow people to speak openly and truthfully, allow the freedom to assemble and ask the government to fix problems (that it can fix), and be able to hold it accountable in the case of overreach. And it would not inhibit a citizen's expression of religion; religion being clearly contextually defined as a monotheistic faith tradition that can recognize the supreme Godhead as America's King. Again, it shouldn't be a controversial topic, but Satanism should not be covered as a 'religion' by the First Amendment, and to pretend that this was in any way the Founders intention is patently absurd.

But this government would be so confident in its people to hold true to the Promise of America that it would go much, much further. The First Amendment covers all the rights afforded to free men as a birthright by their Creator. Although God leaves us this inheritance, it is up to us to hold true to it. This government would understand that it is up to individuals to defend their rights if someone came looking to take them. It is up to individuals to understand their rights so that they may find them important enough to defend themselves. Self-defense of your rights against anyone who would try to take them from you is as fundamental as the rights themselves.

It is a necessary right of free men, if they are to be truly free, to keep and bear arms when necessary. If you do not have a right to self-defense, you don't truly have any other right, for it is merely a statement of freedom without the gall to make it so. This government would enshrine such a right so that it could ensure that no power on earth could ever truly defeat the promise of America. In short, the government would not be God; it would be the only thing that it could be: Just. Giving each what they are due and what they are owed according to their ability to keep the promise of America.

Justice is a word that only makes sense if there is a standard by which to judge it. The word is inexorably linked to judgment and, therefore, a standard. That is why justice is often depicted in the image of the blind-folded Lady Justice, who holds the 'scales of justice' in one hand. The blindfold captures the fact that justice must be unprejudiced. This does not mean that justice must be unbiased by morals, rules, or laws. It means that judges cannot be personally invested in the outcome of the decision; they must truly be dispassionate about the outcome to allow true justice to prevail. The scale is a two-fold depiction: 1. that human affairs are highly complicated, no one is perfect or perfectly innocent, and that in most deliberations on justice there is culpability from both factions. But 2. And more importantly, the scale symbolizes the ultimate standard upon which human behavior can be judged; it tilts one way or the other. And if it hangs in perfect balance, there is nothing for Lady Justice to judge.

Perhaps it escapes the notice of most, but Lady Justice holds something else in her other hand: a sword. This is perhaps the most intriguing part of this depiction. It means that justice is not merely a decision-making exercise. It means that the decision rendered in justice demands something of the unjust and their injustices. More than speaking to the rights or duties of the state, I think that this speaks far more to the depths of the human heart. Whether we are three or ninety-three, when we encounter injustice, there is a welling in the heart that cannot be ignored. Whether we throw a tantrum like a three-year-old or have a more metered response in our maturity, it is the same intrinsic response. It is a rational response to want to put things right, even if rationality gets easily blurred by calamitous emotions. A sense of personal justice is so intrinsic to the person that it becomes intrinsic to the society in which that person lives. Which brings us to the state. The state, in its duties of executing the deep human desire for justice, wields the sword.

Hammurabi's Code, often touted as one of the earliest legal tomes, attempted to set just laws for all of Babylon. And by logical extension, we needed to set just punishments that the government would oversee. I suppose in a perfect world where men were angels, we'd have no need for government, and we would be able to exact justice in our daily lives. Perhaps our modern society, corrupt and through the looking glass, is a good example of why you don't want a government holding the reins of justice. There must be a higher standard still. Often, human beings, when taking justice into their own hands, allow their wrath to consume them. This is how the Hatfields and McCoys come to hate each other and blame each other for the slew of injustices that they are both responsible for. But humans can also wield forgiveness and even mercy, if they so choose. To take more than you are due is a temptation, and if you fall for it, you are unjust. Those who will allow you to make it right aren't just; they are something higher still. But the state is not a human being that you can look into your eyes and have compassion for you. It can only wield the sword. That fact, along with the fact that relative governments arbitrate to you what is 'justice' according to their own narrative, is one of the most obvious arguments against utopian ideologies.

The idea that justice could exist in a vacuum or on a continuum is absurd. Today, a popular deception is to add the word 'justice' after your political and social projects to try and legitimize your own sense of right and wrong as a universal truth and standard. The term 'social justice' is bandied about in such glowing reverence that everyone seems to neglect the fact that the term itself actually has no real meaning. What most modern activists are conveying when they use the word 'justice' is simply 'their point of view,' which is an injustice in itself. Even so, if one wants to define justice as 'what sounds right in the zeitgeist of the culture,' they are setting the standard of justice based upon the prevailing opinions of the day. It was Chesterton who said, "He who marries the spirit of the times will soon find himself a widower."[14]

It is a sad time in human history when we need to be reminded that ascribing to the popular and prevailing narrative does not make one just. Without the ability to defend one's rights, we do not have any rights at all. This is why the Second Amendment is so important, but also why, in order for the Second Amendment to exist, we must first have the more fundamental right of justice—and that justice cannot mean what feels right but actually what is right according to the law of Nature and Nature's God. If someone breaks into your house, you must have the right to defend your family and your property against this immediate violation of your rights. This framework exists because we have the more fundamental right to justice, which would exonerate the victim's use of force as defense and hold the victim's actions as just retribution for the violator's actions. The definition of Natural Law is "a body of unchanging moral principles regarded as the basis for all human conduct." Those unchanging moral principles come from God's law and how God declares that we ought to treat one another in justice. Without this understanding, the legal system does not make sense and slowly begins to erode and then completely break down in relativism. I will let you be the judge as to where AG Garland's Justice Department is within that progression. Just know that this won't be the last corrupt DOJ if you continue to do nothing. You must begin to demand God's law over man's law as an essential part of your sonship and citizenship.

America is an exceptional country, brought forth upon the Earth by extraordinary people. It was a unique time in human history that did not rhyme. By all historical comparisons, George Washington should have become America's first king and begun a monarchic dynasty like all his predecessors, who found themselves in the same position. The people begged him to take the crown, and his placing that crown in its rightful place has resounded volumes to the content of his character. He made the words that Thomas Pain wrote in Common Sense come to pass; he placed the Crown of America on the Constitution, which sat upon the Bible, and thus, for the first time in human history, properly ordered the government in its relation to God and his people. By his humility, this could take place, so that this crown could be divided among the worthy sons of the King who would defend these divine gifts against all tyrannies and principalities of the Earth.

Are we upholding this vision in our country today? Every indication would say no—there is a new movement trying to become the animating soul of America. In the next chapter, we will explore the rival who seeks to conquer the sons of the King and bring them under its own rule. I, for one, do not plan to assent to this exile. Will you choose to stand with God or against him? Because what is occurring in the world today is as simple as good and evil. Do you want God to rule you, or the best that a Godless humanity can muster? We can no longer pretend that this decision can be put off or avoided. If we are to survive as a nation, we must defend our sonship. When God told Abraham that he would destroy Sodom and Gomorrah for their wickedness, Abraham asked him if he would destroy the righteous with the wicked. Would he spare the whole city for fifty righteous men? Forty? Thirty? Twenty? God said that if there were just ten righteous men, he would spare the cities from destruction. You, me, and at least eight more must stand up. Otherwise, this age will end with the destruction of the greatest country ever to exist and the descent of the world into the reign of Godless men who will dictate to us our rights. In our exile, we will lose our royal sonship and not have the right or power to call upon our heavenly Father to restore the rights we are no longer worthy of wielding. Heed these words for the sake of your soul and the soul of America:

> *"God who gave us life gave us liberty. Can the liberties of a nation be secure when we have removed a conviction that these liberties are the gift of God? Indeed I tremble for my country when I reflect that God is just, that His justice cannot sleep forever."*[15]
>
> —Thomas Jefferson, 1786

CHAPTER 7

The Soul of the Global Communist Movement

> *"The first step in liquidating a people is to erase its memory. Destroy its books, its culture, its history. Then have somebody write new books, manufacture a new culture, invent a new history. Before long that nation will begin to forget what it is and what it was... The struggle of man against power is the struggle of memory against forgetting."*[16]
>
> – Milan Kundera, from *The Book of Laughter and Forgetting*

There is a competing ideology looking to extinguish the soul of America and become the animating force of our society, our politics, and the world. The Pilgrims, and indeed all of those who came to the New World, were seeking to set a new table in America. It was to be a Christian table, no doubt, because the peoples that came here came from Christian England. It is also worth noting that those that came to America thought that England had gone pear shaped; it was now not Christian enough, and something drastic had to be done about it (hence the whole starting over in a foreign land decision ... calling themselves 'pilgrims'). Scores of religious sects, along with a contention of more secular opportunists, came to America. In coming, the religious zealots could not escape the more secular opportunists any more than the more secular opportunists could escape the cultural mores from which they all came. Yet they all had one thing in common: they were ready to risk everything, including life itself, to forge a new path in the American wilderness.

The more secular opportunists, too, would accept the fact that the American table to be set was to be set by the culture that would spring forth from the religious communities that they traveled with. As angry as it may make modern atheists, America was founded by Christians. Eight of the original thirteen colonies had official Christian religions. The five that didn't (Delaware, Rhode Island, Georgia, Pennsylvania, and New Jersey) had explicit open calls for religious toleration of the various Christian denominations (no open calls for Islam, Buddhism, or Zoroastrianism). 'Freedom of Religion' is cited often in the modern legal system and used loosely in modern parlance. The religious toleration of the earliest Americans, though, was exclusively in a Protestant Christian context. Their fellow Christians, the Catholics, were a debatable addition to the list. One would have to be delusional to think that these Protestant groups, as disparate as they may have been theologically, came to the New World to found a 'commune of free religions' with no limitations. They were not deluded that the table they were setting was the table of a Christian America, and all were welcome who would cross the lentil of the Christian home in which that table was set.

The fact that this is a controversial statement today shows that, as clear-eyed as these early Americans were, we have come to live in full delusion of the concept of freedom of religion. In 2023, the Supreme Court heard a Texas case from a Satanic temple arguing that any law that restricted abortions violated their religiously protected sacred rights. That's right; the 'freedom of religion' is supposed to extend to a Satanic temple wanting to perform human sacrifice through the act of abortion, and we are supposed to pretend that this is what the framers meant by 'free exercise thereof' in the Constitution. Thank God Satan lost his case, but shame on us as a nation for allowing him to try it in our courts! The founders couldn't imagine a post-modern world in which the fundamental rights of Americans were being expressed for the purpose of tearing those rights down and destroying them for everyone else. What house can stand divided against itself? And what house would willingly agree amongst themselves to dismantle the home? Perhaps there is something greater at play here than meets the eye.

This forgetting of our Christian founding is not one of people losing the old traditions through the fog of time. Nor is it the fading of outdated fads or the displacement of the old ways in the wake of new advancements. It is a deliberate power that has worked for a very long time to dislodge Christianity as the national hegemon and replace it with a new vision. The American table was a table of Christian morals and justice, but it has now become a table of relativism and tolerance. Our moment in time has a schizophrenic duality in the sense that we live in between the changing of the guard, and no one can quite define the good from the bad, the freedom from the slavery, or the coming from the going. For the first time in American history, a majority of people decry the moral law of Christianity without realizing that our system is a product of it. Too often today, people are 'interpreting' the Constitution and American law by redefining basic concepts like freedom of speech, religion, and the right to bear arms.

The modern relativist uses the same words and terms that the founders used, because that gives him legitimacy. But he purposefully redefines the meaning for his own end, which gives him power. It is not a game of moral clarity, reason, and just jurisprudence; it is a game of winning and losing. We all know that you cannot abuse a system like this and expect it to remain in good health. But here's the thing: to destroy this system is the feature, not the bug. Because it is a game, ultimately, of usurpers getting a seat at a table that they have no right to sit at. It is a simple sleight of hand that has worked so well, the turning of Christian charity into the false virtues of niceness and tolerance. The usurper's values are not aligned with the home in which the table is laid. But the argument goes, 'Why can't we be tolerant?' The Christians think that, in charity, they will evangelize the usurper and bring him into their ranks! They think that they are bartering in good faith with their fellow travelers. But the usurper is not there to receive God's mercy through His faithful; they are there to use whatever means necessary to win.

Of course, in the end, the first usurper is allowed to stay. Then, because the usurper now has a seat at the table, he now has a say. If the Christians do not hold the standard and allow the standard to become a 'middle ground' between them and the usurper, in which direction is the narrative going to be pulled? Slowly, one-by-one, this usurper is able to invite more and more guests who have no claim either. They are even further from the Christian ethic that laid the table, but nonetheless, in tolerance, we must accept them and slide further toward the 'new middle.' There comes a day, and we are living in this moment, when the Christians will be openly fighting to keep their seat at that table and their voice part of the definition of the new middle.

They will have to endure slings and arrows to remain at the table—set in the name of Christ—by their forebearers. Because the table has now slowly become, through the very deliberate method of ideological creep, the table of liberalism and tolerance. The new guard will keep the lentil post and sign the same, as well as the dishes and silverware. But they will declare victory over the table—that they shunned the snooty and judgmental Christians for their exclusionary ways. In triumph, they will boldly proclaim that no group will ever be disinvited. They may even come up with a slogan like, "Diversity is our strength!" Sure, diversity can be a great strength, but only when, despite the diversity, we stand united toward a common goal. And sorry to tell you, comrades, being united in destruction does not mean you will be united in reigning over the ashes.

Over enough time, the invitation to sit at the table becomes easier and easier to traffic, until the integrity of the table's company is utterly lost. And that's when it will happen; when there is nothing left to fight for, the ring leader of lies and division himself will appear and sit at the head of the table that has been redefined into oblivion as the 'table of tolerance.' And that, my friends, is how Satan has come to sit at America's table; it has always been an inevitable outcome of the path that we are on. We began upon Christian principles, were usurped by the relativism of the limitless modern liberal movement, and now that everyone is tolerated—even Satan himself—there will be a new guard that will come to rule the table that mirrors God only insofar as it is the inverse of goodness. When 'freedom' becomes 'do whatever you want,' or when an act is marked virtuous based on whether or not consent was exchanged, there are no redeeming qualities to the table you have set. It is the same mockery as 'playing chess without rules,' and presuming that the result is 'freeing.' And as a result, the comfortable and secure home that Christianity built comes crashing down around America's table. A Godless dinner party is left in the chaos, wondering where it all went wrong.

There is no escaping the fact that man, by nature, worships. Said in a more secular way, we are beings that, by nature, must be oriented toward something. It is a part of our telos, or design. In a right-ordered world, we are oriented toward Truth, Beauty, and Goodness itself. Put in a more religious way, we ought to be oriented to God (defined as the Creator who is Truth itself, Beauty itself, and Goodness itself). If we are not oriented toward God, we will orient ourselves toward something else: our job, our passions, our delusions of grandeur. But this is not a zero-sum, either-or game. The human condition itself is a strange duality in the sense that we are "ensouled bodies." We are a biological animal, for sure. But last time I checked, lions weren't questioning the existential meaning of their intellect. Along with our intellect, our ability to see intelligibility in the world and our ability to reason to new conclusions is a great and unique gift. But it is neither a gift without a giver nor a gift without an ultimate, orienting purpose. Denying this reality is the basic materialist's position, and it is as absurd as thinking that fruit cakes magically appear in the mailbox and that Aunt Martha doesn't expect you to come visit next time you're in town. When we lose our orientation to the good, we cannot come to rest in some naval gazing position as the center of our own neutral universe. When we abandon our orientation toward God, no matter what we claim as our new orientation, we simply get pulled into another force that we must contend with.

Just like in any good saga, there is a protagonist and an antagonist in the grand epic tale of this story we find ourselves caught up in, what I like to call "The Existence of Everything and Your Role in It." Most people today prefer to live in the realm of conceptualizing the 'powers' of 'good and evil' without attributing these to the actual powers and principalities from which they derive. Whether you are comfortable with using such triggering terms as 'God' and 'Satan' or want to be more abstract about it, there is no denying that we are seeing two great forces collide in our current time, and the distinction between the two is becoming more obvious by the day.

The people who came to the New World knew well the forces of good and evil and how to form a cohesive ethic that could: 1. make sense of the world; 2. the good that created it; 3. the evil that pervades it; and 4. their role in the struggle between good and evil. They didn't invent this ethic; it had been passed down through the millennia as a matter of faith called Christianity. These pioneers of the American wilderness were seeking to live this ethic out to its fullest by relying on God, their divine sonship through Jesus, the Holy Spirit, and the teachings of Scripture to provide for them the path forward through this world and onto Heaven. Not a marketing spiel, just some basic facts. Amidst these pioneers were those who did not fully embrace the Judeo-Christian framework; this is true as well. But they were all fellow travelers in one unique way: they were all steeped in the Western Canon. Included in that canon are the ancient leading thinkers of Athens, who, as it turns out, were really onto something. Good 'ol Uncle Aristotle, a full three centuries before Christ, had already laid solid groundwork in the pagan world.

The Mosaic tradition, Aristotelian realism, and Thomistic moral theology are so steeped in the Western Canon that they might be compared to the background radiation that envelops our universe. Within this canon, the existence of an ultimate Good from which the universe derives was unquestioned. The idea that we were personally linked to this Good because we were created in its image was a given. And the fact that we have moral recourse in our lives to that Good, and we will have to answer for the conduct of our lives, was a foregone conclusion. These very basic abstractions are the 'water' in which these pioneers 'swam' to use modern phrasing. It is out of this conceptualization that you get 'the rights of man,' 'endowed by our Creator,' and that rights granted by God 'shall not be infringed' by government.

The Constitution is no accident, nor is it the logical and reasonable outcome of any other peoples that might spring up and overthrow their former leaders. History is littered with examples that prove my point; the 'enlightenment' French being the premier example. The Constitution was the product of a full-throated embrace of the Good which created and gave order to the universe. It is the product of faithful adherence to His justice and His laws and living out a life of service to that Good. And it is ultimately the product of people who lived and moved this way regardless of their government—and their government was made better and blessed because of it.

To fail to realize this is to assume that the comfortable family home, the warm and secure hearth, and the table set with the love of God happen naturally as part of societal formation, mere accidents that occur by virtue of being creatures who exist near each other in this world. Our society, violently divorced from our past by the injection of a new animating spirit, throws off the thankfulness for the order that was so hard fought for. Most shamefully, we throw off the discipline and responsibility that are required to maintain such vaunted norms. We do so to our peril, just as every other generation before us, by their disobedience, found themselves exiled into the wilderness to contend with the spirit who prowls there. He too is seeking safe distance from the Good, for this spirit too refuses to serve the Good from whence it came. This outer-land spirit is the high priest and keeper of the soul of the global communist movement. Although that is not what he calls it or what he calls himself.

Relativism is the denial of all truth. It is utopia in the purest sense of the word. The Greek word from which utopia derives is literally translated as 'no place.' Conceptually speaking, one can imagine such a world without truth and imagine the complete liberality that would result. But in reality, a world without truth cannot exist. This is going to get dense for a second, but bear with me. In philosophical speak, relativism is a self-refuting premise, meaning that the definition of relativism is a contradiction unto itself. To say that 'there are no truths' is really to say that 'there is ONE truth ... and that ONE truth is ... that there are NO truths.' Do you see the breakdown in the logic? Know this well, because it can help you discern the interloping soul that is trying to replace the soul of America. There is no question that there is truth in the world, because to accept the other position is absurd. In philosophy jargon, this is called the via negativa: to view the thing backwards. "Is there truth in the world?" This cannot be definitively answered with undeniable certainty. That is to say, by human reason alone, we cannot arrive at, see clearly, and define Truth with one-hundred-percent certainty. We can know it is there and come to know a great deal about it through our reason, but our reason alone cannot truly and fully see God for who and what He is. But if you ask the opposite question, you CAN arrive at a definitive answer. If the question is posed, "Can the world be devoid of truth?" You can definitively say, 'No, it cannot.' To say the world is devoid of truth is to establish the "truth" that there are no "truths." The via negativa proves that there must be at least some truth in the world, even if we can never know exactly what that is. Okay, rapid fire philosophy class is dismissed. In conclusion, the real question is: what is the nature of truth, what does it mean for my life, and how can I live in accordance with it?

This is the most basic breakdown between the soul of America and the soul of the global communist movement. The soul of America has an answer for what truth is, and it centers its worldview around that truth and what it means for life and how to live it. The global communist movement rejects that there is any truth in which life, meaning, or existence should be centered. Because it holds the false premise that a being designed to be oriented can simultaneously become its own orientation. Those who think that they are the arbiters of truth or that their unique perspective is the 'rightest in all the world,' all think that they have 'liberated' themselves to become their own orientation. They fail to realize that if they do not orient themselves toward the good, they merely become 'captured' by another gravity well. In the metaphysical universe, there are only two points of orbit: those of light and good and those of dark and evil. There are no alternative modes of being that we can fall into. If you are foolish enough to become a naval gazer, you are also probably foolish enough to believe the lie that you are the center of your very own universe.

Relativism is Satan's most precious lie because it allows him to capture people who think they control their own destiny. The animating soul of the global communist movement is the utopian state of relativism. A false nowhere place that cannot exist, but from this place of madness, there is nothing you cannot imagine and nothing that can be denied to those who wish it so. In the Biblical tradition, it is said that Satan was an angel of God who was of very high rank and very powerful. Shortly after the universe is put into motion and God shares his beatific vision with the angels, Satan is said to have rebelled in disgust, particularly on the part of humans being elevated eventually into the realm of Heaven. The famous attribution to Satan is the Latin term non-serviam, or "I will not serve." He turns a third of the Heavenly Host (a third of the angels) against God's vision, and they are cast out of Heaven. A work that captures this moment is one that the early Americans would have known well; that would be the poem Paradise Lost by John Milton. Milton describes the moment that the utopia of relativism is born, as Satan wrestles with himself, and what is to become of an angel that has lost God's favor:

"Farewel happy Fields
Where Joy for ever dwells: Hail horrours, hail
Infernal world, and thou profoundest Hell
Receive thy new Possessor: One who brings
A mind not to be chang'd by Place or Time.
The mind is its own pl'ce, and in it self
Can make a Heav'n of Hell, a Hell of Heav'n ...
... Here we may reign secure, and in my choyce
To reign is worth ambition though in Hell:
Better to reign in Hell, then serve in Heav'n ..."[17]

—John Milton, *Paradise Lost; Book 1*

A mind not to be changed by place or time. In other words, no amount of reality that this mind bumps up against will prevail in swaying it from its delusions. Because one must accept mad premises from the start to live in a place, that is really a 'no place.' This line too is a powerful insight: better to reign in Hell then serve in Heaven. Sun Tzu says that the most dangerous enemy is 'an evil enemy, who will burn his own nation to the ground to rule over the ashes' (slight paraphrase). The belief in God, in goodness, and in an ultimate truth to whom we are all accountable is the soul of America. Relativism is the soul of the global communist movement, insofar as it is the closest thing to an anti-God; the nearest a concept can be to an inverse of the existence of truth. This is the 'liberation' from which a movement can move forward with a theocratic assurance in itself, overcome every moral accountability, justify any atrocity, and push every other objection aside to assert dominance and power. There is no bridge too far or violence too great; every means necessary must be employed to ensure that 'the revolution' is seen through to the end. The destruction of a standard of justice levels the playing field to a mere power struggle, and the one who is willing to abandon every standard (save for the amassing of their own power) wins in the end.

I hope that pitting these two animating ideologies against each other in this way is eye-opening and helps you to see more clearly the battle that we are fighting. It is a spiritual battle, or a battle of 'powers' if you will. And it is going to be a classic good vs. evil story; that is to say, it is not going to be a nice-off where we win them over with kindness and good will. No, we will have to go to (at least ideological) war against the powers of evil and be ready to defeat them and drive them from our lands to preserve the good. It is a battle for the soul of the nation and whose future we will live in. You must choose which side you are on. Do you believe that there is truth in this world and that it is worth defending and rallying around? Or do you want to live in a world where Godless men think they can change the very nature of reality by simply wishing it so? I will not choose the path of trying to make myself the center of an imaginary universe. I will not choose the path that leads to perdition, destruction, and madness. I will choose the hard path—the path that requires discipline, grit, integrity, and the courage to stand for the truth. I will choose the path that leads to God. And along the way, I hope to leave the world and our country in better shape than when I found them.

If you cannot make yourself worship God, then at least orient yourself toward the concept of "The Truth." If you cannot make yourself read Scripture, then read Aristotle and be a scholar of the Western Canon. If you cannot be a person of faith, be a person of such high integrity that you would stand up for the rights of man and stand against anyone who would use those very rights to undermine the freedom that these rights give. Because you are up against those who would make stumbling blocks out of your integrity, holding you to a standard that they themselves have no belief in. You are in a battle with people who have declared themselves your ideological enemies and have declared war on you. They will shout any slander, or coo any praise, or do whatever is necessary to win. Those who believe in God have proven that we will live in peace after the war. But the left has proven by their own madness that they will not stop until they have complete hegemonic control of our society—and your life. In the end, you will have to repeat every single party line or join the right in the gulag. To those of you who think you can avoid this conflict by becoming a 'Kuiper Belt traveler,' someone in the far reaches of the orbit around the good (or evil) that you encircle, be warned. The fight will be brought to your door, even if you post the square, and fly the flag, and support the thing. Eventually, if you are not in ideological lockstep, you will find yourself on the other side of party lines and in the crosshairs yourself.

This is not a crazy political battle being fought between radical factions on the extremes. This is the fringe of the left eating the Democrat Party, and the last remaining vestiges of American traditionalists sounding the alarm.

It will not end in mudslinging, agreeing to disagree, and then a 'return to normal' where Congress fights about how much funding we should throw at the next foreign war. This is the beginning of the end of the soul of America being the dominant voice at America's table. Everyone who still holds some semblance of being grounded in truth needs to wake up and stand firm. Otherwise, we need to be prepared to parrot our new overlord's talking points or become political prisoners for refusing. It is best to heed the words of Sun Tzu: "If you know the enemy and know yourself, you need not fear the result of a hundred battles. If you know yourself but not the enemy, for every victory gained you will also suffer a defeat. If you know neither the enemy nor yourself, you will succumb in every battle."[18]

I began this chapter with a quote from Milan Kundera, who was, oddly enough, a communist. It seems like the delusion of collectivist ideology runs very deep; Orwell himself was a socialist. How or why these great authors can so eloquently speak to the evils of totalitarianism and still believe in collectivism is beyond me. We will explore how these two things are inextricably linked in the next chapter. The reason that Milan's quote is so pertinent to our time is because it is prophetic for what is happening in our culture today. Solzhenitsyn, who was a political prisoner in Soviet Russia, saw the takeover of the soul of Russia by the global communist movement firsthand. In The Gulag Archipelago, he wrote: "To destroy a people, you must first sever their roots."[19] You must erase their memory; then, you must replace it with a new one. Nothing encapsulates this more than the narrative surrounding the American flag, the symbol of our nation.

Nike was set to release a shoe with the 'Betsy Ross' flag on one of their myriad, standard release campaigns; it certainly wasn't a 'deeply patriotic statement' from a company that epitomizes foreign wage slave exploitation. Colin Kaepernick, famous for refusing to stand for the National Anthem at National Football League games, claimed that this flag was offensive. Since then, the narrative has been that the American flag itself is a symbol of systemic oppression and racism. If you fly the flag, then you are the embodiment of what the flag symbolizes. Do you know of any other country that hates its own flag? This move was one in a line of movements that have morphed into the justification to call our country evil. That it was never an idealistic, shining city on a hill. That it was no better than any other colonizing, oppressive regime in history. From Howard Zinn's absolutely heretical book A People's History of the United States down to the blasphemous 1619 project, it has been a deliberate re-writing of history to make people hate their roots and disbelieve that this country was founded on anything substantive for the happiness and flourishing of humanity. We should know our history and why the American system is better than any other, but we should also realize that we aren't arguing with people in good faith over the fundamentals. This is a power struggle—nothing more than our declared enemy trying to radically upend the worldview of the youth so that they are wholly incapable of relating to their parents and the generations that came before them.

When the right defends the country, the left throws America's failures in the right's face and asks the right to justify them. People on the right, stop taking the bait! The point is not the point; winning is the point. They are not here to argue with you; they are here to win, and boy, how they are winning. Reagan once said, "If you are explaining, you're losing."[20] He is exactly right; they don't care about the truth; they care about winning so they can burn it all down and rule over the ashes. There is no other country in the world that is educating its children to hate their own country and history. The right can win by passing a one-page piece of legislation that says it is illegal to disparage the country while educating children; the penalty is a lifetime ban from education for breaking the law. Let them hiss, wail, and cry. And then move on and win some more.

A new history is being unfolded before our very eyes, a new culture, complete with all the literature, accoutrement, and elites who have control of the institutions of power. Preaching hatred for America is not ultimately about turning the people against the country; it is about demonizing their opponents to the point that the people give their allegiance over to them. Just think how the narrative has changed in the last decade on citizenship, monetary theory, economics, social programs, government intervention, and even the nature of men and women. And as an observer, one would be led to believe that this is not only the majority opinion, but that it's always been this way! The nation is in the process of forgetting what it is and what it was. This is not happening because the communists are right, better, or have a greater track record of success. It is because they have made a battle plan, declared war on us, and are engaged in that war in plain sight. And unfortunately for us, we haven't gotten around to putting our pants on yet. We haven't been training, learning, and preparing ourselves for an ideological struggle for the soul of the nation.

It is said that strong men make good times; good times make weak men; weak men make bad times; bad times make strong men; and strong men, once again, make good times. In this struggle, this ideological struggle for the soul of the nation, there will be plenty of bad times in which strong men are made. Will they be Nietzsche's Übermenschen? The men who usurp all moral codes, all cultural mores, and truth itself to wield power? Or will it be the humble men of truth and God who prevail? It is up to you. In the end, you must decide if you are on the side of God or the side of the Godless. Because, as Solzhenitsyn points out, "the line between good and evil runs through the heart of every man."[21] Ultimately, these ideologies are not mere abstractions; they are actions, movements, and moral codes played out in the lives of individuals. Those individuals form cultures, societies, and governments and create the histories of a people. Understanding the root of an ideology is important, but ultimately the question is, what are you going to do about it?

Are you on the side of the visionaries of a nowhere utopia, or on the side of those who can create a reality of liberty and justice for all? Are you on the side of the central planners, who will stop at nothing to see 'the revolution' succeed? Or are you on the side of human rights, human dignity, and human flourishing? The choice is yours, but you no longer have the luxury of going without a choice. For in the end, the global communist movement is just a tool to destroy our country and to put into play a greater mechanism by which the WEF can centralize the world under their power. The date is set, and the game is afoot. We must be able to beat the communists here and re-establish the soul of America if we ever want to defeat the WEF in their global ambitions. The winds of change are stirring, and it is true that we cannot change the winds of this age or the forces that have already been set in motion.

The only question you must answer is this: in which direction will you set your sails?

CHAPTER 8

Why There Are No Communist Governments

Imagine for a moment, if you will, a mentally ill person who is paranoid. He is convinced that the Illuminati are listening in on him. This isn't a trick scenario; you know the person is clinically mentally ill and that he is suffering from his own delusion. He is convinced of his conclusions, and his cork board is full of pins and red string, proof that he is being monitored and tracked by a secret society. He knows too much, you see? He tells you his entire elaborate scheme to prove to you that he is being watched. Knowing that he is mentally ill and suffering under a delusion of his own making, you have pity and want to help. What do you do? Do you tell him the truth? And how will he take it? If you tried to reason with the person and tell him that he is not being spied on, he could only come to one conclusion: You're in on it! You're one of them! Because in the game of illogic, from his unreasonable perspective, his logic makes perfect sense. It is the same premise when you argue with a collectivist true believer about whether or not communist governments work.

Do you remember the 2010 Scorsese film Shutter Island? It was a mystery thriller where two U.S. Marshals, one played by Leonardo DiCaprio, are investigating a disappearance at an insane asylum. At the end of a very entertaining saga, you find that it was just one giant psy-op. DiCaprio's character is a patient suffering the delusion that he is a U.S. Marshal; his doctor is 'playing' the role of the other U.S. Marshal; and the staff is letting the 'investigative fantasy' play itself all the way out to see if they can make him realize it is all in his head. There is a moment of lucidity where the patient snaps back to reality, but it is revealed that this isn't the first time they have done this exercise. It is also revealed that this is his last chance; if he falls back into the mania, he will have to be lobotomized for the safety of himself, the staff, and his fellow patients. Although ambiguous at the end, it seems that he slips back into the fantasy character by calling the doctor by his imaginary U.S. Marshal name. Great concept for a movie, but in real life, I think that might be considered patient abuse. Of course, it's the 2020s now, where we affirm people's mental delusions about themselves. So, I guess the 'Shutter Island' treatment was just ahead of its time.

I bring up this movie not for a film review or a prolonged discussion on psychology and potential treatments. Rather, it is the perfect analogy for having an argument with someone about whether or not a communist government can work. It is granting the asylum patient his delusion and then arguing within the internal framework and illogic of his madness. The term 'communist government' is a contradiction in terms; it would be like referring to a man as a 'married bachelor.' If you grant the premise that a man can be both single and married simultaneously, you have forfeited the meaning and the definition of both words. You can continue to have a conversation about married bachelors, but you now have to adopt the new maniacal definitions and subscribe to the internal illogic of the argument. The defense of communist governments is like defending the reality of a leprechaun's gold. In order to even be talking about the gold's whereabouts, the premise that leprechauns are real had to be granted along the way. Don't be the person who grants the premise that leprechauns are real, and you won't have to have ridiculous arguments about the redistribution of the leprechaun's wealth.

The second there is a hierarchy of government, the state fails to uphold the most basic tenant of communism: to hold all things equally and in common. The commune, by definition, must be run by the collective; the second a 'leader' is appointed, this breaks the collective decision-making process. As soon as someone is placed in an unequal position of 'leadership' above the 'proletariat,' he is no different than the bourgeoisie that he overthrew! There are no communist governments—only totalitarians who preach communism for the sake of their own dominance over the people. There have been tyrants and despots throughout history who have strong-armed the people. But none have been more effective at paralyzing populations with guilt-inducing rhetoric than the self-avowed communists. The language of communism allows the despotic regime to wrap its ideology in tolerance, peace, and the promise of future prosperity. They get to vilify anyone who opposes them and kill them for the sake of 'the revolution.' No measure is too obtrusive, and no edict is too strict; it is done for the sake of the people, you understand. They can literally kill millions of the nation's people in the name of saving the nation! Whatever this is, whatever this specific type of government is, that may be up for debate.

What is certain, however, is that the people were never in control of the USSR. The people of China are not now in control of their own destiny. And the people of Cuba do not hold all things in common. None of these people have the right to ask their leaders to change a single iota for the sake of the revolution. These are all slave states, and yet we nonchalantly refer to them as 'communist' as though that in any way describes what is happening. When we do, we are granting the asylee the premise that he really is a U.S. Marshal. We are arguing about what to do with the leprechaun's gold. We fall into the trap of arguing inside the illogical premise that a country can exist as a commune.

Sometimes reality is stranger than fiction; one of the examples of a contradiction in terms is to be a 'gentle torturer.' I can't think of a more hilariously accurate contradiction in terms for a 'communist regime.' Marx defined communism as the 'dictatorship of the proletariat.' The most basic concept of communism is that all material goods are held in common, but in what context could that work? If three siblings held their parents' estate in a trust, this arrangement could be handled in a 'communistic' way. Imagine that the parents gave equal ownership of the family's vacation home to their children. The three children, now with families of their own, continue to enjoy the home as a vacation and retreat destination. They lovingly plan around the needs of the whole family and the other siblings and their family needs, and it is just a lovely tribute to the memories of the parents who left such a wonderful legacy and gift to their family.

But what happens ten generations later? Now you have direct and indirect heirs, cousins, degrees of separation, and who knows how many people who, in some respect, still hold all things in common. Does everyone still have an equal say? Should everyone have an equal say? Are all contributing to the maintenance of the home (each according to his ability, of course)? What if some take according to their needs but are needier than others? In this case, there would obviously be many algebraic functions to determine who and by what percentage each heir is entitled. Not to mention an accounting system for who contributes and who does not. And, most importantly, there would need to be a designated person who could force votes, prioritize the home's needs, and make coherence of the chaos of hundreds of people "sharing something in common."

The point is, three people can have a conversation, make decisions for their future, and then enact those decisions. But what if it's a hundred people? A thousand? Or 330 million, perhaps (just to pull a random, maybe meaningless number)? The idea that the rabble can make a unanimous decision in which all are happy and can perfectly feel equality of outcome is patently absurd. You have to put someone in charge. And therein lies the problem: the second you put someone in charge of the commune, you have created a hierarchy that—by communism's own definition—cannot exist.

Many regular, everyday people espouse communism, and I think they are sincere in their beliefs. Every person in the bong circle wearing a Che shirt is a true believer. I think even the American politicians and bureaucrats who advance collectivist sentiments in government are sincere, albeit sincerely misguided about what they are sincere about. Conceptually speaking, communism sounds nice, especially to those who perceive themselves as poor and oppressed, especially if they believe their circumstances are the fault of society or the government. The allusion of grandeur that can be conjured up by communist rhetoric is hard to deny, and we should not try to make flat and simple arguments as to why communism is a bunk idea.

Although it is a good "gotcha," saying that communism has failed every time it has been tried is not a good tactic. This is an especially bad line of argument when you are talking to true believers. They are completely justified in answering with the classic line, 'That's because real communism has never been tried!' Did you catch where the breakdown of the argument was? The second that the premise was granted, that communism can be tried at a government scale, you assented to the unreality of the whole argument. There is no logical way out of an illogical argument; you can engage in a Socratic dialogue to the point where true believers talk themselves out of an illogical argument. Eventually, they have to quit beating the dead horse they claim to be riding, abandon that horse and their tactics, and go about finding a new one that doesn't require violence to function.

Beyond the contradiction in terms of 'communist government,' there are many flaws in the arguments for collectivism more generally. One of the primary premises (and fundamental flaws) of collectivism is that equality of outcome can be achieved among people in a society. It is the premise that we will share all things in common so that everyone has exactly the same outcome in life as everyone else. What is often missed in this argument is how this outcome has to be achieved (because it cannot organically happen), and that is by social engineering. Social engineering that must be decided upon and carried out by somebody. Somebody who will be in charge, and the second you do that, you have hierarchy, and thus you have abandoned the pure state of communism where we hold all things in common.

This is one of those pieces of the communist puzzle that pulls at the heartstrings of men. Since the time we were two years old, we've been preaching fairness. If you put one cupcake in front of two kids, you won't have to wait; both will advocate for outright ownership first, and then fairness as a razor close second. Now, I'm not dogging fairness; I think that it should be the aim of any public endeavor (including politics, which, by root etymology, simply means how the public aspects of the polis or city-state ought to operate). But this equality of outcome is a very juvenile level of fairness, one that cannot begin to apply to all aspects of life. As such, it is utterly hopeless in trying to rule over the lives of people. And ultimately, the very attempt to implement it undermines the very reason we were trying to do so in the first place.

Communism is ultimately an ideology that requires an act of faith to accept, and that act of faith is that, somehow, we can make everyone equal. That we can bend the human will, intellect, and capacity into a perfect state of being and harmony in the world with every other human will, intellect, and capacity. And sadly, as a religious ideology, it has promises that pull at our heartstrings and sound, oh, so fair and good. But it is as illusory as a unicorn, because ultimately, the promises of communism cannot be brought into real life in the real world—especially through a government. The pure equity of communism as a theory will never be able to square itself with the nature of man. Nor can the desire for equity reconcile itself with the fact that a government, by nature, is hierarchical.

If there is a public park, everyone should have fair and equal access to it. The nature of this arrangement is one that we are all familiar with in America, having many city, state, and national parks. To have this arrangement, we all assented to it being public land maintained by the local authority, thus being under their jurisdiction, and thus we have abandoned pure communism, where we hold all things in common. But the public park is a good display of fairness nonetheless. However, if I develop a park on my own private land, the public will not have the same equal and unfettered access. I could charge admission for people willing to pay a premium to go to my park, or I could keep it to myself and my family. It would be my prerogative, because it is my property. A property that I built using my own private funds. But this would be an unforgivable sin, according to the true believer. The argument would be that the workers were exploited by me to achieve my vision and that they deserve to claim ownership over what I designed and funded—and then paid them to build for me. Now, the person capable of such things is enemy number 1, and what he has must—in the name of fairness—be distributed among the people. This is according to the sentiment and claim of communism, but by whose decree? After all, we hold all things in common.

A communist government cannot exist because once the government has a single staff member, that comrade holds a position of power over everyone else, and now all things are not held in common. The abolition of private property is a core concept of communism because it is absolutely contrarian to the concept of equity. But the illusion of no ownership is precisely that; the concept of ownership does not disappear like a mirage. It just means that the state, and whoever controls the state, owns everything. It is by design that the WEF's first prediction is that you will own nothing. There are no communist governments—only totalitarians who preach communism for the sake of their own dominance over the people. Ultimately, what happens is that the totalitarian regime preaching communism to maintain their power seizes everything, because there is no natural mechanism in the world to produce an equality of outcome, no matter how many children, how few cupcakes, or how many slices you can cut them into.

I can create fairness in limited scenarios, but only in my limited capacity of ownership. But try and scale this to a universal truism, and you will find yourself breaking the legs of the nation to achieve fairness with the crippled. The doctrine of universal fairness can only go in one direction. The cupcake must be cut into pieces. The business owner's business must be seized, and the landowner's land must be broken apart and occupied. The child does not care by what means the cupcake came to the table; he just wants his portion. When you pretend that this can work as a form of government, you are pretending that you can consume what isn't yours and what you did not produce and be morally superior for doing so. You also pretend that there will always be someone else's cupcake to divvy up. This is why dictators who preach communism eventually run out of other people's money and resources; there is nothing being produced by a system that can only divide.

This is another contradiction in communism; it assumes that the incentives of production will not go away in a world where there is no incentive to produce. It assumes that the personal responsibility of ownership will transfer into a world where, by virtue of holding all things in common, we don't truly own anything. Without an incentive to produce things and the personal responsibility to care for yourself, your family, and your community, you don't have a society. You have a construct that uses the lives of people to achieve its own ends.

This is why we must be precise in our language; the next time someone refers to a government as being communist, reject his premise. It is an oxymoron; the second someone places himself in charge of the commune, he has rejected communism for hierarchy. These people are nothing more than a totalitarian regime that is preaching communism for the sake of their own power over the people. Now do you see why, when you grant the premise of a communist regime, the true believer is one-hundred-percent right when he says, 'True communism has never been tried?' The leprechaun, riding his unicorn, hasn't found the right rainbow that leads to Mount Olympus either. Don't have a conversation about whether or not the destination at the end of the rainbow is Mount Olympus; just reject the totalitarian leprechaun from the start (with all that gold, he's probably one of those evil capitalists anyway).

Lebron James is a natural athlete, a true competitor, and (regardless of the g.o.a.t. conversation) a generational basketball player who, for many, will be the greatest player of their lifetime. I don't agree with a lot of things he says, but that has no bearing on his abilities on the court. We are nearly the same age, and I only mention this to say that we will live concomitant lives; we will be born, live, and die in the same country and time period, with so many of the same opportunities and privileges. The contrast between the two of us, however, is proof that equality of outcome would rob us both. When I was fifteen, I couldn't ball like Lebron when he was fifteen. I damn sure can't ball like him now! And when we are both old men, I still won't be able to ball like him. The very real comparison, as two Americans living in the same country at the same time, could be proven on the court (if I ever found myself in the pitiable situation where I had to play Lebron one-on-one). If that ever happened, the outcome would be undeniable, and it would be undeniable no matter when that happened during our lifetime. Even if we were both out there on walkers, he'd still effortlessly beat me. Do you know why? Because we are not equals! There is not a universe in which I could organically become an athlete that can do what Lebron James can do, either by natural ability, practice, or combination. Lebron will beat me at basketball every time, despite being born at the same age and time. You know how I could beat Lebron at basketball, though? If the NBA made him wear ankle weights, shoot on a smaller rim, walk and not run on the court, only jump flat-footed, and wear blinders. That, and then give me a point for every time I dribbled the ball. Then, maybe, I could beat Lebron at basketball. As long as we did that fifty percent of the time, we'd have fairness, right? I'd be able to beat Lebron! Or would I? This would produce an equality of outcome, but would it be fair? Most importantly, would it be just?

When you try to take the juvenile concept of fairness and make it into a truism by which people are ruled, you can only create misery with it. You can only create lesser outcomes, not greater and better ones. That is the Faustian bargain of trying to create equality of outcome, which is why the Founders of our country so vehemently rejected the idea. Our country was built on a different principle of equality: equality of opportunity. This is the only equality that a government can promise a people. Equality (not equity) says that Lebron James can excel and become the best basketball player, and entrepreneur, and athlete, and public figure, and, and, and. There is nothing outside of him that limits him. He can be whatever he wants to be, and he does not have to worry about whether or not I can keep up. And I, conversely, can have my own thoughts and beliefs, my own life, liberty, and pursuit of happiness that are not in any way contingent upon anyone else's successes and failures.

I know there is one person in the back raising a hand right now. "What about the slaves?! They didn't have equality." Yes, that is true, and there is no sidestepping the awful practice of slavery. I wish that Jefferson's rebuke of slavery was not edited out of the Declaration of Independence (the nation's birth certificate); it made America's promise an impossibility for many Americans until after the Civil War. However, I will point you right back to the previous chapter: the American form of government was hypocritical for its allowance of slavery because it was violating its own standards (which are God's standards). In time, the Founders knew that the hypocritical nation would have to either overcome its hypocrisy or collapse because of it. I am glad that it was the former. We hold slavery to be unacceptable by the very principles on which this nation was founded—principles that are unique among the constitutions and nations of the world. It is a strange irony that ostensibly the best government to ever exist can be held in such contempt for its inherited errors—errors that the rest of the world did not have the courage to eradicate by their own constitutions, principles, decrees, and standards. No leftist seems to be outraged at any other country's historical practice of slavery, nor current ones, for that matter.

Hypocrisy cannot exist where standards are being met, and the rest of the world has horrible standards that are being met while America is trying to live up to God's standard. No one is surprised by that certain leader of a certain country who has enslaved millions of his own countrymen because of their religious views. You know who I'm talking about; I think everyone was surprised to find out just how much Winnie the Pooh hates Sunni Law. We cannot rightly call this leader, his government, or the country hypocrites. That's because he is matching the standard that he has set and what the rest of the world expects. So again, I will pose the question to you from the last chapter: do you want God or the best that a Godless humanity can deliver? Stalin had no problem with slavery; Lincoln did. People are still slaves in China today, and they aren't in America. That is the difference between the despots who would enslave you with communism and the promise of America.

The difference between communism and Americanism can be summed up by the meme with two pictures side-by-side: a lion in a zoo and a lion in the wild. One is completely taken care of, fed, cleaned up after, and in a safe and secure environment. The other one is free. Choose wisely. There is one last point about communism that is important to the overall thrust of this book. We have discussed a few examples of tyrants who preached communism for the sake of their control. There is a main difference between these historical examples and the new regime concocted by the WEF. Many of the so-called communists in government, as well as those in NGOs and activist groups who advocate for socialism, are being financially underwritten by the WEF. This would, on its face, seem like a very foolish thing for the WEF to do. Why would they subsidize what would appear to be their competition? Just like the economy, the media, the culture, and the other moving parts of this world, they just see the collectivist vision as one major aspect of their overall plan. The true believers in Marx believe that communism is a global project. They would not rest until 'the revolution' had taken over the whole world. In a weird, through-the-looking-glass way, the success of the WEF as the tyrant over the whole world, preaching communism for the sake of dominating the people, is a self-fulfilling communist prophecy.

The true believers, when confronted with freedom or rule by the WEF, are going to willingly allow the central planning WEF to rule the world simply for the sake of being able to say, 'True global communism has finally been reached.' There are literally millions—if not billions—of self-avowed collectivists, that is, true believers in the various ideologies of collectivism, be they fascists, socialists, or communists. They range from the poorest of the poor to the most influential politicians. They are all useful idiots for despots who preach their message to gain power. Because no matter how sincere these true believers are in collectivist equity, forming a 'communist government' is a contradiction in terms, like a gentle torturer or married bachelor. Collectivism demands that all things be held in common and in equity; the second that a hierarchy of government is established over it, you have abandoned the very principles upon which it claims to rest. Therein lies the modus operandi for the greatest trick in the history of mankind. Sure, Castro, Mao, and Stalin all made great runs manipulating the ideology of communism for the purpose of wielding their power. But the WEF doesn't want a country; they want to rule the world. Unfortunately, all those clamoring useful idiots will celebrate that the world communist movement has come to fruition. But it will be the only thing that a government preaching communism can be: a LARPing despotic regime that demands hegemonic control by whatever means necessary.

The groundwork that the WEF laid in the communism department will have paid great dividends to them in the end. They will have billions of scared subjects who will be happy to be the lion in the zoo, too scared to adopt the mantle of freedom. They will have thousands of communist politicians who will gladly sell out their fellow man and become the WEF's network of regional delegates.

They will prove very useful as mouthpieces of the expert class and the league of nations. They will already have the right disposition: central planning is best, the party is always right, and every form of tyranny is an acceptable method of preserving 'the revolution.'

As an ideology that cannot truly come to fruition as a means of governance, communism will prove to be a short-term benefit to the new world government. Peace, prosperity, and the rest of the utopian promises of communism will always be just beyond the horizon, and they will have (hopefully) a few dissidents to blame. It will help hide their ineptitude, their failures, and the failures of their relativistic ideologies that lead them to believe that they can make a utopia despite the realities of ... well, reality. Yes, the idea of communism will go a long way, maybe even as far as a thousand-year reign. They know how powerful and destructive a force it can be to bring a nation to the brink of failure. They know the internal illogic of communism requires an act of faith in order to be assented to. If you are trying to displace religions and competing philosophies, a political vision that can double as a religion is a powerful tool of domination. And they know that the only way that a so-called communist state can work is if there is total hegemonic control, but that won't be a problem. In the new world order, there will not be an East and West Germany. There will not be a competing country that your dissidents can run to. There will not be a competing narrative or a competing medium in which to speak. They are making the gamble that they will be able to do what no previous tyrant preaching communism could do: see 'the revolution' through to its global end.

Two of the most influential books of the twentieth century warned of total global domination: Orwell's 1984 and Huxley's

Brave New World. Orwell predicted the outright tyranny of 'big brother,' while Huxley predicted a soft tyranny of the people through Soma and satiation. The lines between these two books will become very blurred if the WEF's 'predictions' come to pass. There will be plenty of carrots and sticks for each of us as we are asked to enter the zoo cage, as we are asked to get in the pod, own nothing, and eat the bugs. I hope that this book will help the world see these enticements clearly for what they are. And I hope that this book will serve as a guide to identifying their game, rejecting their premises, and helping our age to back out of the illogic of their arguments before it is too late.

CHAPTER 9

The Marxists – The Ultimate Useful Idiots

Perhaps the worst concealed conspiracy in the history of the world is that the communist movement is here in America. That one is no longer in the "theory" stage; they've been here for a long time. Hell, we have avowed, self-identifying collectivists in Congress! And it goes without saying that being a collectivist (ideologically a top-down central planner) is a pre-requisite for wanting to work as a bureaucrat in the fourth branch of government. There are no communist Republicans, so far as I know. They are all on the left, and the establishment Democrats can call them the 'radical left' or the 'fringe left' all they want to; it doesn't change the fact that the patients have taken over the asylum. The country has slowly been sliding to the left over the past forty years, a bit like wading out into a shallow surf. But ever since the 2016 election, it feels like our country has finally found the edge of the continental shelf. We have been so jarred by the progressive's narrative that most people can't recenter themselves due to the whiplash. And notice I did not say the Democratic vision for the country; it is the full-blown, neo-Marxist vision.

The goal of the global communist movement is to continue 'the revolution' until every person is under communist rule. Until, basically, there is no other alternative to communism. This is an ideological struggle, one that has a religious adherence component to it. It is not necessarily the communists' desire for a one-world government; that push is coming from a different direction. The communists are here in America, and they now animate the Democratic Party through the American arm of the global communist movement: the progressives. These are the people who espouse grievance policy and victim mentality and have used Marxist critical theory, most recently through "anti-racism" and modern gender theory.

The purpose is to burn America down so that they can reign over the ashes. I know that sounds harsh, but it is true. They say that America is a systemically evil place that has never been good and is in need of (in Obama's words) "fundamental transformation." I don't think that they have any common ground with American patriots. I don't say that necessarily to people on the right; I'm talking to every single independent, moderate, and liberal who is in the middle of that divide. I am speaking to everyone who does not absolutely agree with every tenant of the radical, progressive left. While the conservatives might allow you the freedom to live in the middle, the progressives will not. If they win out in what they consider to be an ideological war for the soul of the nation, you will have to declare your allegiance to them or join the conservatives in the gulag.

Collectivism as a modern social phenomenon took on its modern form in the late 1800s and culminated in the establishment of many communist regimes throughout the post-World War II era, with the USSR and the PRC chief among them. All the useful idiots speaking about, advocating for, and eventually succumbing to the ideology of communism only served to help despots come to power in these countries. They were politically useful idiots, for sure. And now the entire nation has to experience the misery of despotic totalitarianism.

The global communist movement is more of a religious doctrine than it is a prescription for government, because, as we discussed earlier, the doctrine of communism is an ideology that cannot produce what it advocates: that governments should be communist. Asking a government, which is by nature a hierarchical structure, to be a mechanism of complete and total societal equity makes as much sense as demanding that all bachelors remain bachelors—but also get married. Communism as a doctrine is really good at creating chaos through critical theory and stirring populations to grievance. As a political doctrine underpinned by theological adherence to its beliefs, it is also a way to claim a feigned moral superiority in politics. It is a powerfully destructive force in society, beyond the death and carnage in the wake of the regimes that carry the name 'communist.' It is the perfect international mechanism for a regime that wants to centrally plan the world and must tear down successful economic systems to achieve their ends.

The people who sincerely believe that communism is a force for good, or are true believers, are going to find out the hard way that they were the ultimate useful idiots to a global hegemon that used the doctrine of communism to bring every country and people under its rule. Not for the purpose of peace, prosperity, or human flourishing, but rather to establish their global totalitarian regime. From there, the doctrines of communism will be used to guilt societies into submission, be the justification of their central planning, and be the noble 'revolution' that they must protect from any political dissident who dares challenge their hegemony. They will be able to achieve, in theory, the global communist vision, but no hierarchy can actually achieve the global communist vision in practice. It is a mechanism for despots to gain power, just like it always is. Don't be the WEF's most useful idiot. If you are a communist or a communist sympathizer, heed the words of Michael Jordan: "Stop it. Get some help."

Regardless of how the party started, the Democrat Party has now become the party of the progressives. Although the greatest amount of social damage came through the 'liberal' movement in the latter half of the twentieth century, the global communist movement got a toehold much earlier. We will end the chapter on how the liberal movement is connected to and most responsible for the blooming of progressivism that we see today. The Democrats became the party of the 'progressives' during what is dubbed the 'progressive era' (1890–1920). It was a great propaganda move by the global communist movement, which converted the term and used it for their own devices. Before the Wilson presidency (1913–1921), a Republican president used the term progressivism. Teddy Roosevelt assumed the post of president in 1901 after the assassination of President McKinley. Despite the political arguments as to why, TR was on McKinley's ticket because of his 'progressive' platform. (It should be noted that McKinley was killed by a so-called 'anarchist.' Leon Czolgosz, though, was connected to many people and organizations in what was becoming the anti-American underground. It was the beginnings of the global communist movement without an official title; they were the 'disaffected workers' that had already begun to undermine the country. I point this out because the people who were plotting to establish the Fed and create voluntary socialism in America are the people he had true grievance with. The T.O.D.s, the tycoons, were the ones causing the 'inequity' he claimed to avenge in killing the president.)

TR became one of the most popular presidents in American history, meaning that he was truly loved by the common American people, while the elites wrote op-eds about how terrible he was. This 'yellow journalism' was as popular as 'fake news' is today, and it points to the same problem of journalists forming conclusions and steering the facts conveniently toward them. Gee, I scratch my head to come up with a modern example. I digress, TR's progressivism was based on holding together American principles and bringing them into the modern age. Remember, this was the height of the social upheaval that was caused by the Industrial Revolution. Armed and violent conflicts broke out between workers and factory security teams regularly during this time. TR's 'Square Deal' platform saw the breaking up of monopolies, factory work reforms, and the establishment of norms and standards for pay and treatment of workers. He was a veteran of the Spanish-American War, oversaw the building of the Panama Canal, and founded the National Parks System. He was, you might say, an America first candidate (which used to be very non-controversial in American politics), and that meant he had equal regard for American business and the American people. He was so influential within the Republican Party that he began to change the tenor and tone of Republican politics (and the establishment couldn't have that).

In 1908, the established powers-that-be schmoozed him out of running for what would have ostensibly been his third term. They promised him the ability to pick his replacement and bring him into the party's future policy positions. But they didn't. TR became so angry with the Republican Party that he challenged Taft for the Republican nomination in 1912. It was a bitter primary between TR's loyalists and the obviously corrupt Republican establishment. But the powers that be managed to achieve the herculean effort of pushing Taft over the finish line (or rolled more like it! Ha. That's a 'Taft was fat' joke). TR began his own Progressive Party and ran as the third-party candidate. Although it was known more commonly as the "Bull Moose Party," it was officially the Progressive Party. His 1912 campaign still remains the most successful third-party run, winning twenty-seven percent of the popular vote.

It is worth noting that there was an attempted assassination during his campaign, in which TR was shot in the chest. He proceeded to survive, make it to his destination, and deliver his speech with a bullet in his chest. The would-be assassin was deemed insane; he claimed the ghost of McKinley appeared to him in a dream and told him to do it. Of interest, though, was that he tracked TR across the country, from Louisiana to Wisconsin, over the course of weeks on the campaign trail. For context, Southern states still lynched people, and Wisconsin was one of the few states that did not have the death penalty, so you be the judge of how lucid he was. Whether he was also a collectivist sympathizer or a plant, the whole situation was not on the up and up, and it lets you know just how much power the men behind the curtain had already obtained. Ultimately, TR's success would prove to be a dire turning point for the country and the permanent redefinition of progressivism, from moral American reform to full-blown allegiance to communism.

The outcome of the 1912 election was that the Democratic Party came out victorious. In 1913, a rabid central planner, socialist sympathizer, and open racist assumed the office of president. He re-segregated the White House service staff as one of his first actions as president. He also screened the very first film at the White House, called Birth of a Nation. Originally, it was released to Southern audiences under the title The Klansmen. The film was a dramatic account of the heroic founding of the Ku Klux Klan. His plan for a League of Nations and his famous Fourteen Points sound eerily similar to some modern 'predictions' that have been made for 2030. Things like how the world should run under a single economy and that no two nations could have private diplomatic arrangements without the consent of the council. Although he had strong rhetoric against the Bolsheviks of Russia, he considered himself and his newly defined 'Progressive Agenda' to be akin to the socialist movements of Europe, primarily the socialist parties that were just coming to prominence in Italy and Germany.

Woodrow Wilson, the global communist movement, and the Democratic Party irrevocably redefined the word progressivism in America to be on the political left, where it has stayed ever since. To make the argument that today's Democratic Party would be 'unrecognizable' to Wilson is to be naïve. He would recognize it as the logical extension of what he was able to implement in his time. The shift of American progressivism away from American values and into the values of the global communist movement is a through line. Formed within the Democratic Party, this line links the disparate anti-American movements of the Progressive Era, down to Woodrow

Wilson and the redefining of progressivism, through to FDR, LBJ, Barack Obama, and even down to "The Squad." This shift into communist ideology is ultimately the shift away from God's law and into the realm of relativism.

If you spend any time in the political space today, you will quickly realize how the ideas of the right are demonized by the left. Every person to the right of Barack Obama is a Nazi, a racist, a sexist, a this-ist, a that-ist, and every other -ist in the book. According to the left, they do not deserve to be a part of polite society; if they speak their ideas publicly, they deserve to be cancelled. Although there are a few brave souls out there fighting back, the right has been much slower in their demonization of the left. It shows that one side is more serious about winning the conflict than the other. But the weak Republicans will say they are 'standing on principle' or some nonsense. As though when you show up to the knife fight and a gun is pulled, the 'noble' thing to do is charge into gunfire with your knife.

Whether we want to admit it or not, we are in a polarized political struggle, and it is not because the Republicans have become more radical. The progressives have obfuscated their main aims and goals for half a century behind the mask of liberalism, but now that they don't have to hide it anymore, they are speaking plainly. **And the plain truth is this: the Progressive Party cannot achieve their vision as long as God is America's King and We, The People, adorn our little piece of His crown.** There is no simpler way to put it. They will demonize their opponent and ratchet it up to eleven until they have achieved their vision. It is not going to cool down anytime soon, and trying to ignore it is only putting the lid on the pressure cooker.

We are in a hyper-partisan struggle; we are the demons in the progressive's narrative, where they are the angels of Utopia. Right now, they are attacking the Christian conservatives because they are the easiest targets. Just like in the cautionary tale, they are counting on independents and moderates to stand by and do nothing because they are not part of the particular group receiving the progressives' ire. Every niche group is hoping that, in the end, they will be able to bargain with the progressives to save their own skins. But there will be no bargaining; they will come for everyone who does not assent to their vision of heaven on earth. After the right is gone, they are going to eat the middle too. Then they will eat the self-styled "liberals" who are on the left. They won't stop until they have complete hegemonic control and no opposition whatsoever.

So, whether you are a traditional Catholic who has earned an FBI surveillance detail by attending Latin Mass or a Bill Maher liberal being ostracized by your own comrades, you better realize that they are coming for you. Not for the crazies, not for the fringe, and not for 'those guys on the other team'—for you. They are coming for you, and they will not rest until you say, two plus two equals five, or until they send you to 'colonize Mars.' It is time that every non-progressive in this country, as disparate as our worldviews may be, stand up against the poison that is progressivism and drive it from our shores forever. We must become their demons! We must embrace our role and become the Demons of Utopia. Because once we as a country are able to pass back through the looking glass and back into reality, we will realize that being demonized by the progressives was our only proof that we were actually ever on the right side of things.

The progressives, building on the liberals before them, have made an art out of shutting Christian conservatives up in this country. They have done so by weaponizing the Christian faith against

Christians for the purpose of achieving their political ends. What the Christian conservatives have failed to realize is that a holy war is being waged on them. Most Christians follow the God, family, and country model, so they do not equate God and government. The progressives cannot see that, by abandoning God, they have made a god out of the government and a religion out of politics. In a strange way, neither realizes that they are in a holy war against each other, because while both are focused on political issues, neither sees that their religious underpinnings are at war with each other. It is time that the right become much more engaged in politics because of their love for God. The right needs to be convicted to restore the promise of America for moral reasons and begin to have a more cohesive vision. A vision of being a good American because they are trying to be a faithful Christian. I hope that this might be a good launching point for connecting those dots.

Gen. Mark Milley, retired chairman of the Joint Chiefs of Staff, proved himself to be an abject disaster for the military. During a Congressional hearing, he had a 'viral' moment when he said that he wasn't even sure what 'woke' means. In the days of the Cold War, military personnel would read The Communist Manifesto so we could better understand our enemy. Conversely, Milley had the servicemen reading about 'white rage' so they could properly feel their guilt during struggle sessions. If anyone embodies the injection of wokeness, it's this guy. Which is, of course, why his statement was so absurd. The left is trying desperately to avoid defining it or allowing it to be used as a label, thus the obfuscation. Clay Travis of Outkick the Coverage gave a pretty good definition to the term woke. During an exchange with Stephen A. Smith, who was feigning ignorance, asked him to define it. Travis said 'woke culture' could be defined as "identity politics matters more than anything else." That is a good definition because it is getting more to the heart of what woke is. Being woke means adhering to an ideological framework. It means more than 'someone with dyed hair and piercings, prone to protest' (although we all know that would be the picture next to the word in the dictionary). I would define woke as:

Woke ('wōk) adjective – 1 – political, The religious adherence to the political doctrine of progressivism.

Which would beg the question: What is progressivism, then?

Progressivism: the fusion of moral relativism as a theological lens and collectivism as a political philosophy, acted out by whatever means necessary for the purpose of complete hegemonic control of a society.

You have to understand this framework for the madness that is the left to make sense. As moral relativists in a moral society, they will moralize the people and claim that their point of view is the more moral one. They will tell Christians they aren't good Christians unless they are nice and tolerant. These, of course, are not virtues of Christianity, but it's been a very powerful and useful tactic to silence those they have declared their enemies. They will puff people up, shout them down, stroke their egos, or indulge their fantasy just as long as it accomplishes the goal. That is why they are constantly contradicting their own viewpoints on different social issues. It's not hypocrisy to believe that black is white and white is black when you're a relativist. The point is not the point; winning is the point. And the more you can make your opponent focus on the point, the more winning you will be doing. It is about power and control; that is the god in their framework, and political activism and bureaucratic control are their modes of operation toward what they worship.

This is the framework for all people who hear the doctrine of communism, accept it in their hearts as lord and savior, and then go about doing something about it. The hypocrisy is lost on them that, as they put themselves in the leadership roles of the communist project, they have adopted a hierarchy contrary to their new religion. Either they are too ideologically enamored to notice, or they never intended to make good on communism's promises. Meaning that from the start it was always meant to be a vehicle for their power; the religion of communism is simply the opiate for the masses that they now control. This is one of the primary signs that proves that progressivism is just the American arm of the global communist movement. The alignment of its timeline with the emergence of the global communist movement should be a clear indication that these two are, at least, inextricably linked. As the end of this age draws near, time will prove that they are one and the same.

The period of time from the end of Civil War Reconstruction to the end of World War I was the height of social and economic upheaval caused by the industrial revolution, and the communist movement took every advantage of the newly created 'working masses.' They also took advantage of the fact that the world was, for the first time, becoming "global" in the modern sense of the word. Through mechanisms like the stock market, the multi-national corporation, and the coalescence of wealth in tighter and tighter rings of influence, fewer and fewer people had control of more and more. The T.O.D.s began placing progressives in power, funding their campaigns, and bringing them in as the 'political partners.' Although paradoxical, the move was actually quite genius. It worked extremely well in the case of President Wilson. And it helped to form that sense of partnership—that the T.O.D.s were 'down with the struggle' and allies. It was a sign to the global communists that these elite were part of 'the revolution' if only silent financial partners in the mission. But in the end, it was the T.O.D.s who got exactly what they wanted. The vetting process for picking these progressive candidates ensured that they weren't getting pure ideologues who would turn on them.

By the proletariat politician agreeing to partner with the bourgeoisie from the start, they knew what they were getting: a politician who would preach collectivist rhetoric for the sake of power. A match made in utopia! Like-minded central planners doing the bidding of the inapparent kings of the world. All the while, the politicians preach to the crowd that they are working to reign in wealth and socialize the economy. The perfect cover for the power behind the throne who wanted just that: a global economy over, above, and more powerful than any country. As time went on, they would expand those governments and fill them with little Faucis—I mean, despots—I mean expert bureaucrats—spouting collectivist ideas for the sake of power. But those little urchins will know from where their power derives and, ultimately, will assent to the proper authority when the time comes for the WEF to take over the world. The ultimate useful idiots.

We have had two progressive presidents in U.S. history and two more presidential administrations that formed alliances with the progressive movement. Now, we have the height of the WEF's version of the progressive vision: one complete shill of a human being who claims to be president, is in control of nothing, and has ushered in the rule of America via the 'experts' in the fourth branch of government. Woodrow Wilson and Barack Obama were our two true progressive presidents. FDR was much more fascist ideologically, but he found some of the progressives' aims and tactics to be somewhat useful. LBJ's administration found similar convenience and cover for their own aims and ambitions during the radical progressive movement of the 1960s. The complete shill is Joe Biden; clearly someone is steering that ship, and it's not 'the Big Guy.' Wilson, the patriarch in this unholy alliance, foresaw a day when the 'expert ruling class' would engineer governments and societies.

The common man would be ruled by bureaucrats in Washington who were so smart that they could centrally plan our lives. They would become our moral betters, who would correct our thoughts and opinions by telling us how we must live—all for our safety and protection, you understand. If COVID taught us anything, it's that the progressives have reached their aims! Regardless of where Wilson stood on communism, he certainly shared the theology of relativism: that reality is a construct and can be reimagined into whatever image can be conjured up in the mind of man. This idea is as old as the Garden of Eden; the serpent's enticement to Eve was that 'ye shall be as gods.' Wilson certainly felt that the world was ours to remake in our image and that there was no limiting principle in that statement. He was willing to twist words, manipulate arguments, and do whatever it took to 'liberate' America from the grip of the Constitution. The Constitution was meant to be a foundational document, terra firma, for the formation of our country. That stands in the way of the progressives' goal of reforming the country in their image.

So, Wilson set about waxing poetically on the 'true nature' of Americanism being 'stifled' by the Constitution. He claimed that the way the Founders thought about politics was outdated and not able to lead a modern nation in modern times. Listen to the mental gymnastics he is willing to go to in order to justify his stance:

"The Constitution was founded on the law of gravitation. The government was to exist and move by virtue of the efficacy of "checks and balances." The trouble with the theory is that government is not a machine, but a living thing. It falls, not under the theory of the universe, but under the theory of organic life. It is accountable to Darwin, not to Newton. It is modified by its environment, necessitated by its tasks, shaped to its functions by the sheer pressure of life. No living thing can have its organs offset against each other, as checks, and live."[22]

Wilson is injecting a relativistic, Godless way of interpreting a document very much founded on the Natural Law. This is what many left-leaning judges in the judicial system do today, pretending that in any way the people who wrote the Constitution did so to protect pornography, flag burning, or the private citizenship of corporations. I'd have to conclude that Wilson was pretty 'woke' and was dreaming about enacting the policies that are now coming to fruition. His rhetoric sounds like that of modern pundits, who imply that the Constitution is somehow racist or that we need to abandon our founding documents altogether because they are outdated. This is right in line with Obama's platitude of wanting to "fundamentally transform" America. In reality, the Constitution was to be a grounding force for the organic operators of the government. The way to stop corrupt men from corrupting our government. The Founders would have never seen the 'government' as a single organism the way in which Wilson describes it. Wilson's words reveal his own bias and worldview, as well as just how un-Christian and un-American his philosophy is.

Now, over a century later, the progressives are finally getting their way ... and it shows. Although Rudi Dutschke, the West German radical socialist, coined the term "long march through the institutions"[23] sometime in the late 1960s, he was describing an ongoing process that had infiltrated America far before that. There were true believers in the government well before the social revolutions that occurred in the 1960s, but it was still a wildly unacceptable position to the general public; communists were still closeted members of society. There had to be a new tactic that would separate people from their trust in America's promise and their faith in God. It had to be able to guilt people into accepting the left's positions without being able to use collectivist arguments and rhetoric. In short, they needed a pervasive ideology that the American people could stomach while it eroded our country. And thus, Modern Liberalism was born.

Modern Liberalism: an ideology which redefines the primary virtue of Americanism as unmitigated tolerance of all behaviors, dispositions, ideologies, and world views. This ideology asserts that it is the obligation of the American experiment to incorporate and tolerate all viewpoints into itself. This ideology practically functions by viewing the past with skepticism; insisting that the old ways were formed through superstitious religiosity. Therefore, the morals and morays of our society must be redefined to comport with the modern world. Its promise is that this unmitigated freedom of the individual to think, behave, and associate as they please without limit will lead to true personal freedom and a flourishing society.

Dutschke was connecting the dots, showing that this modern liberalism was a part of 'the revolution; it was just the latest iteration of it in this new age. There is just one fatal flaw in the definition above: there is no limiting principle. There is no end to what can be redefined into oblivion in every new age. In Dutschke's time, it was a new age of radicalism—flag burning and spitting on soldiers. Communists were demanding toleration for their poisonous speech. The free love movement and the denigration of the American people through drugs, satiation, and the abandonment of faith. In a very short period of time, moral relativism as a more tolerant, more just, and more open society supplanted the promise of America and the various Christian denominations as the national grounding force. It vilified faithful people as bigots, intolerant of their fellow man, and too dumb and stupid to step into a new and modern world. It mocked American idealism and true capitalist principles as the economy soared to new heights and began to globalize. It primed the pump for the moral ambiguity of countries, creeds, and mantras; no longer did we have a unique American ethic, and people were happy about it. You don't want to be judgmental, you see. Modern Liberalism was released on the American people as a neo-communist primer, and it worked perfectly. Now, most moderate Republicans espouse some form of modern liberalism, meaning that the most radical hippy in the late 1960s is now just a run-of-the-mill Republican. That's how far we have slid to the left in the last sixty years.

Modern liberals are also moral relativists by nature, with a unique design enhancement: they find their superiority in carving out arbitrary guard rails, or 'bridges too far' for themselves and society.

This way, the liberal politician will push for 'reform' but not have to 'go all the way.' The other enhancement is that the liberals got to pretend to be a part of the 'classical liberal' tradition of Jefferson 'and others.' This was an appeal back to liberalism spawning from 'enlightenment principles,' although no one can quite seem to define what those are exactly (you will get as many different definitions as the number of people you ask). And it made modern liberalism sound American and part of the American tradition, even though they can't quite put a finger on how "defending pornographers" is "Jeffersonian."

The Modern Liberals were here to do one thing: to ask 'why not?' in a morally relativistic yet morally superior tone. They were here to put "Wouldn't It Be Nice" by the Beach Boys on repeat. Wouldn't it be nice if we could maintain a moral society if we lose our faith in God? Wouldn't it be nice if we could just foot every bill, fund every war, satisfy every need, and spend more than we take in each year in taxes? Wouldn't it be nice if we could cure poverty and every injustice? Of course it would! Only a bigot would say no—and you're not a bigot, are you? We (the progressives pushing modern liberalism) just need you to give up your freedoms and your money and trust in the government to solve problems for you (the government we are reforming in our image). We need a new three-letter agency to fix that. They were here to ask 'why not?' in every sphere of life. Because, after all, they are progressives, and the progressives believe that the personal is the political. Why can't we have prolific sex and erase the consequences through hormonal drugs and abortion? Why can't we pretend that there is no real difference in makeup between men and women? Why can't we do whatever we want in the privacy of our homes as long as we're consenting adults? Why, why, why? You're not a bigot who wants to steal my happiness, are you? We (the progressives who push modern liberalism) just need to rob the American people of their taboos and their traditions. We need to rob the states and local communities of any of their local sovereignty. We have to vilify anyone who would try to set a moral standard. Those types are just close-minded bigots. Look how smart and tolerant we are!

They have called us bigots for sixty years, while they have driven our country into the ground and are barely holding onto that power as the new radicals stand poised to rend it out of their octogenarian hands. It is all part of the same machine, and the new operators will push these progressive reforms to heights that even modern liberals will never have imagined.

Moderate Republicans are liberals who drive the speed limit, as the saying goes. Liberals are merely progressives who drive slightly over the speed limit. That is, they consider themselves 'radicals' and 'progressive' but still think they are grounded in principle. Self-styled liberals are people who won't assent to the moral law but still think that some things are still morally "beyond the pale." It simply means that they think their outlook is right; the way that they see the world is right. Their perception of good and evil is the correct lens with which to view the world; in other words, they are the arbiters of their own truth. In short, they are moral relativists.

Bill Maher is a perfect example of this. He has scoffed at every Republican who has ever appeared on his show. He made an entire movie about how 'dumb' religious people are and how 'dumb' religion is in general. He has made a career out of being a middle finger, but he is ultimately pointing that middle finger at God, a moral code, and anything else that he sees as 'stifling his freedom.' This is the perception that freedom is license rather than liberty. It is a cheap and fleeting view of the world, and it has no historical basis in American culture or politics. It obviously has failed Bill Maher, as he finds himself aghast that the new generation is outflanking him to the left and pushing him out of his own party.

Committed modern liberals today are caught in their own trap; they want to continue to preach their 'you do you boo' doctrine, but now they are shocked to find that the generation supplanting them is tearing down the arbitrary guard rails that they put up! How dare they breach the guidelines we felt were beyond reproach? Bill Maher has cursed at, derided, and bullied people on the right his entire career. Now that he is being cancelled by the progressives that his liberalism fostered, he has the audacity to look over his right shoulder and say, "Can you believe the kids these days?" Yes, Bill, we can. Thanks for calling us bigots when we told you this is exactly what would happen. Thanks for calling us bigots still and pretending that there is not a pattern of behavior here that began with your broken, anti-God, and therefore anti-American, ideology.

Here is a last, tongue-in-cheek analogy that I will use to sum up the last sixty years. Compare politics to a modern family's vehicle safety and maintenance. The conservative dad who bought the family car is the one who recognizes the rules of the road and the maintenance requirements of the vehicle. The conservative dad says that, for the good of all fellow travelers, we should all follow the rules of the road and keep our cars well maintained. This makes the family consider him stodgy, old-fashioned, fuddy duddy, and so forth. The liberal is the mom, who gets to drive the new, nicer car (that dad also paid for). He can drive the old one. She drives it irresponsibly, questions every rule of the road, never changes the oil, all the while blaring "Wouldn't It Be Nice" by the Beach Boys. It is the conservative dad's responsibility to keep the liberal mom's car on the road, but he is never allowed to interject his opinion on safety, maintenance, or driving. The progressive is the activist son, who gets the brand-new car with an even bigger car payment than mom's car. Dad's still driving the old clunker. The son ends up speeding through the ditch in a school zone. But he has an ally in the liberal mom; it's two against one, and the conservative dad is not allowed to ever comment on, give advice, or demand safe driving or good vehicle safety or maintenance from either of them.

If the conservative dad ever points out the simple fact that the oil needs to be changed and that reckless driving is dangerous, both the liberal and the progressive stick their heads defiantly out the window and shriek, 'Why do you care so much? Why can't we just live our lives the way we want? What an idiot!' The liberal mom's car doesn't get far; her car breaks down after she puts diesel in the tank, but she finds some way to blame everyone else for her failures. The progressive son, on a handful of cheap amphetamines, flies into the school crosswalk, mows down eight kids, and blames society for all of his failures. Then the liberal mom turns to the conservative dad and says in exasperation, 'Who could have seen this coming? Can you believe what our son has done!' The conservative dad has to pay for the liberal mom's tow, the progressive's damages and legal fees, and is not allowed to be a part of the conversation as to how we might keep this from happening in the future. And that is the final outcome; the right never gets to offer solutions; their voice is to never be heard. At best, the liberal gets a seat at the table, but it is really the progressive voice and solutions who will win in the end. The progressive solution is to redefine his crimes out of existence and walk away from the courtroom holding the gavel and judging the world (which he claims failed him). Thanks, liberals; they couldn't have done it without you!

I don't have a 'new found respect' for Bill Maher because he's angry at the urchins his generation influenced—he's only angry that they don't respect the arbitrary guardrails he set. There should be no remorse for the liberals having blown up the original and rightly set guardrails in the first place, and we shouldn't be looking to 'restore' America to a relativistic and liberal 1990s culture. If the right ever begins to make headway, mark my words: the progressives will pivot back to a Clintonian moderation for the sake of preserving 'the revolution.' This should not be an acceptable position of stasis for the American people, no matter how enticing the 1990s sound as compared to our current madness. Modern liberalism was always just the progressive movement masquerading as liberalism. If we allow it to retake the dominant narrative, we will only delay the WEF and their plans for a Great Reset. And our children will not thank us for that, not while they are navigating their future as it approaches the brink.

It is important to understand where the politics of the global communist movement fit into the overall picture of the WEF's plans. Mostly, because we are fighting a battle on two fronts. If we are able to expose the WEF for what they are (T.O.D. psychos who want to rule the world) and defeat them, that will be great! But we have to defeat their useful idiots as well, the 'junior partners' in their globalist endeavor. We have to drive these morally relative, power-hungry ideologues away from polite society, political discourse, and ever having institutional control again. We have to punish professors and teachers who poison our children's minds with collectivism and moral relativism. Because the truth is, they will always be somebody's useful idiot. In today's day and age, they are especially dangerous. They are walking the world into the hands of the T.O.D.s, who have the power to control the world's politics for the next thousand years.

But they will sleepwalk into anyone's power grab; they are equal opportunity offenders in this regard. We are a unique nation with a unique founding. We have a soul, and it is not the soul of the global communists. And most importantly, we are not a liberal democracy with a morally relative ideology seeking to return to a liberal normalcy. We are Americans with a promise from almighty God! We are His sons and heirs, and it is our sacred duty to uphold a society of brave and courageous people who would go to war to avoid the captivity of collectivism or the slavery of tyranny. Don't be a useful idiot; don't be the liberal mechanism by which useful idiots gain outsize power; and don't be a squish who can't make up his mind. Be the alternative that your country needs you to be. It's our only hope.

CHAPTER 10

Whose Future Will We Live In?

Machiavelli's seminal work is *The Prince*, which often gets a bad rap for being cruel. I think that one of the biggest disconnects for American conservatives reading *The Prince* is that they have accepted several liberal lies. The first is that a Christian is a hypocrite if he is a shrewd politician, even though Jesus himself asked his disciples to be 'wise as serpents and innocent as doves.' The other lie that is improperly foisted upon Christian conservatives is that niceness is a virtue. This is a lie to make Christians feel guilty if they oppose the liberal worldview or disagree with their policy points. It does not exist to make people nicer or more tolerant. It is the liberal's cudgel to put Christians and conservatives in what the liberal deems their 'proper' place. That is at the political 'kid's table' while the 'adults in the room' slowly push the country left. The same tactic is being used when the left calls the right 'racist.' If you called Nick Fuentes a racist, he would say 'thank you!' and not be offended in the least, because he's racist. The trope is used against someone who is not a racist because the person slinging the insult knows that the person will be offended! You should be nice to your friends, and for the most part, you should be nice to strangers. But there is no room for niceness in a bare-knuckle brawl. Nor is it 'nice' or noble to continue to fight with your bare fists when the other guy pulls out brass knuckles.

The term "Machiavellian" has become synonymous with people who use any means necessary to get what they want. But if you actually read *The Prince*, I don't think that this is what Machiavelli was actually getting at. He has a lot of good advice for appeasing the people, honoring promises made in negotiation, and keeping one's word to curry favor with allies and maintain a strong national front. Sure, a fair bit of his advice is morally questionable and really only applicable in the feudalistic context of the Italian city-state system. However, Machiavelli's key insight into politics was that people vying for power in a political sphere are enemies, and enemies, by definition, are not friends. We don't live in a world today governed by political parties who are debating the best way to get to our common destination. We live in a world today where the political vision of the left has made itself an enemy to whoever would oppose it. And enemies—well, they are at war with each other. The first person who recognizes this and can master the situation has a far greater likelihood of winning. To be Machiavellian, in its proper context, should mean to be shrewd, to be wise as a serpent but innocent as a dove. In deeply polarized times like this, I think we do Machiavelli and ourselves a disservice by thinking of *The Prince* in a purely negative light.

Alexandra Pelosi, Nancy Pelosi's daughter, once described her mother by saying, "She'll cut your head off, and you won't even know you're bleeding."[24] This is the type of moral relativism that proves which side Nancy Pelosi is on but does not necessarily make her 'Machiavellian.' In her own mind, I'm sure it does. But if her own daughter says this about her, then the only thing she took away from The Prince was the line "it is better to be feared than loved,"[25] and then took it so far out of context that she owes Machiavelli an apology.

As I said, progressives do not have moral standards and only care about yours insofar as they can turn them into a stumbling block for you. If we can be wise as serpents and find ways to beat them on the battlefield, we will not be abandoning or betraying our moral, conservative, or Christian values. We will just actually meet them where they are, beat them at their own game, actually win for once, and begin to push back on the culture war that is being waged on this country. That begins with the right having a vision for the country, and that vision cannot just be to 'stop the left.' I bring up Machiavelli because I think that he gets a bad rap as a 'mafioso type,' and that is simply not true. But also, because it would be easy to vilify the members of the WEF and the collectivists with the Machiavellian stigma. In doing so, we would abandon our own ability to fight back in the ways that we need to. I would call the WEF members and the collectivists Machiavellian with great reluctance because I think these people are way, way worse.

There is a categorical difference between shrewd and evil; Alexandra's quote above is exhibit A. I do think that the left would do whatever it took to win, morals and the rest of it be damned. We do not have to be that way in dealing with them, but we cannot also pretend that we can 'nice' them into submission and that we can 'win them over to our way of thinking.' They are counting on you doing this, by the way. They prepared for battle and counted on you showing up to have a conversation. Because in that scenario, it is much easier for them to cut your throat before you realize you're bleeding. Then, when you are indignant, they will tell you that you can't fight back. You have to 'stand on your principle' and 'lose with dignity.' Meanwhile, the point was not the point; the point was winning. And who walked away with the W?

I spent many years in relationships with people who exhibited non-clinical sociopathy. It was the water I swam in, and so I didn't know any different, and my normalcy bias told me that what I was going through was fine. Often, when people are describing narcissists, sociopaths, or psychopaths, they are described as having a 'lack of empathy.' I'm no psychiatrist or psychologist, and I realize that all of these terms are used improperly and should only be used to describe diagnoses and not behaviors. I also know that it is popular to use these terms on social media videos to describe people you don't like, and that is not appropriate either. But people use these terms recreationally because they do comport with patterns of behavior, and they become the mechanism by which we can talk about such things.

Although it is true that people who are full of themselves (or insistent upon the world bending to their will) lack empathy, it is a little bit more complex than that. After years of trying to negotiate with, appease, or otherwise maintain the relationship, there are at least two components that I see; the first is that it is a strange, inside-out dissociative disorder. I mean that you always seem to be speaking to their 'front office,' as though their authentic self is always behind the veil. When they need to, they will appear authentic, but the illusion of aloofness and the illusion that something is brewing under the surface are useful tactics. These can be used to create mystery and tension where there is none, but ultimately it is a way to hide oneself from exposure or vulnerability, and it is a survival mechanism that was learned through some past trauma in their life (after all, hurt people hurt people).

The second thing I notice is that they recognize the niceties and norms of behavior around them, and they weaponize them against the people that they are in relationships with. I have described it as a moment of 'enlightenment' in their mind, whereby they recognize that someone's good will and social norms can be used to manipulate them. The manipulators just have to be 'brave enough' to step outside of the fray and hold themselves outside of those norms. This creates a superiority complex in the person's mind.

This phenomenon plays out in the mantra 'people are dumb and follow cultural mores; I will not follow the mores, and in my enlightenment, I am free to use the mores against others for the purpose of my power.' Because if the world is relative and the norms of a society are not based in morals, then it is just an arbitrary jungle where every creature is locked in a death struggle with every other creature. In such a world, it is nothing more than a power struggle, and only the most powerful, the apex predator, wins in the end. It is a light switch moment that, unfortunately, is very hard to reverse. From there, the only change you see is a change in tactic, and the longer someone persists in this mode of operation, the harder the reversal and the climb back out to normalcy.

I want to draw this distinction because it is the difference between the Pelosi caricature and the path that we need to take. I truly believe that this one life experience has done more to prepare me to write about this particular political moment and this particular movement. I can attribute my recognition of manipulation and abuse to it. I can attribute my strong sense of justice and rejection of moral relativism to it. I can attribute my love of reason and philosophy to it. And I can attribute my ability to see systems to it—to recognize the system that you are in and recognize if it is designed for a mutual relationship or one-way dominance. I spent years coming out of those manipulative relationships, having to relearn what it meant to have a normal relationship. I can tell you I am never going back into that realm, either to be the abuser or the abused. I am still working to continuously improve my ability to have flourishing relationships. But once you have seen it, you cannot unsee it, and you cannot unsee it whenever you encounter it in the world. So here we are.

THE SLIPPERY SLOPE

The slippery slope argument is a logical fallacy. It assumes a causal chain from an original event, which cannot be proven with certainty, will happen. Something like, "If you don't get into a good college, you will be poor the rest of your life." It is fallacious not because the logic is necessarily faulty but because it is operating from a false premise. The example above requires you to assume the false premise that a traditional education from an elite academy is the only way to become wealthy. It is important to note that slippery-slope statements are not necessarily always false; they are just not always true. The left has become masters of the slippery slope. They have perfected the art of creating slippery slopes and then accusing the right of being irrational for seeing them. By creating slippery slopes, the internal logic of their arguments becomes sound. Thus, the conclusion, in an incestuous way, moves from the realm of absurdity into the realm of foregone conclusion.

The frustrating part of being told that the slippery slope argument is a logical fallacy is that we can very clearly see that it is the intended outcome of the progressive agenda. The big push in the Vietnam War era to protect flag burning as an act of 'free expression' was never just about that one act of heresy. The Great Society legislation was never about truly providing economic relief to the poor. And the Green New Deal is certainly not about making the world a sustainable and cleaner place to live. It is just a first precedent—a first push off to gain momentum to get where they wanted to go all along. If it is not painfully obvious by now, it certainly should be. The expansion of progressive ideology has not come because there is broad support for their ideas. I think that if you laid out the entire progressive agenda, WEF and all, you couldn't get ten percent of the country to buy into it. Yet it pervades every corner of our society today. How can this be?

The progressives are relentless in introducing a seemingly innocuous piece of 'common sense' legislation, setting that as precedent, and then relentlessly pursuing more and more extreme precedent through legal action. Progressives demand 'common sense' gun restrictions on assault weapons. The point is to disarm us completely; you know it, I know it, they know it, God knows it, your dog knows it, even the village idiot knows it. Disarming people abiding by the law has proven time and time again to increase crime, and all the data points to this. But that doesn't sound as compassionate as trying to eradicate violence. We must, in the name of compassion, eradicate every scary boomstick that we can get our hands on. Right?

The Progressives railed against free speech restrictions in the 1960s. There wasn't a word offensive enough or an act of 'free expression' blasphemous enough to be outlawed on a college campus. Now, the same progressives who have gotten all their depravities legalized are creating limited free speech zones and 'safe spaces' on college campuses. They want to make your words illegal, in total contradiction to their original premise! You can call it absurd or a contradiction. But the point was never the point; winning was always the point. We have to recognize this, meet them where they are, and defeat their power dynamics without becoming depraved by their internal madness.

Republicans have, for far too long, been the party of inaction. "Vote for me, and I will get the government out of your personal life." Which just means they aren't going to pass legislation and set precedent while the progressives will. Even when Republicans are in power or move the needle in the right direction, what inevitably happens? The country slides to the left. The idea that we can deny the progressive's false premise is proving to be a false premise itself. When your enemy is at the gate and declares war on you, you are not at leisure to deny your enemy his war. If you are in a fight and your opponent pulls out brass knuckles, you are not at leisure to 'stand on your principles' and 'fight fairly.' The fact of the matter is, you won't be standing for long, and your opponent will clean out your wallet after they beat the crap out of you. The idea that our political leaders can 'take the high road' and not stoop to the progressives' level is a cheap out. They are basically saying they'd rather do nothing while the world burns, rather than do what is necessary to stop the arsons.

The Congressional Baseball Game takes place every year. Because the Democrats have to follow the rules of baseball, the Republicans usually win. In 2023, the Republicans beat the Democrats, 10-0. But that is not how the modern Congress works. The Republicans show up to Congress in their pressed uniforms, their rule books, their regulation equipment, and every intention to play by the rules. The progressives show up in dominatrix leather, bats wrapped in barb wire, and a sniper just in case (too soon?). The lefties burned the rule book (along with an American flag) on the pitcher's mound during the time when the National Anthem used to be played. We don't do that anymore, you see, after the left defined it as racist and banned it.

The Republicans take the field and await the first Democratic batter to step up to the plate. But lo and behold, the Democrats rush the field and start swinging their bats wildly at the Republican players. They call them racists for not allowing them the 'free expression' to play baseball in their personal lived experience. The rules, after all, are racist too and a patriarchal construct; they cannot be relied upon as a source of truth. The Republicans retreat to their dugout and watch as an angry mob of Democrats stands shoulder-to-shoulder on the basepath. They insist that unless the Republicans agree to let them 'win,' they will continue to 'play baseball' according to their 'rules.' Or whatever other 'rules' they need to get what they want. 'This is a crisis!' they shout. Now you tell me—at what point will insisting that these lunatics play by the rules resolve this situation?

I am not suggesting that the Republicans do anything extra-Constitutional, nor am I suggesting that we try to beat them at their own game with their tactics. But we do need a vision of our own to combat theirs and the courage to not only get the buy-in of the American people but also have the courage to re-establish it in our laws. We can pass a law or an amendment to the Constitution that bans collectivists from serving in government. When we have power, we can find out who helped Jeffrey Epstein "epstein" himself and actually investigate January 6, but not before we get to the bottom of what happened in the 2020 election. We can fire radical bureaucrats, declassify and dismantle the CIA, stop flying pride flags at the embassies, or really just follow through on any—any of the promises from the campaign trail. We can route CRT from schools, put our country first, or, how about ... anything? But as long as Republicans' fear of being called racist supersedes their ability to be clear-eyed opponents to the progressives, they will be too afraid to ever come out of the dugout. Pretending to stand on your 'dignity' because you think that you can deny your enemy's brawl—well, that's just weak sauce.

We must fight the culture war. We must insist that the American Way is worth defending, even against barb-wire, bat-wielding weirdo perverts in 'gender affirming' vegan leather. It is time to undo the damage done by this evil ideology and recognize that it is diametrically opposed to the American form of government and the American way of life. Most importantly, we must be unafraid to call it out for what it is. The progressives will use any object as a cudgel to hold you to your own standard for the sake of taking all standards away. They will destroy this country, and they will gladly burn it all down to reign over the ashes. That is the premise from which they are operating. Although it can be argued to be a false one, it is the real driver in the land of make believe, where all their ideas create utopian paradise. Let's stop granting them the premise that utopia is achievable. Whether they are sincere in their stupid ideas or just malevolent enough to use them for their own ends, every progressive is willing to brawl. It's high time we judiciously drive them from the field.

The ballgame analogy is often used for toxic relationships;

a toxic person doesn't want you on the field playing the game and following the rules. They want you in the alley behind the field, playing by their rules (or their toxic dynamics) and playing whatever version of 'trash ball' they are playing. Ultimately, in a relationship, you can invite that person back to the field, but if they refuse, you cannot force them. Eventually, you will have to put up an appropriate boundary between the two of you and go your separate ways. That way, you don't put them in a position to drag you back into the alley to play trash ball. Although you can depart from a relationship, our current political situation is a little more precarious because we are trapped in the same house permanently together. We are in a struggle to maintain the rules of the game, while the progressives are seeking to permanently redefine the game in their image. One will win, and the other will have to assent. That, or suffer the winner's new rule regarding dissenters.

TWO VISIONS FOR THE FUTURE OF AMERICA

It's easy to forget in the crazy chaos of modern politics, but Obama was hesitant to support same-sex marriage officially in his 2012 re-election campaign. The Obergefell decision that redefined marriage was in 2014; just look at how crazy things have become from 2014 to 2024. It is tempting to want to go back to social and political norms from ten, twenty, or even thirty years ago. But were things truly better during Obama's first term? Or were things just hidden that are now in plain sight? Does that hold true for Clinton's presidency too? Although I'd take a Clintonian Democrat in a heartbeat over a progressive, the sickness is the same in both camps; we do not know an age without relativism being a part of the social, cultural, and political dialogue. We need to be able to ideologically decouple liberalism and progressivism for the sake of political clarity, but there is no way to decouple either from the underlying premise of both ideologies.

We cannot forget that the slow relativizing of our society throughout the last century, through liberalism, is how we got here. Like the slow, clicking machinations of a roller-coaster car climbing the hill, liberalism was the mechanism by which relativism crept in and began to erode our standards, degrade our education and understanding of our freedoms, and inject unsustainable programs and bureaucratic agencies that centralized our government. That was the necessary slow-build in order for the inevitability of gravity to race us down the other—progressive—side of the tracks, where there is nothing stopping the relativists from running away with our country.

Although we have become nostalgic about the normalcy of the nineties, we cannot set our sights on going back to the beginning of the end—the'morals adjacent,' 'wouldn't it be nice if,' society. It may end this particular wild ride, but that would be like staying on the rollercoaster after it pulls back into the station and naively thinking that it won't roll back out again. We have to get completely off this ride if we want to ever reclaim a true sense of normalcy, re-establish our country's source of greatness, and create an America worth having.

Shortly after the Obergefell decision, a new term suddenly emerged onto the American lexicon. You are wise enough to put the pieces together when I say that if you criticize the validity of this word today, you become political enemy number one. It is a name that can get books banned. So, for the purposes of strategic ambiguity, let's call it 'gender relativism' for now. When I first heard this word and the basic explanation behind it, my first thought was, "Wow, they didn't wait long to move the goal posts again, did they?"

I made a statement to my friends in 2014, and I was told that I was crazy. I was told that I was being bombastic, stretching a bit too far, and that I was predicting things that could never come to pass. I would like to repeat that statement, nearly a decade after it lost me friends that day. You be the judge as to how accurate my prediction was: "The radicals will fully embrace 'gender relativism' and wield it for the sake of their power. If they can make this claim—that reality itself can be changed merely by wishing it so—what can't they extend this claim to? If you must rely on an expert's opinion to know the truth or someone's interior gnostic knowledge of themselves to truly know who they are, what fundament of reality could possibly be shared among two people? The answer is none, except for the 'reality' created by the one wielding the narrative." It has been a designed answer from the start. You tell me how far off the mark I was now that we get to live in the reality I predicted. And it's just getting started! We are only in the first third of the drop to the bottom on this wild ride. The last ten years have been psychotic, and the next ten are only going to accelerate. Even if the Great Reset ends up going pear-shaped, the next ten years are going to be insane.

By the 2034 midterm elections, we are going to live in a radically different world. And I say that not because I think the left's march is inevitable but because we are either going to live in their world or the snapback of their losing is going to radically reverse the course of this country (personally, I advocate for the latter). Either climate hysteria will drive us economically into the ground or we will be energy independent and never go back. Either we live in a pseudo-global union of governments, or that system is eradicated altogether. Either Harvard is going to be purely an indoctrination credential, or it will open back up its seminary (okay, maybe that last one is a little too hyperbolic, but you get my drift). We will either be towing the party line out of fear and have no freedom of speech and no recourse to our government, or we will live in moral clarity and true freedom decoupled from the relativistic ideologies of liberalism and collectivism. We can have either outcome, but we must fight—and win—against the worst ideas in our society if we want to achieve a better outcome. If we want the best outcome, we not only need to win against the worst ideas in our society but also against the bad ideas that served as the mechanism for introducing those worst ideas. Victory cannot look like a "return to the liberal middle." If that is the case, the globalists and collectivists will just take another pause, infiltrate the ranks slowly, and live to fight another day.

We are poised for a great ideological battle, and we have to know where allegiances lie; if not, we will be dooming future generations to being forever stuck on a rollercoaster that will inevitably lead America back to the brink. In the intro, I stated that war was being waged upon us, and that meant there were a few ways to lose but only one way to win. To give quarter to this modern liberal, relativistic ideology in the wake of a victory over the collectivists is just one of the ways to lose, or at least find ourselves in a temporary ceasefire before the degradation happens all over again. The modern liberal experiment, run by moral relativists (who all called themselves progressives, mind you), has failed in this country. They have had cultural and political control for the last sixty years. In that time, our economy has been hollowed out, our institutions are falling apart physically and ideologically, any sense of moral clarity or patriotic unity is practically non-existent, our spending and our debt is out of control, we have lost our credibility on the world stage, and the entire American project is on the brink of collapse.

And it's not because the Christians were in charge! And it's not because of conservative policies or even the Republican platform. These failures have all been liberal policies, ideas, and the mindset that you can make a brave new world out of singing "Wouldn't It Be Nice" over and over again. They don't deserve a place at the table that must be reset for our country. They can participate in the nice society that we can form in the absence of their ideas, but they cannot be allowed to continue to use American freedoms, granted by God, to undermine the reality of God, the authority of His law, and its essential place in the function of this American experiment.

THE PROGRESSIVE DECADE

There is a very clear path that will emerge in the next decade if the progressives have their way. Although there are many opinions and theories as to how we arrived at the results of the 2020 election, one thing is absolutely certain: the mailing out of unsolicited ballots by various states absolutely broke the public trust in our election system. It does not help the public trust that the legacy media, as though they are a cult, called it the 'fairest election of all time.' It really didn't help that, like an initiation ceremony for a cult, they made every 'Republican' who came onto their shows assent to this claim—live on-air—before they were allowed to continue talking about what they were there to address. Each state conducts its own elections, and in doing so, there is great public trust that they are done fairly and accurately. If we cannot rely on this outcome, the entire system will break down.

In a 2021 Forbes.com article, a Monmouth Poll was cited, which found that eighty-one percent of the country supports voter ID, including sixty-two percent of Democrats. So how did thirty-seven states modify their mail ballot rules ahead of the 2020 election, and how many of those 'modifications' were set as a new precedent? In predicting what will become of the 2024 election, I can only say the Democrats contesting the 2000, 2004, and 2016 elections and the Republicans contesting the 2020 election are going to look like child's play if there are just as many irregularities in 2024. And that is regardless of who wins. The resurfacing of the COVID hysteria in the fall of 2023 is shaping up to recreate the same scenario that we had in 2020, and this should be of deep concern for every single American.

If the progressives have their way, they will continue the new paradigm set in 2020, and despite all odds, whoever is the Democrat nominee is going to barely eek out a win in 2024. What is shaping up to be a clear Republican majority in the Senate will only materialize into a few-seat majority, and those Republicans that are elected will be controlled by an opposition that votes with Democrats on spending and social policy. The House will be reclaimed by a fractional margin by the Democrats.

If the progressives get their way, they will slowly ramp up that majority in the coming decade and slowly create and build a majority in the Senate. The 2028 election will see any conservative candidate beat out by moderate, controllable Republican candidates, and the Republican establishment will return to being the controlled opposition. By the 2030 midterms, if the progressives get their way, they will have a clear two-thirds majority in the House and Senate. The Supreme Court will be radically changed into a progressive bench, and any Republican appointments will be impeached. Then, the Constitutional amendments will begin. The Second Amendment will be revoked, as well as the First Amendment fundamentally changed to exclude intolerable speech. Most importantly, the Bill of Rights will be fundamentally redefined as "government-granted rights." And it will consist of nine amendments after the former Second Amendment is no more. Elections will be transformed into a national endeavor, and the electoral college will be disbanded. Spending will reach a breaking point, and there will be no check on the expansion of the federal bureaucracy. Then, the cataclysm will hit: The Great Reset.

I will not make predictions on what it will be, but it will be an international crisis, and the rallying cry will be for international cooperation to solve it. This will not come from the progressives, but rather from their bosses at the WEF. (The treaty to stop 'Disease X' was rolled out early in 2024; read all about it on the WEF website!) This will radically consolidate the international economy and rend any economic freedoms from every nation on Earth. The world monetary system will move to a single, global, digital currency. The World Bank and the Federal Reserve will be consolidated for the sake of international solidarity, and there will be no paper or local currencies. The European Union will either be disbanded or expanded and renamed, and a call for a global council of governments will be disseminated by every legacy media outlet.

This will be touted as the solution to our problems through social media platforms and search engine results. Unbeknownst to most, the global council of governments will have an overarching 'board' that will set the policy agenda for the global council of governments. The member countries will deliberate upon pre-ordained policies, which they will obey and incorporate into their national laws. And let me be clear—they will incorporate them if they don't want their people to suffer the consequences of their disobedience.

The progressives will lead the charge to make sure that the United States is one of the founding members, which means that we are the first to give up our sovereignty. A conversation will ensue as to whether or not a 2032 election needs to take place. By the 2034 mid-terms, if the progressives get their way, the members of the House of Representatives will be the district representatives, who are elected on the basis of their allegiance to the progressive uni-party. They will be empty vessels to have the rhetoric and policy of the global council poured into; they are nothing more than cheerleaders for the global initiatives. The Senate will continue to be the 'deliberative body' that will pass the global council's laws into our nation's laws. The president will be our global representative and hold a dignitary position. The experts in Davos will craft policies on energy, climate, economy, production, social policy, and even religion. This will be adopted by the global council of governments, and the world will be radically transformed.

Every country will have a controlled, progressive, collectivist-minded government that is beholden to the edicts of Davos. Global communism will have finally come to the world, meaning that a handful of people will be the tyrants of the world, with faithful minions doing their bidding. The progressives will not care; they will have achieved their vision. The world will be remade in the image of the relativists, who will try to redefine the world in their image, and we will be prisoners of their every whim and caprice.

In 2034, if the progressives have their way, this is the future that we will be living in. Transhumanism will have been fully implemented through the lesser devils of 'gender relativism' and trans-speciesism, which, believe me, if the progressives can manipulate to their advantage, will be very mainstreamed. There will be no such thing as protected speech. Dissidents will be criminally charged and sent to work in labor camps that are upholding the vestiges of our economy. Disagreement with the global agenda will be met with swift force by the American arm of the international peacekeeping force, whose enforcement and bylaws will be kept by the global council of governments. Eventually, the global council of governments will be so beholden to the international banking system and the rulers of the global economy that their sovereignty will be nothing more than regional distinctions of the global governance system.

Information will be controlled globally, and a social credit system will eventually be linked to the global digital currency. The WEF, in the name of human solidarity and peace, will control every aspect of technology and allow the use of it as needed by the world's population. There will eventually be one global information system, one global food system, and one global healthcare system, and you will have no choice but to opt-in; it will be criminal to think for yourself, grow your own food, or seek any health alternative. The 'predictions' of the WEF will come to pass, and we will enter a thousand-year reign of the Lords of Davos and their progressive junior partners. Countries that resist will be erased from the face of the earth and forgotten by history. In the name of climate justice, we will be deprived of sovereign mobility; they will take our methods of personal transportation. We will be at the mercy of the WEF to 'rent' our experiences, and our obedience will be the measure of what we are allowed to participate in. Not a single aspect of our lives will be autonomous; they will have complete hegemonic control. That is, if the progressives get their way.

THE AMERICAN DECADE

There are two diverging paths if the progressives are denied their utopian vision. The first sleepwalks us into a period of pseudo-peace before our children are led back to the brink of progressive victory. The second puts us on a path to true freedom. If we are wise enough, we will take the road that has, throughout all human history and in the recent memory of America, been the road less traveled. Broad is the road paved with good intentions, and we all know where it leads. If we allow the Modern Liberal experiment to continue to be a driving force in this country, we will have restored America back to a place where the progressives can burrow in and wait us out, make us stupid and dependent again, and undermine us with our own freedoms. We have to have clear eyes and the courage of George Washington to choose the road less traveled and thus rid ourselves of the poison of relativism forever.

The 2024 primary race heats up, but the defenders of freedom coalesce around a non-establishment candidate. The COVID narrative (or some other scary virus) will have been amped up since the fall of 2023, and there will be a huge push for the mail-in balloting scheme of 2020 to happen all over again. But this time, preparations have been made. The Republican candidate has a team of lawyers ready to file motions in all fifty states. They are ready to sue any state if they attempt to send out unsolicited mail-out ballots. The voters have prepared as well; they choke the donations out of the Republican Party itself. House candidates in their districts and Senate candidates in their states get direct campaign contributions because they ask their constituents not to support the establishment, and they run anti-establishment, America First campaigns. WINRED, the mechanism that lost the 2018, 2020, and 2022 elections, has to either seriously reconsider its politics or completely disavow the voters.

By 2028, the leadership of the Republican Party is completely turned over; there are no more establishmentarians who exist to be controlled opposition. If the Republican candidate runs on a platform of restoring the American economy, making sure that the COVID lockdowns never happen again, securing the southern border (getting it at least back to Trump era numbers), and promising to reign in the FBI and CIA for their abuses of power, they win thirty-five states in a landslide electoral win. A sixty-seat majority in the Senate is achieved, and a sizeable majority in the House— the'red wave' that the squishes could not bring to fruition in 2022. The left will contest the results of the election, just like they did in 2000, 2004, and 2016, but this time it will be a completely different animal. ANTIFA will take over entire cities and regions on the West Coast, and rioting in Democratic cities like Chicago and Baltimore will rage for months. There will be an incident far worse than January 6 during the counting of the electoral ballots. In the wake of this chaos, the path will again diverge in the woods. Allowing the chaos in the name of liberal tolerance will cause all the momentum in 2024 to be lost.

But the defenders of freedom choose a better way. The national guard is sent in to restore law and order and to reclaim sovereign land from an organization that, afterward, is declared a domestic terrorist group. The wailing and gnashing of teeth from the legacy media will sound like the screams from Hell itself, but the defenders of freedom will no longer care; the game has been exposed, and their shrieks and vile name-calling fall on deaf ears. The Democrat governors, mayors, and city councils are completely embarrassed in the wake of this move to restore order and allow the police to do their jobs. Crime is greatly diminished in these cities that have been destroyed by Democrat policies, and the American people living in those cities make a mental note. The new president also makes a declaration, as leader of the Republican Party, that the Republican Party is a party for all people and that any racial supremacist movement is not welcome. No longer will the trope of the 'far right, neo-nazi, fascist' be an arrow in the opposition's quiver. They will not be able to denounce racial supremacy movements, and it will be another win for America.

With the Border Patrol actually doing their job, thousands of corrupt bureaucrats out of a job at the FBI and CIA, and the economy back on track, the 2026 midterms will see wide support in purple districts and an increased majority in the House. Each new House member is America First and considered a Demon of Utopia. They are there to do something about it. If the right can be wise as serpents and innocent as doves, they can destroy the precedents of omnibus spending and the pork barrel forever. They can create a surplus budget going into the 2028 presidential race. The new right has used these advances to their advantage. Relying on the current activist groups that are in place, they empower them to work in areas that the establishment Republicans have abandoned long ago. The gains are substantial, and they are substantial because as the right wins, the left becomes more desperate. They attempt to pass more and more radical legislation that turns more and more parents, independents, and moderates off. The pressure is kept on the enemy, and the left is continually exposed for their radicalism. The race-baiting, the vitriolic confrontations in the hall, and the rest of the left's parlor tricks no longer work. But most importantly, the liberal narrative and the collectivist narrative are tied together in debates, in interviews, and in stump speeches by all the new right's politicians. The American people are awakened by the revelation and take a mental note.

The year 2028 becomes a new political moment, and things radically change. The greatest temptation to take the path more traveled presents itself. Knowing that the level of violence and vitriol is unsustainable, the progressives will make a liberal pivot; they will pivot back to the middle in order to demonize the right as Christian nationalist extremists (or whatever term they feel most effective). This will be a great temptation to pivot off the successful path taken. The establishmentarians will grasp like desperate animals in their attempt to get their way. But the new right has already gained too much momentum and will choose true freedom. They are met with a great deal of election fraud in 2028, but they are able to maintain majorities in both Houses of Congress and pick up broad support among independent voters who are abandoning the liberal mindset because they understand it is incompatible with Americanism.

The legislative wins would be huge in an American decade as well. In that time, the Supreme Court is preserved and strengthened, and many court cases reverse bad liberal precedent and federal overreach. Energy independence is achieved, which untangles our foreign entanglements, and is done simultaneously with a plan to seek out alternative energy sources and ensure that we are never again dependent upon another country for sustainability. We restore the American economy by promoting new manufacturing and new businesses with great tax structures while simultaneously taxing multinational corporations into the ground or out of our country.

Beginning with the most destructive alphabet agencies, slowly the fourth branch of government is dismantled. Regulatory agencies, if they exist at all by 2034, are state-level agencies of the blue holdout states. Local communities educate their own children and decide on the curriculum that they are taught. If we are still spending federal dollars on education, they follow the child to the school of the parents' choice. And, by 2034, we are in a position to finally make a triumphant push to eradicate the Federal Reserve and reclaim our Treasury and monetary system from the Lords of Davos, who had to retreat in fear of the American beast that has awoken. They could not weave their web-like schemes into a world with a strong America as an alternative to their utopian visions. The Great Reset never happens, and the Lords of Davos are exposed for the central planning and conniving cabal that they are, and their empires and their casinos are disbanded, and their wealth is used to dissolve the debt-based economy. Their ties to the CIA are exposed, and the true nature of their evil plans irrevocably breaks the corrupt Democratic Party and the progressive central planners that have taken it over. There is no longer a progressive political alternative, and the liberals who facilitated the progressive takeover are exposed for what they are.

There could begin a new American century where, decoupled from the corruption that once hid in our government, we are free to make good foreign policy decisions, be an ally of integrity, and restore the balance of peace that a once moral America used to command on the world stage. Lastly, to have a true American decade, we must enshrine into our laws that collectivism and relativistic ideologies have no place in American politics. They are declared unconstitutional and illegal. If the next ten years are the American decade of true freedom, we will leave a legacy to our well-educated and patriotic children who will be prepared and ready to carry the torch of truth fearlessly down that road less traveled, and it will have made all the difference. So, in whose future will you choose to live? Now is the time for choosing; this is our time and our moment to stand at the place where two paths diverge in the wood. Both time and Providence dictate that we cannot rest here much longer before walking on to discover the weight of our decisions.

PART III

ALL HUMAN CONFLICT IS ULTIMATELY THEOLOGICAL

CHAPTER 11

The Greatest Conspiracy: The Denial of the Satan Adjacent

The hierarchy of this book is no mistake. It is set up to discuss three realms, which each need their own treatment but are by no means equal parts of a tripart conversation. We began with the economy because, growing out of the material measurements of the world, there is a shadow force that is using the economy to command control of the fight for world domination. But even though economies are measurable in dollars and cents, they are run by people and their ideologies. Economies are made up of brokers, buyers, and sellers, each with their own agendas and outcomes. Extrapolating that out into data is very useful, but it does not get to the deeper level of ideology that is driving that data forward. For a clearer understanding, you have to dig deeper into the realm of politics, and by that, I do not mean the in-fighting and policy platforms of political parties and movements.

Politics, in its basic etymology, means how we live together in society and make decisions as a cohesive cultural whole. In this way, it is mostly political ideology that drives the economic narratives forward. The political deep dive was a necessary discussion as an outer layer that envelops the discussion on economics. The political discussion is also very important because we live in a very polarizing time of clashing ideas. The global communist movement is the predominant force in the political world right now. It is commanding the control of the conflict and directing our future political state away from the standards and moral underpinnings that have undergirded it for nearly two millennia.

And so, there has to be an even deeper level of discussion about the nature of what it means to be a human being, a social and therefore political animal, living in society with other speaking beings. And, ultimately, what the highest form of society is. In the end, we must have a clear vision of the world from an existential, metaphysical, and theological point of view if we want to prevail over the forces that have wrenched power away from us—and now stand at the brink of destroying the old ways forever.

The way out of the current conflict is to understand the ultimate "why?" behind the "what" of society. The title of Part III, "All human conflict is ultimately theological,"[26] is a quote attributed to Cardinal Manning by the writer Hilaire Belloc. Hilaire recalled this 'quotable' from a conversation he had with the cardinal around 1890. Engaging in economic policy without first establishing what the economy is for is like trying to operate a rooftop restaurant on the third floor of a building whose foundation has not yet been laid. To try and decide policy without establishing what the policy is for is like pretending to stand halfway up a stairwell that has not yet been built. A firm foundation of what human flourishing is and what good societies are must first be established, from which all other conversations must take place. Without a foundation from which to build, a true sense of bearing and progress cannot be established. If there is no agreement about the fundamentals, there is no real agreement about anything.

There are many resources through which you can learn about the state of modern economics and politics, and I encourage you to seek those resources out and find good arguments against communism and political collectivism. But what I want to focus on more than anything is coming up with an ultimate solution and an alternative vision. I believe that my contribution to this conversation is to see the throughline that connects these dots back to the ultimate, outer layer of the entire conversation. To help people reconnect with the fundamental modus operandi: the philosophical and theological underpinnings that can lead our world out of its current madness and into a new world grounded in eternal truths about the human condition and the human experience.

I am using leftist language on purpose when I refer to the "Satan adjacent" in the title of this chapter. That way, this book can live up to its dedication and be a thumb in the eye of the worshippers of relativism. But it is also to help set the stage for clarity in what are several, overlapping conversations on what morals look like on a personal, societal, and global level. The truth is, we live in a fallen and imperfect world, and there is not a person alive today who is not guilty of being Satan adjacent at least once in his or her life. But what does it mean to be a good person, and does that goodness lead to deprivation or flourishing? What does it mean to have a good society? What are the right demands that we can make on society? And in turn, what can society rightly demand from individuals? These questions are foundational to forming political bonds. When I use the term "Satan adjacent," I am referring to both personal and societal movements that are not in line with right-ordered ends. It does not necessarily have to be in line with evil or attempt to achieve evil ends. But, as we see in the secular, listless society that we live in, we cannot leave the moral engine of the country in neutral and expect the car to sit still.

It takes hard work to maintain the American status quo, and it takes the vigilance of protecting our freedoms today and educating future generations so that when it is their turn, they can carry the torch. There are many natural forces that will move the car in the absence of moral drive. But one thing is certain: those forces are not going to find the car rolling up toward a higher plain. The only way a neutral car can move is down. This is true in our personal lives as well; if we are not willing to have rigor in our self-control, our passions will control us. But this personal disposition radiates out into the broader sphere, which you influence and which has influence on you. The academic study of this dance between the individual, culture, and time is called anthropology, and it is the fundamental dance that shapes the reality of politics (or how we are to order society).

If societies are ordered in a morally ambiguous way, they do not place themselves above the moral fray in their political decision-making; they simply make themselves Satan adjacent. That society will have morals that go the way of the world, and they will be doomed as a society because we live in a fallen world. It may take decades or even centuries, but society will collapse. The left has been very successful at steering the car, insisting on the car being in neutral. In the liberal haze of the last sixty years, we have found ourselves not moving up to new heights but slowly in the direction that the progressives have wanted to take us all along. Since they are on the way to utopia, which is located precisely in the bowels of Hell, they have been content to let the car roll downhill in neutral, building steam. Now that the progressive movement has come to monopolize the Democratic Party power center, we are going to see them put the car in overdrive to reach their desired destination. We will move from Satan adjacent to being in perfect, relativistic alignment. We can no longer have a neutral position on the morals of the nation if we don't want to go to Hell with them.

To avoid reaching the destination that the progressives are progressing to, we have to stop this shallow politics of "2D philosophies." We aren't going to defeat the idea of radical collectivism with the equally shallow idea that we can be atomized individuals in society with no obligations to each other. We have to stop the madness of thinking that consent is the only moral limit to our actions. And we have to stop giving into the liberal lie that we can leave the car in neutral and, by doing so, maintain the status quo. This lie must be rejected on a personal level as well as in societal standards and norms. It has been used against us for so long and has been so normalized in society that it is hard to know where to begin to detangle this web woven to deceive us. If we want answers—real and lasting answers—we must turn to the wisdom of the ancients to help us find clarity. Because, at this point, we are far beyond a simple economic solution to cure our national ills. And we are far beyond a political solution, too, in preserving our freedom in the face of the global threats that have allied in their war against us.

The battle cry of America that once forged the greatest nation on Earth rings hollow to us now; our watchwords are nothing more than modern platitudes, injected into campaign slogans after workshopping and polling. This is not because we have forgotten what made us great. As a nation, we have forgotten, but our amnesia extends from the fact that our identity was stolen from us in an ideological conflict that goes back over a century. It was done by evil people with evil ideologies who knew they couldn't defeat us unless they convinced us that being Satan adjacent would lead us to true liberality. And all of this political movement and moral decay has been done at the behest of Godless men who think they are gods themselves.

Godless men know that weak men are easier to manipulate and control, and that maxim will be true for all of us. They will have hegemonic control over the Godless communists and over those whom they rule over. They will gladly step into the dictatorial role and allow the communists to be their useful idiots. And they will rule over a moral less and degraded people, so intellectually shallow as to be trapped by their vices with no means of escape. They will make of us a people that couldn't be free even if we wanted to; cave dwellers incapable of imagining shapes behind the shadows. And make no mistake, this is their game, and they will win—but only if you continue to play this losing game and let them beat you at it. If you can be kept adjacent to their plans, they need not ever classify you as a threat.

I know that the 's' word is a very provocative term in today's modern world, but we cannot get clarity about good and evil if we are not willing to draw the distinction between sinners and hypocrites. It is true that God is the judge of the human heart; there is not a single person who can judge a heart as fully as God can. But that's not to say that we are therefore completely blind to the conduct of our fellow man. When it comes to good and evil on a personal level, it is needless to say that no one is perfect, and we have all made mistakes. Our reaction to making mistakes is the difference between being a sinner and a hypocrite. A sinner courageously faces the fact that these mistakes have offended his Creator God and seeks to rectify these actions with atonement and the solemn promise to 'go forth and sin no more.' The hypocrite, from the very beginning, sought to articulate a standard that he had no intention of upholding.

Jesus was angry at the Pharisees of his day, not for their sins but for their hypocrisy. Herod was an interloping king, not of the kingly line of David. The Pharisees were an interloping priestly class, not of the tribe of Levi. They were operating at the behest of the Romans to create a semblance of local continuity within the Jewish people and their homeland, but they were part of the larger political power structure and were ultimately there because they were willing to be the pawns of Caesar. Hypocrites use standards as a means to garner power and control, whether that is to use your standards against you or to manipulate societal standards to their advantage. The standard is not the point; winning is the point. In other words, a hypocrite is a relativist.

Based on the rebukes that Jesus gives in the Gospels, it would seem that He held hypocrisy as a far greater evil than merely being led astray into sin. He forgave sins and offered salvation to sinners. He cannot offer the same to hypocrites, not because he isn't willing to give, but because the hypocrite is unwilling to receive. All hypocrites are sinners, because even the shallowest hypocrite is still adjacent to evil. They are not only engaging in a sinful act but also perpetrating evil in their ideology. In his book, The Gulag Archipelago, Solzhenitsyn has a famous quote that epitomizes not only the human struggle with good and evil but also illustrates this distinction in how someone might respond to such a quote:

"If only it were so simple! If only there were evil people somewhere insidiously committing evil deeds, and it were necessary only to separate them from the rest of us and destroy them. But the line dividing good and evil cuts through the heart of every human being. And who is willing to destroy a piece of his own heart?"[27]

It is true that the line between good and evil cuts through the heart of every man. We must choose whether we are to do good or evil. And we cannot pretend that there is a way to do neither. We will ground ourselves in reality, or ground ourselves in the delusion that, unequivocally, reality is what we declare it to be. That is the fundamental distinction. And from that moment on, we will be enemies with those on the other side. This is the ideological line between good and evil, which is becoming more distinct in a world so divided along this ideological framework. We have to be able to articulate the side of serving reality and the good and form our worldview out of that lens. A theist understands the true meaning of this quote; the progressive understands how to use it as a weapon. Progressives know how to relativize the morals of the situation, assert that their claims are morally superior in the conflict (if that is convenient to their aims), and accuse their opponents of the same level of evil that they are engaged in.

As I said before, as we approach 2030 and the progressives get to run freely in our politics, the line between good and evil will become clearer. If we are unable to be a powerful force for good standing up against the powerful forces who are exposing their evil, then it will be the progressives' future that we live in. If we corrupt ourselves, if we are conflicted in our hearts and they are gray with relativism, we will be torn between two futures until the progressives crush us all. We cannot expect to live in freedom and hold onto our weaknesses and vices. And we cannot expect to identify, stand up against, and conquer foes who will use those weaknesses and our lack of integrity against us.

We have to put down the porn, stop doom-scrolling, educate ourselves on the truth, and prepare for the slings and arrows that are going to be hurled our way. We have to be courageous enough to fight against the enticements and temptations of this world, relativism as a sake of personal convenience, and the notion that we can have a 'liberal' society through relativistic tolerance. Wouldn't it be nice if we could indulge in every one of our desires and delusions and still be good people? Ultimately, we need to see the warped nature of that question in its fullness to realize how pernicious the lie of relativism is and how deeply corrupting it can become.

Relativism isn't just the failure to live up to our fullest potential; it is to reject that it is even our purpose to strive to be that best version of ourselves. It is to warp our striving for the good into our pursuit of the lesser desires of degraded standards. And that is the nature of descending from sin to hypocrisy. A sinner's conscience is stung by his sin, and after repentance, he is able to move forward again on the journey toward his highest self. The hypocrite is relegated to a different path, returning to his favorite sin again and again. Each time, hypocrites must convert the shame of their degradation into an unrighteous indignation of all standards. Each time they do so, it makes the light of truth and righteousness hotter and more uncomfortable, until they come to hate it. And there is the devil, the first relativist, to coo in their ears. To tell them that anyone who would ask them to bathe in the light of righteousness must be evil themselves. You can get pretty damn twisted up in that dynamic, but at the end of the day, a man wrapped up in himself makes a small package indeed.

We live in an age where the grayness of relativism is being contrasted back into its original black and white. We must be prepared to choose a side; we must be prepared to step into the light of truth or into the complete denial of it. The forces of darkness are aligning with each other, and they will be united on their front. We cannot remain a dim gray light and hope to defeat them. We have to be courageous enough to outshine the darkness in our personal actions and our societal convictions. It will be a personal decision for each of us that will shape the society we will live in. In the end, history will play out according to our choices, and we will reap the just desserts of the path that we tread. If you are reading this and are with me this far, I know which side you are on. But there is one more wrinkle that we need to understand in this dichotomy and fight for the soul of our nation. That is the fact that we are fighting not just against the forces of darkness. As we fight against them, we must also be aware that victory can only come if we are able to win over the great disaffected middle.

The Milgram experiment was a very controversial study done by Yale psychologist Stanley Milgram. The experiment was quite simple in its setup. Milgram would be the "authority" figure who sat in a closed room with the test subject. The test subject would sit at a control panel with a microphone, a voltage dial, and a shock button. The third person in the experiment, pretending to also be a test subject, was in the next room. He was said to be connected to electrodes controlled by the dial and the shock button in the other room. The test subject and the other 'volunteer' would meet before the experiment would begin, and then they would assume their respective positions. The experiment went as follows: Milgram (the authority figure) would tell the test subject to read questions into the microphone, which would be broadcast to the third person in the other room. If the third person failed or refused to answer the question, they were to be shocked. If there was continued disobedience, the voltage was to be increased by turning up the dial.

The experiment would continue for several rounds, until either the test subject refused to continue or the voltage was increased to its maximum (deadly) level. If there was any hesitation by the test subject, Milgram was there to sternly assure the subject of his actions and tell him to complete the task. Milgram set up the experiment so that, obviously, the third person was not getting shocked. The experiment was also set up so that the third person (a grad student) would purposely not answer the questions or respond in any way. The only sounds that would come back through the PA system were the sounds of electrical current and the third person's groans (both growing louder and more intense as the experiment ratcheted up).

Milgram wanted to see how far the test subject would go to 'follow orders.' To his shock (pun most certainly intended) and his astonishment, all test subjects continued with the experiment; even if there was discomfort and hesitation on the part of the test subjects, not one refused to shock the third person at least once. Subsequently, most test subjects continued the experiment, turning the dial to at least three hundred volts before breaking down and demanding that the experiment be stopped (three hundred volts causes burns and irreparable damage to shock victims, by the way). Most startlingly, the majority of test subjects carried the experiment to completion, turning the dial to its maximum—a lethal 450 volts.

Milgram was obviously not surprised that most subjects at some point during the experiment hesitated to express discomfort, to protest, and to express empathy for the third person. He was, however, amazed that, when prompted by an authority figure to continue the experiment, they did. When analyzing the meta data from Milgram's studies and those recreated internationally, the range of people willing to carry the experiment to completion was a consistent sixty-one to sixty-six percent, regardless of culture, ethnicity, or social factors. Milgram's experiment was borne out of a perplexing thought that had stumped him for years. He couldn't understand how German soldiers under SS Nazi rule came to commit the terrible atrocities of the Holocaust. How did the soldiers not stand up? How is it possible that not one soldier complained, hesitated, or mustered the courage to say 'stop?' I tend to think that the soldiers were selectively chosen for this task, constantly brainwashed, and duties were regularly rotated to avoid any connection with or empathy toward the prisoners. I would also be willing to bet that many soldiers couldn't cut it and were reassigned. Nonetheless, it is very easy in our comfort today to assume that we would be better than the SS soldiers and that somehow we would be unstained by the moral failings of our leadership. But we have our own atrocities in this age that stain what will eventually become our history.

Milgram's experiment, done in the early 1960s, was designed to test the limits of obedience. His own perplexing thoughts about the SS soldiers were to be answered: were these men truly monsters, or is it possible for individuals to commit monstrous acts because of a normalcy bias? Milgram reluctantly published his findings in a 1974 article, "The Perils of Obedience." Sadly, the academic community found his research findings too alarming. They revolted in the face of the facts. Being honest cost Milgram his job at Yale. Analogous to Socrates, he presented a hard truth, and society gave him his reward. The great disaffected middle, the majority of the people in this study, were simply following orders. They were doing what seemed to be normal.

I would venture a guess that you picked up this book because you follow politics and your spidey sense is tingling in this age of madness. And I would also venture a guess that most of your friends don't like talking politics as much as you do. Most of the people you talk to about current events are reacting to them in real time, while you had seen the writing on the wall months prior. Right now, we are losing the campaign to sway the great disaffected middle. That is slowly beginning to change as parents got a virtual window into what their kids were learning during the pandemic. People are also slowly becoming disenchanted with the left's new gender theories as they shift from the argument of tolerance, and now we get to see the effects of their implementation.

This shift, although hopeful, is not moving the needle enough; if things are left on the current trajectory, it will not be enough to sway the tide on the WEF's timeline. We need to first craft a vision. This vision will work better than the left's vision because it will comport with reality. But the greatest battle we face is convincing the great disaffected middle that it is worth getting behind. And lastly, we need to clearly articulate why the utopian vision of the left is poison, both to the soul and to the soul of the nation. That begins by first knowing ourselves and striving to fulfill our fullest potential in our daily lives. But it does not end there. If there is not a unified vision moving forward, it doesn't matter how saintly we are. Recognizing that relativism is the liberal water we swim in is the first step in tackling both.

If this book is able to help you recognize relativism, I will consider this book to be a great success. I do not like the adage said about education: 'We don't want to teach kids what to think; we want to teach kids how to think.' It is a bit too clever by half, because you cannot neatly separate these things. If, however, you can come to identify relativism, you will be able to clearly see each side for what it is, discern the truth in any argument you hear, and make your own decisions. We need to be people who listen to political pundits, not to be told how to think about issues but to challenge our own beliefs that we have formed through the power of our own reason. This will help you in your personal life, but it will also be the conduit for transforming our political future.

It is true that the normalcy bias is one of the strongest subconscious factors operating beneath the surface in the human mind. You may have heard the term 'lizard brain' before. The human mind is an amazing thing, and built into it are biological and neurological mechanisms that ultimately link to our metaphysical reality that transcends the mortal plain of existence. You may not have a name for it, but this is the basic understanding of, and argument for, the eternal soul. Because of this ethereal plain of existence, we know that man is an animal, and yet an animal unto himself; he has no intellectual equal in the animal kingdom.

The lizard brain is a description of our animalistic brain, which is centered on the survival and propagation of the species. We are constantly bumping up against this part of our brain in our daily decision-making, and if left unchecked, it can give way to poor decision-making and a very short-sighted view of life. When learning how to fly an aircraft, one of the things that pilots must learn is how to overcome their lizard brain. Man is not naturally designed to fly in the heavens. Perhaps to think of heavenly things, but we are not designed to travel hundreds of miles an hour through the sky. When something goes wrong up there, you have to be able to think logically, keep your cool, and solve the problem not as a lizard trapped in a tin can but rather as the brain of a giant steel bird, whose extension is not your flesh and blood but the very craft you are flying. If your lizard brain kicks in, you are going to cling to the stick for dear life and fly straight into the ground. You'll land alright, still clinging to your steel branch like your life depended on it. But it didn't. Your life depended on whether or not you could crawl out of that primal frame of mind and overcome the task that lay before you to land the plane as gently as possible.

Most of us are not facing life-or-death situations on a daily basis or needing that higher mindset training to be the brain of an airplane. Still, we are bumping up against that lizard brain as we make decisions in our daily lives. And we must embrace the mindset training of choosing what is better for our flourishing. The deluxe car or the affordable one? The relationship that's just for fun, or the stable, lasting one? The policy position that pays me a kickback, or the one that will actually be better for our nation? We all got problems, man. The real question is, how are we going to respond?

Many, many motivational speakers are trying to snap their listeners out of their normalcy biases with one technique or another. If we are able to get outside of our own heads and see our circumstances for what they truly are, it can be a radically transformative process. It can move us out of our lizard brains and our lower desires and change our lives for the better. It can help us grow into who we were meant to be and leave behind the old insults and tropes that people told us we were. It can help us regulate our nervous systems and be healthier and more powerful human beings. It can help us recover from old wounds and old hurts and grow stronger because of them. And each time we do, we are crawling further and further out of the pit of nature that we are born into and into man's true natural state. That is to know himself, to know the world as he can know it, and to stand in awe of creation. He can only do so because, by knowing himself, he knows that he is a unique creation—the only one that can see and accept that the Creator is his Creator and therefore his Father.

This is the foundational understanding of the Natural Law, and why we would make an argument for the laws of nature and nature's God. Neither Jefferson nor any Natural Law scholar is arguing for the laws of the jungle to rule over the societies of man. Despite the riveting prose of the Bloodhound Gang in their song "The Bad Touch," we are not merely animals who are at our leisure to do it, as seen on the Discovery Channel. Our normalcy biases are not simply our lizard brain tendencies, although that is certainly the starting place. What we learn along the way on the road of life becomes ingrained in us, sometimes to the point that it becomes a limitation to growth and prosperity. It is no mistake that our youth are being deeply miseducated—not only indoctrinated with the most relativistic ideas, but also being deprived of the educational resources and tools to articulate, hold, and defend an alternative viewpoint. It is not by accident that we have all been collectively dumbed down in the classroom and simultaneously pitted against each other by the media narrative.

Where we live, what people around us accomplish, and what values we see enacted in society all contribute to our normalcy biases. This does not put us in a position to simply blame society for our failings, but I do see why people fall into a life of crime (whether that is dealing drugs in the inner city or moonshine in the backwoods). I do see why people fall into a life of poverty (city or rural). I do see why a sick society would produce disparate and sad outcomes for the majority of its people. Escaping what is said about you and your past is one of the hardest things you will ever do in life.

The normalcy bias can be summed up in a study that was done on a group of monkeys, and this will tie back to the Milgram experiment. In the monkey/ladder experiment, four monkeys were placed in a cage with a large ladder. At the top of the ladder was a nice bunch of bananas. Every time a monkey tried to climb the ladder, the entire cage was sprayed with cold water. Soon, every time a monkey would attempt to climb the ladder, the other three would pull him down and severely punish him for his attempt. One by one, the monkeys were replaced. Each time a new monkey was introduced, he would join in the practice of keeping the other monkeys off the ladder, even though they had never experienced the original spraying water treatment. At the end of the experiment, all the monkeys had been replaced with new monkeys that had never been doused with cold water, but they still engaged in the practice of punishing any monkey who would attempt to climb the ladder and claim the bananas.

This is how normalcy biases, even when they are above the level of the lizard brain, subsist in societies over time. This is why a majority of a population will, under the guidance of an authority figure, go along with what is considered normal, even if they have reservations about it themselves. It is said that only three percent of the nation took up arms against the British in the revolutionary war. Two-thirds of the population were happy to not fight and to see the outcome. We need to be the three percent; we need to be the ten righteous men that can stay God's hand and save the nation. In doing so, we can become the people who inspire that great normal and disaffected middle. We can help our nation strive toward higher ends than shocking those who don't tow the party line. We need to reward and elevate an elite that helps us transcend our basest passions and reach ever higher for a greater and greater standard. We need heroes not only as leaders but also as people who inspire other people to be heroes themselves.

That is how we save this nation—by you being that elite. By demanding that from your politicians. By supporting organizations that foster the American vision. By not supporting those who provide mechanisms for the left to prevail in the battle for the soul of the nation. If we do not, we will see our declared enemies victorious. We will be plunged into a future where we are capable of nothing more than our base passions, where we watch the complete implementation of moral relativism, and where we live in a dog-eat-dog society. Instead, we must begin with a foundation of understanding who the Creator made us to be and live into that reality more and more perfectly each day. If we do so and align ourselves with like-minded people who are carrying the banner of truth, the great disaffected middle will follow our rallying cry.

Right now, the great disaffected middle is following the left in the absence of a better alternative. In the next chapter, The Death of Relativism and All Its Evil Promises, we will explore just how we can train our minds to become warriors worthy of that cause. Saul Alinsky, a very influential progressive through the latter half of the twentieth century, wrote a book entitled Rules for Radicals. This book was deeply influential for the likes of the Clintons and the Obamas in their political careers. Although the progressive movement tries to obfuscate and dismiss it, Alinsky gives a 'tip of the hat' to who he considers to be the OG radical:

> *"Lest we forget at least an over-the-shoulder acknowledgment to the very first radical: from all our legends, mythology, and history (and who is to know where mythology leaves off and history begins — or which is which), the first radical known to man who rebelled against the establishment and did it so effectively that he at least won his own kingdom — Lucifer."*[28]
>
> —Saul Alinsky, *Rules for Radicals.*

I believe that Saul Alinsky knew his Milton, enough to provide this 'tip of the hat' to the devil. I opined on Paradise Lost earlier in this book, and I think that Saul took the devil's words to heart: "better to reign in Hell than serve in Heaven."[29] The first moral relativist was Satan, who beyond being the father of lies is perhaps better summarized in his unofficial motto: non-serviam (I will not serve). He refused to serve truth itself (God), and in doing so, he corrupted a third of the angels, mankind, and himself in the process. By now, you can clearly see that relativism is its own contradiction. One of the things that Satan hates most about God is that he is God's creation and therefore cannot truly deny God in the way he pretends to do so fully. Similarly, relativism must acknowledge the existence of truth in order to falsely argue that there are no truths. In other words, the relativist's argument is saying that it is true ... that there are no truths. Academics and modern progressives will often try to claim that this 'arm-linking' that Alinsky does with Satan is just a quip, a wink, and a nod. That he knew this dedication would piss off those stodgy Christian conservatives. But you also know by now that this glib approach is part and parcel of the progressive method of thinking. Lying, glibness, and sinful social calculus are all acceptable tactics to win hegemonic control.

Denying the existence of right and wrong does not make right and wrong disappear. And pretending that good and evil don't exist in politics is a sure path to societal perdition. There is a very common breakdown in today's society between our actions and the repercussions of those actions. It is a breakdown in liberal logic that inevitably comes home to roost. The liberal lie is that we can manipulate or eradicate moral standards altogether, and that only positive and good outcomes will result. In other words, you can leave the car in neutral and it won't be at danger of rolling back downhill. In my humble opinion, this is the result of a person's actions bumping up against a moral standard, and instead of attempting to understand the purpose of the standard and the good that comes from it, an attitude of aversion is adopted instead. G.K. Chesterton analogizes this in what has now been dubbed "Chesterton's Fence."[30] The concept is that an unknowing person encounters a fence that is built across the road he is traveling down. How obtrusive and stifling, how limiting and cruel! In indignation and ignorance, the fence can be torn down, but once done, the entire society will reap the repercussions and be obligated to deal with the ramifications. If the fence was protecting the town from wild beasts, then exactly who was freed in the end?

Chesterton's conclusion is that change should not be made until those demanding the changes fully understand the reasoning behind the standard in the first place. I would take it one step further and say that not only must understanding be involved, but a clear and present future state must be presented as a better alternative. We can either assent to the moral standard or pretend that our particular situation is exempt from it. Exempting oneself is the non-serviam spirit of the OG radical, and once that position is adopted, the fundamental rules of the game are changed. At first, the game was meeting the standard; you meet the standard and course correct when you fail to do so. When it became a game of exemption, however, meeting the standard was no longer the rule of the game. People who watched you exempt yourself from a standard are not going to respect your new 'standard' in an attempt to live up to it; they are going to find a way to exempt themselves from whatever standard is in their way. This becomes an endless deviation further and further from the original standard that was set, until there are no standards and no one even attempts to live up to them. This is where we are in the modern liberal experiment.

The coup de gras of the liberal lie is that people who participated never stopped believing in their own moral superiority within their arguments for their own exemption. Because of that, they justified the exemption not as an exemption but as a new, nobler, gentler, kinder standard that was better than the old one. In doing so, they could stand on their own "moral high ground" to deflect any naysayers. This moving of the goal posts is the exact same mechanism that the progressives are using, except it is radically accelerated.

The new feature of progressivism is that it has become much more efficient because they have abandoned moral standards altogether in the new game of power, winning, and losing. They can accelerate the shifting of the goal post and never answer for contradiction or hypocrisy from their previous positions. The old-school liberals like Bill Maher find this infuriating—the idea that the progressives have no appreciation for establishing and maintaining their own moral high grounds from which to argue their moral superiority. In the liberal's mind, progress means deviating within a perceived reasonable degree from the old standards. This "corruption without destruction" allows them to feel in control and morally superior. As long as the divide is narrow, you can stand in the precarious position of having one foot in each world.

Progressives are arguing from pure relativism; their moral high ground is the denial of every truth claim—save their own. That is why it manifests as pure destruction and disdain for the old standards. It is total corruption for the sake of destruction, in order to manifest not as "James Dean" but rather as the Devil coming to sit at America's table. But when you fundamentally change the rules of the game, you crack that divide wide open, and there is no amount of mental gymnastics that will allow you to have one foot in each world. The old school liberals can feign indignation all they want, but in the end, they cannot be mad when their game is redefined by the generation that was fostered with their liberal mythology. Liberal legend said that if you go into a dark bathroom and look in the mirror and recite the lyrics of "Wouldn't It Be Nice" by the Beach Boys, you will be transported to a new place where you are morally superior in all of your decisions. What in the world makes these indignant liberals think that the mythology of future generations would be any less spectacular?

We cannot pretend that this is a sustainable way of thinking or that it is an acceptable middle ground to fall back into. As Hamlet put it, "There are more things in heaven and earth, Horatio, than are dreamt of in your philosophy."[31] (Emphasis added to drive home the point that Horatio's limited worldview could not, by its very nature, be the solution to everything; even his philosophy must rest on something greater still.) The denial of the Satan Adjacent is one of the great mistakes of our age. We cannot be a nation of moral microcosms that are all going in disparate directions unless we want to create an environment where the progressives win. In this, I must make a distinction: I am not referring to every Democrat voter who supports his side as an evil person; in fact, I hope that the use of my progressive language is an indication that I am not lumping the Democrat voter in with the perniciousness of the Democrat party leadership. Blue Minnesota and upper New England are good examples of mostly well-meaning people who are trying their best to be laissez faire and support the Democratic Party out of that lens. But, in doing so, they fail to realize they are supporting a party that is hell-bent on the downfall of our society.

I would wager that most Democrats today still think that the liberals are the dog and the radical tail is wagging at their behest. The Republicans in the nineties were victims of this; they did not realize that in their championing of the multi-national corporation as a blessing of 'capitalism,' they were the party of the wealthy elite, inadvertently advocating for their power in the name of 'free markets.' They were the party of war, supporting the incursions in the Middle East in the name of 'freedom' and 'security at home.' The vast majority of Republican voters do not hold the old war machine views today, and at least in Ukraine, the war machine is only finding support from the left. A shift, similar in tone, is beginning to take place within the Democratic Party. Now the left is the party of the elite, especially the tech elite. They are doing so in the name of 'safety and security' and protecting people from 'hateful speech.' They are now the party of Palestine and not Israel, which used to be a pretty non-controversial and bipartisan topic when we as Americans supported our only Middle Eastern ally. This shift in the Democratic Party has a twist of its own, as the progressive wing of the party slowly wrenches power away from the octogenarian liberals of the party. It is becoming the party of collectivists and authoritarians because they are now carrying moral relativism to its ultimate and logical conclusions.

If there is no right or wrong and the only metric of success is power, then it is only about winning and losing, and to the victor go the spoils. To the victor as well, goes the power to set the narrative. Central planners must have compliance in order to truly be in power. It was not a moment of triumph in which Nietzsche declared that God was dead (and that we killed him). It was in line with his concept of the Übermenschen: that the man who could separate himself fully from the social and cultural mores of a society was then powerful enough and 'free' enough to do as he truly wills and control his destiny. The Übermenschen is the epitome of the 'strong man' of relativism. This seems absolutely crazy to me, but that is because I know there is a God and I'm not him. I also have a Christian worldview, where my own internal culture is one of love for God, love of my fellow man, and giving to all what they are due. If a culture bases its mores on that premise, then Nietschze's entire case falls apart. Because if that were the standard, to rebel against it would be to rebel against the good of yourself and humanity. It is this rebellion, both against the good and the refusal to accept a standard of good, that is the fertile soil created by a Satan adjacent culture.

We live in a crazy time where people deny God and pretend that morals and cultural mores are complete and total constructs incapable of being defined as good or evil. That is a scary place from which to try and create culture, society, and the governments that reign over them. I don't want that, do you? It sounds so wise to say, 'live and let live.' But if we live in a you do you and imma do me society, we live in a world without limiting principles. It would be like living in the internet. Of course, there are a great many things online: wonderful resources, the ability to connect, and the ability to learn. But also, on the internet, there is ubiquitous porn, illegal dark web transactions, and all manner of degraded ideas as well. It is easy to turn your phone or computer off to escape from it. But when you try to break every single barrier of society down, you end up neighbors to a meth lab, a woke church, a brothel, and a monastery. What kind of society is that? Not a great place to raise a family.

There have to be limiting principles of society on which all agree in order to create society in the first place, cultural cohesion, and a community that is acceptable to all members. The American culture is breaking apart because it is getting ripped in opposite directions—and one side is ripping off the bigger piece of it. We have to be able to articulate the vision of America, the soul of America, and what that means in terms of policy decisions in today's day and age. We cannot keep pretending that the progressive ideology is not rooted in evil. And we cannot keep pretending that modern liberalism isn't adjacent to that. If we are not standing for the truth, calling out relativism, and fighting to reclaim the old standards that made our country great, we are nothing more than the Satan adjacent ourselves.

Jesus himself said, "If you are not for me, you are against me."[32] What he is articulating is that the dispassionate become engaged in whatever is around them; they will do whatever is normal in the time and place in which they live. It is akin to Milgram's findings; there are a great many people who are not actively seeking to question authority. In order to defeat the left, we must not attack the Satan adjacent per se. But we must ideologically clash with the progressives and convince the normal middle that our side has the true answers. I want to dive much deeper into the philosophy and metaphysics behind that in the next chapter. But in conclusion here, I want to drive home that our frame of mind in finding solutions is a two-front war.

Many people write into various mailbags on podcasts. A great portion of those are young people asking for dating advice and asking for help or resources to stop looking at pornography. Still, many others are writing in to ask the pundits what their thoughts are on the MWGTOW movement or characters like Andrew Tate. The reason that these alternative voices are popular is because they are speaking to the reality of our degraded society. They are articulating the actual state of things on the ground in the dating scene and in the divorce courts. It is true that we have a deeply broken society, and it disparately impacts the youth of our country, who have to try and navigate their futures within that hellscape. I find the responses from these political pundits to be deeply dissatisfying.

Most of the time, the pundit will meander through an answer that is relevant on some political or ideological level but ultimately land on the 'you need to improve you and focus on that' approach. The reason I find this so dissatisfying is that it does nothing to address the actual problem that they are facing! The dating scene is deeply messed up, the relationship scene is worse, and divorce—heinous enough all by itself—can leave men destitute at the whim and caprice of the woman. Through the waves of radical feminism that have rotted our cultural mind, the entire relationship dynamic between men and women has become nothing more than a deeply skeptical encounter where each engages the other with nothing but usury and self-service on their minds.

Now, the young men are just as culpable as the young women as soon as they assent to participate in the broken system; I don't want to make it sound like I'm being unfair to one sex over the other. But that is the current state of things. If we don't have a clear vision of what to do to fix that, then we shouldn't ask people trapped in that state to 'do better' or 'suck less.' There are only two ways you can have credibility in asking for their self-improvement: if you are doing it yourself, and if you are willing to put some skin in the game and try to change the brokenness of the current moment. It requires both; which is why it is so vital for us to have our own alternate vision to combat the WEF and their useful idiots who are attempting to lead us into utopia.

There was a particular young man who wrote a mailbag question where he said he was not sure if his current girlfriend was 'the one' and was asking for advice. I thought the advice was good, which was to stop thinking of some dream girl in your mind and look at what you've got. It would be an appropriate question if there were two real women that you were choosing from. However, the ethereal mistress in your mind that might be out there does not actually exist; the person you are going to date and marry exists, and she is her own person. Although I liked the advice, I couldn't help but think to myself, 'Why is that young man dreaming about some perfect future state where he is married to an imaginary (albeit perfect) woman?' The answer to that question is my point: we all have stars in our eyes and lumps in our throats when we think about the perfect, erudite, wonderful future state where we have eradicated all evil and we live in an idealistic America that is so perfect ... it's just another form of utopia. The truth is, it is easy to point to the failures of the left and to the absurdity of their ideas. Everyone seems to have a podcast now where the libs are 'owned with facts and logic.' But we are going to lose bitterly if that is our only plan of attack to take the country back. Those of us who want to save America cannot view her like the 'soul mate' in our minds. And too often, we speak so abstractly about capitalism, conservatism, or American patriotism to the point that we aren't really saying anything more than platitudes about a nowhere place.

We have to stop tolerating this rhetoric from politicians and coalesce around a vision that is going to bring the fight to the left like never before. Because at that point, we are not just standing athwart history yelling 'stop!' (the definition of a conservative according to Andrew Bretibart). Being a conservative should mean that we are true to American principles and so wise in them that we can craft a vision in any age. That requires us to be better ourselves, but we are emboldened to do so because we are going to reap the benefits of it in a society that demands that from everyone. People who are skeptical that living a saintly life will get them to Heaven are going to have a very hard time living a saintly life. In turn, they are going to have a very hard time getting into Heaven. If Heaven is just a nice idea or a warm fuzzy, then no one actually takes seriously the steps to get there. Don't ask people to do better in order to entertain ethereal visions of grandeur. Rather, give people the path to victory, and they will be inspired to rise up and be the courageous men and women they need to be. At least, that is what I see as the main thrust of the problem.

Most young people are far more conservative in their mentalities than generations past. But they also live in the total degradation of liberalism, and the keys to escaping have been purposefully hidden from them. If our political rhetoric remains nothing more than empty watchwords, we will continue to get empty-suit politicians who will be too weak to lead the insurgency. I cannot stress enough the power of the alternative vision; it is our only hope in this dark time. That vision begins with reclaiming the original vision of the people who founded this country, demanding it as the standard for this country, and being brave enough to battle for it in the political arena.

Dismus was the thief that hung on the cross next to Jesus. He would have never found the courage to repent of his sins if it were not for the example that Jesus showed him. Dismus saw the vision and was inspired to follow it; in turn, he received the promise that 'this day you will be with me in Paradise.' Now, we can't guarantee anyone a free ride to Heaven, nor do we want to craft a relativistic utopia of our own. But if we come to the table with nothing more to offer than 'the libs are a total ick,' we are not going to provide the inspiration needed to avoid the Great Reset. We have explored the economic and political woes that have befallen us in this age. In order for us to resurrect the vision that formed this country and reclaim our country from the relativists, we must go back to square one. We must explore who we were created to be and thus craft a vision for the future of America. In doing so, we will find out what that means in today's battle for our own souls and the soul of this nation. So, let's get to work.

CHAPTER 12

The Death of Relativism and All of its False Promises

> *"A nation of well-informed men who have been taught to know and prize the Rights which God has given them cannot be enslaved. It is in the region of ignorance that tyranny begins."*[33]
>
> —Benjamin Franklin

If we want to defeat the progressives, we must be able to articulate an alternative vision. That begins not in 'gotcha' bylines and pointing out their hypocrisy. Instead, it begins with understanding our own vision on the deepest levels. We have to begin with the first principles that the last one hundred years have failed to pass along to us. The left are relativists, plain and simple. The libs are 'relativist lite' and the progressives are worshippers of relativism. If their worldview is true, that the highest form of human existence is to be Godless, moral less, and worshippers of utopia by navel gazing and worshipping the uninhibited self, then America was a mistake that deserves to be rightly overthrown. If their worldview is true, then God is dead; we killed him, and that makes us heroes. Those are giant ifs, though. If atheism is true, if there is no God to whom we can orient the standards and morals of man, then we are doomed to live in the left's future. Not because the left is correct, but because their worldview is one in which correct and incorrect do not exist; forget about right and wrong, or good and evil.

In such a world, there are no rules, and the most cohesive group of tyrants deserves to win and rule, just like the largest male in the herd. If atheism is true, then relativism and collectivism are "correct" in the sense that they are at least as valid as any other philosophy. It also means we are doomed to always argue with the left on their terms. Again, giant ifs. Where are our terms of debate?

Millennials were taught the bare minimum of classical literature but certainly were not taught ancient philosophy. I can't imagine how lacking the education system is now, but our terms of the debate are somewhere in that vacuum. If you take the time to understand who Socrates, Plato, and Aristotle were and what each taught, I think that you would be amazed at not only the cogency of ancient philosophy but, in the end, find yourself completely disabused of any of the modern philosophies that fill the zeitgeist of our times. At least this is what happened to me when I began this journey to rediscover the soul of America. As it turns out, you can get ninety-five percent of the way to the American vision by simply reading Aristotle. There are a few extra steps at the end, but if you are an agnostic who struggles to accept any or all religions, this might come as a relief to you. If you are a person of faith, I hope this comes as a relief to you as well. It means that there is much more that unites us than divides us as human beings before we ever get religion involved.

The philosophy of Aristotle is known as 'Aristotelian Realism.' The greatest moral theologian of all time, St. Thomas Aquinas, referred to Aristotle as 'The Philosopher' in his seminal work, Summa Theologica (The Sum of Theology). In a funny twist of events, Aristotle was lost to the West for over a millennium. It was not until the first crusades that Christians rediscovered The Philosopher through, none other than, the Muslim tradition. The ways of divine Providence are but art, which though canst not see. This, in turn, ignited a great academic tradition in the Christian realm. Now, if you read a modern textbook, you will find that these were the 'dark ages' before the great 'enlightenment.' Which is to say, it was the time when the Christians were doing the deep work of reinvigorating the soul of the West, while the humanists were working on a great marketing campaign. In the end, the powers of the world claimed all the credit for the great art and literature that resulted from that work.

Think about any art class you took; did you learn that the techniques and strategies for creating art came out of the ordered tradition of the Christian faith? Or did you instead learn about Salvador Dali's sexual kinks? What about in science? Did you learn that the entire scientific tradition rose out of the university, created by the Catholic Church during the so-called 'dark ages?' Or did you learn that the evil Christians turned Galileo into a bald Rapunzel? When have you ever heard anything positive about the Christian influence on the world? Perhaps that is a question worth exploring, if it hasn't yet occurred to you to look into it. There are many worldly, relative philosophies that rested on the laurels of the Christians who advanced science, political philosophy, and the modern nation state and took victory laps on the work that was done. But in their degraded state, they were unable to maintain or recreate the decadence that surrounded them. And the proof of this is in two republics that, by historical terms, were almost twins.

The Christians who founded America revolted against the British Crown. They went on to form a limited government that bound itself in its governance to the laws of nature and nature's God. That government went on to become the greatest to ever exist among the governments of man. Conversely, the "enlightened" French revolted against their crown roughly a decade later. They formed a Godless government, outlawed religion, and were so 'reasoned' and benevolent in their rule that it became known as the 'reign of terror.' They are now on their fifteenth government since storming the Bastille and just can't quite seem to get it right. Choose truth, and you are blessed by Providence. Choose your own delusions of grandeur and suffer the consequences.

Many modern Americans try to attribute their 'liberalism' to 'Jeffersonian Principles,' which they claim were an outgrowth of 'the Enlightenment.' This is a baseless claim with no real grounding in history—and certainly no grounding in American tradition. Ask a hundred scholars what the Enlightenment is, and you get a hundred answers. Come back tomorrow and ask the same question, and you'll have two hundred answers. It can be at best described as a period of time (the 1700s, basically), but there are no doctrines or eternal truths that come from this period of time. Just romanticized prose—persuasive only to those who are already inclined to like that particular author's opinions.

The people who would one day become Americans bucked the system. They rejected the relativism of the enlightened period so vehemently that they left civilization behind in search of the truth. So, what did come from the Enlightenment? During this time, we had great works of art and great romantic literature. But in its decadence, it was corrupted by the rising humanists, the relativists, who came to claim their spot at the table and slowly began to push their way in. It was, as the expression goes, the good times that made weak men. As this dilution was taking place, the great art, literature, and ideas that came from the Enlightenment period began to get more and more disparate from each other, and they began to forget (or choose to push out) the foundation from whence it came. It was the beginning of corrupting the greatness that was built before it. And it has been doing nothing but devolving ever since. It was the 'scholastics' as they were called, who in previous centuries had built a great ethic for Western civilization. Never before in recorded history did we have such a robust conversation, producing such a succinct and thorough marriage of philosophy and religion.

This phenomenon is often referred to as the marriage of Athens and Jerusalem. It provided the order and social practicability of bringing this into the political sphere. We often point to the sixteenth, seventeenth, and eighteenth centuries as turning points in world politics; during this time, many preachers and politicians on both sides of the pond were on the same page, preaching the natural rights of man and the God-centric sovereignty of his freedom. Although this is a turning point in world politics, it comes only because it is high-pointed by the work done by the scholastics of the thirteenth, fourteenth, and fifteenth centuries. The scholastics were later demeaned as nerds and bean counters who spent their time debating silly things like 'how many angels could dance on the head of a pin.' But it was that great tradition that built the liberal arts and modern academia into the vaunted institutions that once existed. Unfortunately, it has now devolved into a gaggle of dolts who can't discern the difference between a person with a penis and a person with a vagina.

Modern appeals to 'the enlightenment' are humanist, relativistic platitudes of modern relativists trying to adorn the mantle of Western civilization with their terrible ideas. The Enlightenment was sold to us as a 'golden age.' But how would the people who lived through it describe it? There was obviously a great deal of political upheaval during this period. The nations of the West were reimagining their governments and societies. I am sure it had much the same tenor as our time—polarized, chaotic, the feeling of living constantly on the edge. Many intellectuals during the Enlightenment were atheists, or at least trying to rationalize how to 'humanize' (remove God) from the political, social, and scientific spheres. This social schizophrenia between the old ways and the new ways probably produced a feeling of growing desperation and uncertainty—a feeling that the political ground was moving beneath their very feet. And I bet that in many cases, the political dialogue of the time looked a lot like Charlie Kirk speaking with radicals on today's college campuses (the only difference, of course, was that the radicals were an even smaller minority).

Those who are trying to vaunt their own ideology by invoking the Enlightenment are making a disingenuous claim. They are attempting to deny the Christian foundations in the realms of art, literature, science, and politics that blossomed before and produced the Enlightenment period. At the same time, they are attempting to claim that those achievements are the products of their own ideology and that the 'enlightenment principles' are a cohesive ethic that can be divined from the relativism they are espousing.

When people call themselves "humanists," they are simply telling you they can't stand the thought of God or living up to a standard. So, they are nothing more than relativists who sugar coat all their relative ideologies in that saccharine cover. That of being a 'believer in and supporter of the human endeavor.' Which is ultimately to say, they are useful idiots just like the communists. Because in the end, just like in all relativistic endeavors, they are proven to be the interlopers they are. Relativism as a plain of existence is itself the slippery slope. Thus, everything it touches will eventually slide down to the ultimate nowhere place of relativism.

The prime example of relativism's inevitable conclusion is Hell itself. Living relativism out proves in time that it is the weak position, not the wise and higher form of human existence. It is much harder to accept responsibility for your actions and your family's success than to leave it to society or others to prop you up. It is a much harder path to be disciplined in your life endeavors than it is to demand a good life while refusing to do good. Somebody has to take up the slack when there are slackers. When the slackers outweigh those willing to bear the weight in a society, it will inevitably collapse. And the relativist, who has claimed all the credit for the good times, proves that he is the weak man in the end who cannot uphold the institutions that require work, rigor, and discipline to uphold. He finds a way to blame anyone and everyone else for the failures of society. And he will be most brutish with the ones that he knows, deep down, are the strong men who can make good times again. In desperation, he devolves further into his relativism because it is all he knows. He cannot, because of his hypocrisy, choose to climb out of the madness that has become his little kingdom unto himself. As the madness consumes him, he will insist that society celebrate his bravery and demand ever more allegiance and control. This is the current moment we are experiencing, no?

We too have a similar decadence of the so-called Enlightenment period. The liberalism of Europe has always outpaced the liberalism of America, and in our post-globalist, neo-liberal worldview, people cannot see the distinction that makes America different from the liberal democracies of the West. It is as though we think that we have all been in the collective bucket of 'Western liberal democracies.' Maybe because the education system taught us the lie that America came from the relativism of 'the enlightenment.' I wish they would have told us the truth: that America was founded in opposition to it.

America rejected this liberalism of the Enlightenment from the start, and that is why we were able to produce a radically different, much more successful, and ultimately better country than anything Europe could muster. We are now in a moment where the nation is torn. Do we preserve the foundation that made our country uniquely great among the nations? Or will we return to the temptations of liberalism and relativism, those ancient forms of barbary that have ruled over history all these long years? The chaos of this modern age will not rest until we have chosen.

The liberal arts used to be a pursuit of classical philosophy—a pursuit of the truth rather than narrative. It used to be a pursuit of those things that enrich the human mind and lift the soul into its higher functions. Today, the liberal arts have been hijacked by relative philosophy, which justifies relative psychological rhetoric. Most modern academia thinks the liberal arts today are centers for indoctrination into popular narrative. Most professors have only been taught post-classical heretics and condemn the classical to their students. And these dullards, elitist in their opinions of themselves, stand on the shoulders of giants and think they are flying. Post-classical philosophy has poisoned the collective mind of Western civilization against itself. This is a strong opinion, I realize. But how else do you explain the cultural suicide of America and the West more broadly? It is because we were fed a pack of lies from people who claimed to hold the scepter of truth. They are nothing more than interlopers, introducing a poisonous ideology in the name of 'real freedom' and 'real flourishing.' America did not spring forth from the Enlightenment. France sprung forth from the Enlightenment.

Jefferson was the ambassador to France during the 1789 revolution. Jefferson gifted the new leaders a large frame with a copy of the U.S. Constitution on one side, and the other side was blank. The obvious gesture is that the French Constitution and the U.S. Constitution would be kindred spirits in the fight for human freedom. But, in the end, France could not produce what our Founders produced. It all came back to the fact that the French married themselves to the mistress of the age, while the Founders married the American government to the wisdom of the ages. The rest of this chapter will explore the philosophical tradition that underlies our form of government. It is this original vision that can (and must) defeat the left, moral relativism, and all its empty promises. So, where do I begin? By putting Descartes on the stand, of course.

Epistemology is the study of knowledge. I know that this sounds ridiculously broad. It is not just one sweeping, deep thought that ponders all human knowledge at once. Think of epistemology as the science of understanding the products of the human mind (thoughts), whether the human mind can form valid perceptions of our surroundings (i.e., knowledge), and lastly, whether our knowing can be certain or if it is merely an abstraction in the mind. Your thoughts are certain; after all, you are certainly thinking them. Even before asking if you are even 'real' or live in 'reality,' you know that you exist because there you are ... thinking about existing. Descartes posited, "I think, therefore I am,"[34] and although that is logically fallacious (begging the question, circular reasoning), it shows the real, inextricable relationship between thought, existence, and humanity. Epistemology is a good jumping-off point from which to begin because it is the foundational premise of not only philosophy but the whole body of human knowledge. Thus, it is important for understanding the human condition and humanity as a whole. Whether or not human knowledge is useful is the first premise in choosing between truth and relativism.

Start by thinking of something very basic: two plus two equals four. Why is this true? Because if I have two apples in a basket and I put two more in there (and nothing else happens), I will have four apples in the basket. I can see the real effects of two plus two equals four, and I can extrapolate that out to a principle of mathematics called addition, wherein if I had two of anything and added two more, I would have four. It is universally true about any such circumstance. But seriously, how do I know this is true? And how would you go about proving the apples, or addition for that matter, even exist? What if they are just your opinions about how the world works? What then is human knowledge, and can it be true, or is it simply the perceptions of a mind that cannot get outside of itself to see the world for what it really is?

Such questions must be asked, but they are not endeavors that are ends in and of themselves. We want to answer these questions in order to get to deeper truths. Modern philosophical schools hold these naked extrapolations out as an end instead of a means. A relativist would ask these questions dismissively and not inquisitively in order to make his opinion equally as valid as anyone else's and therefore make him 'right.' But the proper disposition is to answer this question in order to provide a foundation from which you can build out.

If human knowledge is an accurate representation of the world around us, and we can use that knowledge to effect real change in the world, then it is a useful tool. However, if it is merely the extrapolation of an overactive imagination, thinking it sees what is not there, then it is a frivolous exercise. There can be no in-between. The question of whether or not we should take knowledge seriously underlies every hard science. If, after all, knowledge is subjective, what is the point of even talking about experimentation, scientific facts, or objective reality? Despite all of the hypothetical doubt, the fact of the matter remains: humans take themselves seriously, and they base all of the decisions of their lives off of their knowledge. In the land of make-believe, we can pretend that the usefulness of knowledge is up for debate. But in the right-here-right-now, there is no debate. Scientists talk about how right they are in their knowledge, as do professors, doctors, lawyers, and Presbyterians. No one discredits their own knowledge, not in words and certainly not in deeds. We believe that our knowledge, and knowledge more broadly, can be certifiably true. And, because we are humans, we think that knowledge from our own private perspectives is the truest. But this is an anecdotal example. What does the science say?

In order to answer the question as to whether or not human knowledge is true or useful, we have to turn back to our old friend, the via negativa. Epistemology is not provable in a positive sense. You can't measure, point to, or otherwise grasp the certitude of human knowledge. It is not a 'thing' to behold. However, you can prove its existence by trying to disprove its existence. This thinking backwards to go forwards is a fascinating aspect of human ingenuity. Is human knowledge certifiable? Do I know that I can, with certainty, know something? And even when I know something, is that knowledge an accurate rendering of the thing that I am claiming to know? We cannot answer this prompt with absolute certainty. And it is at this point that modernity stops thinking. See? All are just relative abstractions. There is no knowledge to see here! If knowledge is relative (meaning there is no certitude to knowledge), it is all just subjective opinion and cultural norm. But is this true? Is knowledge just an abstraction, or can we truly know something? This is a fundamental question; if the answer is no, then nothing matters. But if the answer is yes, then there is a lot of work to do.

That is why you must begin with epistemology—the very thought of thought itself. Because what is the point of knowing if knowing has no point? The question can only be answered by disproving the inverse of the question. Now let's ask the opposite question: Can I know, with certainty, that nothing can be truly known? Not without being my own contradiction. To say that certifiably nothing can be known is to say that you know one thing, and that is that you can't know anything. Or, said another way, you know one thing for sure: that you don't know anything.

This is what you would call a self-refuting premise. Although it cannot be positively posited that human knowledge is certain, the alternative is absurd. The via negativa proves that we can, with at least some level of certainty, know something. We will not have perfect knowledge of the entire world or the universe, but we can come to know a great deal about it through observation and our reason. The much more efficacious exercise would be to apply our observation and reason to studying ourselves and the human condition. In this realm too, we might not have a perfect knowledge of the inner workings of man and his metaphysical ends, but we can come to know a great deal about what it means to be human, what it means to be a good person, and what it means to live a fulfilled life.

One of the new progressive tactics today is to deny mutual understanding of a situation by invoking one's own 'lived experience' regarding the matter. Observations and reason be damned, I do what I want to do and claim no responsibility for the repercussions. It is the relativist lie that everything is ultimately an illusion. This is done so that they can make the claim that you cannot 'impose' your version of 'reality' on the whole of humanity. The only problem with that is they have no problem doing themselves what they have, by their own relativism, forbade you to do. Because the philosophy was never the point; winning was the point.

And therein lies the problem: after one establishes that our knowledge can be of substance (although not perfect), what is this knowledge for? Does it reveal that humans are made for far more than this mortal coil and animal existence, or does it mean that we are just Übertierisch? Not Nietzsche's Übermenschen (supermen), but simply 'super-beasts' who are at leisure to do whatever we will with this knowledge in pursuit of our own tribal power and control over the world? If relativism is true and knowing is only an extension of our diminutive search for power, then evolution made a horrible mistake in the human brain: the conscience.

If knowing is merely an extension of our animal search for power, then the wisest and fittest humans would descend back into the trees and live as savagely as the animals. For civilization, love, decency, morality, and any other "truth" are mere figments of the human imagination. And if that is true, then the imagination becomes a hazard to survival. Nothing more than the illusions of a cursed but common beast oppressed by its overactive imagination. So, if (and a giant if at that) this is true, then the relativists are right, and as the sorely mistaken losers who think that we owe our fellow man dignity, we deserve to be eradicated through the survival of the fittest. This is a fundamental dichotomy that the relativists muddies time and time again in their pursuit of power. Because they will invoke your standard to hold it against you, and then immediately abandon all standards as soon as it is convenient for their next power play. Because the point was not the point, winning was the point.

We are never going to get the progressives to say they are Godless relativists. First of all, most radicals have been properly indoctrinated and therefore couldn't articulate a clear philosophical vision, even if they believed in one. Second of all, they scoff at your standard and any other as a tool for power. But the power for you is not only to understand your vision but also to understand what you are up against when you are speaking with someone. When you can recognize relativism as the driving ideology in someone's argument, you can quickly delineate whether you are speaking to someone in good faith or someone who would slit your throat before you knew you were bleeding. This is only going to become more and more of a relevant superpower because the left is only going to get slimier in their rhetoric, and their mental gymnastics are only going to increase until, if they could take bodily form, they would look like a person possessed.

Either there is something that sets humans apart from animals, or there is not. If there is, a philosophical conversation of merit and meaning can ensue. If not, then we are merely upholding a farcical view of a reality that is not reality at all. One of the most frustrating things about talking to relativists is that they will use any glib argument to run away from your arguments. They will say things like, 'We are just biological animals with sex drives. Ergo, we can't hold humans to any sort of sexual ethic.' But that is only when they are rationalizing their policies for debasing the culture sexually. The second a man acts this out, he gets 'me too'd' by the exact same people! The relativist will argue that 'we need ubiquitous freedom of thought and freedom of expression to be able to be "free" enough to make our own decisions.' This is to justify their lack of adherence to any sort of standard. But the second someone, of his own free volition, chooses to be a Christian—well, his opinions must be removed from the conversation. If there is no common understanding between two people, this back-and-forth almost looks like a coherent conversation. But it is a conversation about second and third principles that come from different first principles. And if we can't agree on the most basic definitions of what the second and third principles are for, then there is no point in pretending that dialogue is taking place in that context.

Relativists don't have first principles because they have no principle at all. They are moving the goal post each time they make an argument, moving from whatever premise they need to in order to justify their current position. This cannot produce a meaningful conversation, but it can produce a sense they are ahead of the game and wise enough to contextualize an argument when done well. The left has gotten away with this for years. Bill Clinton's famous line on abortion was "safe, legal, and rare." We all see how that has shifted over the years. The same shift is occurring with the redefinition of "undocumented immigrant" and "newcomer" in the illegal immigration discussion. Understanding the ultimate 'why?' behind the 'what' is currently the right's greatest lacking. The left has abandoned the 'why?' altogether. They have adopted the slippery slope argument as their first principle, and they will continue to drive the country down and left until we are able to articulate the reason that we need to go up and right.

Epistemology, as the basis for all human thought, must rest in the fact that some things are true whether we like them or not, or whether we personally know them or not. It is the glue that holds things together and makes conversation possible. It is considered one of the four main branches within philosophy, along with ethics, logic, and metaphysics. I would argue you can't have a conversation about the other three branches without establishing strong epistemic arguments first. Truly, a conversation of any substance would not ensue without knowing whether or not what was being said was even useful. Before we talk about truth in an ethical or moral sense, an argument must be made that things can actually be true. The same goes for logic; if there is no agreement on the terms of logic, there is no point in talking about whether your knowledge is logical.

Going back to the basics, we are left alone with ourselves and our thoughts. What is the purpose, or the telos, of human thought? Even this is shaky ground to start on. At their most basic, our thoughts are directed toward survival and are directed up according to need. Maslow's hierarchy of needs begins with the physiological needs (food, shelter, and clothing). Once these are met, we strive for safety and security. Then we can move on to the psychological (intimate relationships, feeling accomplished, and self-esteem). At their highest, humans then strive for self-actualization, or becoming the best version of themselves. Even this model strains itself in the overlap; there is a lot of human interaction in this hierarchy and therefore many opportunities to find the most selfish human thoughts clouded by others' needs.

When we are infants, all our thoughts are self-centered. A baby's survival is completely contingent on other people, and it is true that our foundational thoughts revolve around self-preservation. But something begins to change as we develop our intimate relationships, develop families of our own, and mature as human beings. We develop empathy, and a slew of other emotions that cloud the simplicity of selfishness. Although some species exhibit loyalty and selflessness, these are exclusively survival techniques hardwired into their brains; I mean to say that they are helping to preserve themselves by adopting a 'herd' or 'pack' mentality. Another example of what seems to be selflessness in animals is the maternal instinct, whereby the mother makes sacrifices in order for her offspring to survive. This seems like a noble thing for an animal to do, but the bird that carries food back to the nest doesn't perceive the world that way. The only thing that perceives nobility, sacrifice, or chivalry are human beings when we see such things.

This is much more telling of the observer than the observed. It means that we are wired differently, that our relationships mean more than herd protection, and that our relationship with our offspring is much more than pushing them out of the nest when the last worm is gone. The bird is doing what it was hardwired to do; it doesn't have a choice in the matter. Nor is the bird deliberating about what it should or shouldn't do. The fact that our brains function in such a radically different way speaks to the fact that our human thoughts are not designed for the mere survival and procreation of the species. There are layers in the human mind that speak to a higher telos, a higher purpose. As Maslow says, the highest need is self-actualization, something that the bird literally doesn't have the brain space for!

Maslow's hierarchy, although a two-dimensional scale as a theory, actually has a 3-D component to it when put into practical terms. Each of the needs is satisfied in accordance with the individual's capacity to fulfill that need. Animals 'live in the moment' insofar as they are trapped in the battle of survival; they are going from one moment to the next, looking for the next interaction where they will have to choose fight or flight. They do not have the intellect to be able to think of higher things, but even if they did, they would not have the capacity.

Archaeologists look for things like the construction of tools (not just using a stick but tying a rock to a stick with sinew) to discern late primates from early humans. They also look for art, division of labor, and the rudimentary elements of early farming. Each 'innovation,' if you will, provides greater capacity within the clan. But I would imagine that the interpersonal relationships of the earliest humans were still very brutish. In every age, as civilization, innovation, and discovery make our lives easier and easier, we are being given a moral responsibility that the caveman did not contend with; as we have the capacity to be better, we ought to do better. It is such a predictable shame that the radical left dyes their hair and screams at the sins of the past. Neither history nor the judgment seat will be kind to morally debased people whose eye sockets are bulging with the beams of their own hypocrisy, and all they can do is scream about the splinter in their father's eye.

As human capacity increases, we are able to think of higher things. The less time you are spending surviving, the more capacity you have to ponder what ought to be rather than surviving what is. The cynical people who are seeking to rule the world understand this principle very well. It is why they have been robbing us and the children of America of their capacity by dumbing us down, making us poorer, and increasing our reliance on the government. Scarcity lowers the mind into survival mode, a place where hope and vision are dim and distant lights (if they are there at all). As the WEF gains more power, you will see policies that outlaw self-sustainability and push people away from having either the capacity or the knowledge to provide for themselves. They are going to submit us to desperation and offer their rule as an alternative. It is also why our children are being educated so poorly and indoctrinated so heavily; if they cannot think for themselves or create even the capacity for survival, they will be loyal subjects without the means to survive on their own.

Perhaps one of the Founders' greatest blunders was thinking that a society would ever abandon the first principles of our country. The principle from the Franklin quote I started with is: "A nation of well-informed men who have been taught to know and prize the Rights which God has given them cannot be enslaved. It is in the region of ignorance that tyranny begins."[35] It is imposed ignorance; make no mistake about it. The nation's bias toward relativism and away from God has also been intricately crafted. Divide and conquer! When the agnostic who still believes in the Western moral civic code is repulsed by the Christian who holds to the same civic code, how are they to stand united against a common threat? Especially when that threat purposefully cloaks itself and its power. It disguises itself as a faceless sea of seemingly disparate and contradicting arguments. We have more capacity as a human species than any other in recorded history—but to what end?

Individually, we are caught up, anxious, and emotionally invested in world events we can't actually do anything about. And what are the people who can do something about it—doing about it? Exploiting it to cause more fear, unrest, anxiety, and hopelessness. We become more depressed and anxious, more reliant upon the soma that is pumped out by Big Pharma. And ultimately, we become less capable of facing adversity when we are the subject of the news story. If we want to do something about it, we must begin by not having ethereal and theoretical knowledge in the palm of our hand because of our smart phones. It begins with growing our own individual, actual capacity. And it begins with imposing that upon the world with a clear vision and demanding that from our leaders and the world. It begins by turning around—by being the individual who is not headed with the herd toward our relativistic destruction. When going the wrong way, the most progressive thing one can do is to stop ... and turn around.

In this polarized landscape, it is easy to see which way is out. In the modern liberal landscape, it felt as though everyone was going in his own direction and doing his own thing, and it was much more of a confusing endeavor. Now that they are just blatant and open about it, the silver lining is that we don't have to wonder if the person is confused by his philosophy. We know that the leadership of the left is going to Hell on purpose, and they are not confused about what they are doing. If we are wise enough to recognize relativism when we see it and together pull in the opposite direction every time it is pushed on us, we will begin to win. When we win, our country will do better. When our country does better, we need to be able to articulate what we did and what is possible beyond that.

When we have shown an alternative for the country, the great disaffected middle will be empowered to stop following these Godless relativists on the road to perdition. The more we articulate our vision and the better the country gets, the more capacity we will all have to reach for higher things and explore what ought to be. And in the end, we can reclaim the American vision of a limited government whose allegiance is to the natural law of man and the Creator that gives them. Ideologically, this is where we must return. I do not know what those policies will look like or what other challenges may come up (like AI) that are just now coming over the horizon. But the first principles matter, and we have to claim the first principles by which we can legislate and navigate whatever challenges a future age may present.

This is not a desire to 'go back in history' to some historical time when we assume things were better. It is a desire to go forward and see America live up to her standards and be the best version of herself that she can be. But what the relativists will never admit, nor will the Creator ever foist upon us, is that there is only one window, one perspective, through which this vision can be seen and exacted. If we are asking to 'revert' in any way as Americans, it is to throw Overton out of the house, reframe the window, and insist that we as a nation look through it to find our future, because that one will be the only future worth having. Any other will be the downfall of the soul of America. The country may well survive into the future with the same name and borders, but the idea of true human freedom granted by

God and left alone by the government will have been erased from the face of the earth.

Epistemology, ironically, is the most known subject in philosophy, even if it is the hardest to grasp and the hardest to prove. As the legend goes, the oracle at Delphi prophesied that "none were wiser than Socrates." Socrates, in his humility, took this to mean that no human on this side of the river sticks could ever obtain true and perfect knowledge. However, this didn't stop Socrates from asking his famous questions or seeking after what knowledge humans can know. It takes this type of humility, this lack of hubris, to approach epistemology from a realistic standpoint.

I say epistemology is the most known subject among human beings because we live surrounded by it and in it. Epistemology questions the simplest experiential phenomena that we encounter every day: time, life, self, being, etc. These are all so fundamental to who and what we are and how we see the world that we have intimate experiential knowledge of these things, even if we do not have an academic understanding of them. Aristotle would argue that this experiential knowledge is only seemingly knowledge and that merely experiencing epistemological realities is not in itself a philosophical exercise (and I would agree). The default human position is to take in stimuli around them and make decisions as they pass through time. The philosophical endeavor begins when we humble our pride and critically examine our choices.

As it turns out, we can come to know quite a lot about ourselves and our place in the cosmos when we do so. Edifying your choices with philosophical exercises will eventually help to form a clear pattern of behavior that can be defined as an ethical standard. But it does not end there. For we can come to know that we are part of a world that has an ultimate standard and an ultimate standard bearer. And in that world, we can judge the standards of individuals and societies as good or bad. But first, you have to dare to know and to pursue knowledge, not as a means to confirm your biases. Instead, you have to be humble enough to be formed by the knowledge you take in and never stop pursuing the truth, which, after all, is the ultimate use of knowledge. To know a fact is not to be any wiser; to know the truth is the end of knowing at all. The faster you can discern useful knowledge from the rest, the quicker you can get to the truth.

In his Confessions, St. Augustine says, "What is time? If no one asks me, I know; if I wish to explain it to someone who asks, I do not know."[36] And thus, the science of epistemology must contend with the strange paradox of being so experientially close but being intellectually far and, in some ways, intangible. We can be sure that we have an intellect because we are surely thinking about things that our pets are not. We are engaged in relationships with each other in ways that animals cannot fathom. This raises the question as to what the purpose of this intellect is. Does it exist merely for our pleasure and our power, like a cheat code? Or does it ground us into a deeper reality that is beyond us? As Augustine alludes to, we can have knowledge of things like time even if we cannot come up with a succinct definition of it.

I have coined a term that I call 'The Philosopher's Paradox.' When you study philosophy academically, you get into the weeds really quickly. People are complex and diverse; their entire lives and their accomplishments and failures are even more so. The philosopher's paradox is that philosophy is not an exercise in and of itself; it must serve the purpose of making sense of the human condition, human interaction, and how we are to find meaning and purpose in that framework. Philosophy can become so opaque in its extrapolations that it no longer serves these ends. Philosophers dedicate their lives to exploring all the extrapolations and what-ifs that might happen when or if this or that happens. It is a noble exercise, and it is a necessary part of establishing first principles and vetting that principle from every angle. But we don't live from every angle; when we are trying to make a choice, we cannot possibly start from the beginning every single time.

If philosophy is to be useful in your everyday life, those deep existential questions must already be answered. If you are answering deep existential questions to decide whether or not to get out of bed, it will be dark before you have come to a conclusion. In this way, we do have to rely on a great many underlying philosophies in order to go about living our daily lives and making choices. This can be the lifting up or the undoing of a person, whether or not the fundamental premises that they are operating from are good or bad ones. This is the first disposition of how we operate in our everyday lives, and it fits hand in glove with another crucial aspect of the default human position.

Aristotle begins his Nicomachean Ethics by observing that we naturally make what we perceive to be the 'good' choice. People do what they think is best, based on their past experiences, their biases, and the underlying philosophy from which they are operating. This default position does not guarantee that we will make the best choice, but it does guarantee that we will feel moral superiority in our choices, no matter if they are good or not. Trust me, even Hitler thought he was making good decisions for Reich and country. The only way that we can know whether our choices are actually good is to have a standard by which to judge them. It is a philosophical endeavor to answer what that standard is and to determine how we can best live up to it. The alternative is to deny it all through relativism. This will not, however, change the fact that you have accepted the philosophical underpinnings of relativism. Regardless of which path you take, you will have chosen to believe one way of thinking over the other. You will have made the leaps through the first premises of relativism in your assumptions, your decisions, and your life, and you must bear the consequences of that.

As your way of life pervades a society, that society must contend with those consequences as well. It is time for us to reject the path that we have been fed and the pathway to our enslavement, where we are ruled by the T.O.D.s. In order to do that, we must have a radically different approach. The one that makes America radically different. The one that caused our forefathers to abandon the comfort of the liberal West in favor of a wilderness where they could be free from relativism and its false promises. A real somewhere place where they could pursue the wisdom of the ages and lay it down as the law of the land. They did just that, although, admittedly, we have allowed that land to again go fallow. It is our time, our moment, to be courageous enough to pioneer back out into the wilderness and reclaim our heritage from the people who have stolen our history and want to carry us off into exile forever. I promise you, that fallow ground will be rich soil for the rebirth of the nation and the rekindling of an American soul that has no equal among the nations of man.

CHAPTER 13

He Places Before You Life and Death; Choose Life

What does it mean to be a good person? Is being "good," even when we define it, conducive to human happiness and flourishing? Or is it an imposition that limits our existence? These are questions that have haunted the human condition since our very beginning. Unfortunately for us, these have been vacuous questions in our schizophrenic, modern age. But lucky for us, someone much wiser than the modern academic elite took up the task of getting to the bottom of this deep, existential mystery. Socrates was the OG philosopher of Greece, and he taught both Plato and Aristotle. As far as we know, he never wrote anything down. He asked questions in a methodical way, moving on by questioning one's beliefs or opinions about something and working down to the first premises. Always seeking the truth, he often frustrated his interlocutor (speaking partner) because they had to answer 'why' upon 'why' until they were talking about fundamental things that had never consciously crossed their mind.

The truth is, the questioning goes back to the normalcy bias of people, which is born out of the society in which they live. First, the family; then, the community; and lastly, the nation in which they live. These things are all connected, and they all matter in the formation of a people. This is because, regardless of their normalcy biases or cultural practices, people do what they think is best. There is a great deal of one's own personal bias that goes into one's decisions, but the fact remains that we do what we think the herd will find normal. But we can break this conditioning of always blindly following the herd and its ways. That is to say, if we have the tools to do so, we can shape the biases of the herd. We can begin to move our society from a position of default to one of design.

In 1487, during the dedication of the temple pyramid of Tenochtitlán, Aztec priests sacrificed more than eighty thousand men, women, and children by removing their hearts from their chests and hurling their bloody corpses down the steps. Tenochtitlán was the Aztec god of the sun and war. The Aztec people believed with great sincerity that this was a necessary sacrifice the people must make to keep the sun strong, the rains coming, and the people in peace. How many Aztecs, the priests included, questioned the morality of that one act of terrorism? They were generations deep into the worship of this false god and sacrificing humans. The Spanish were horrified at these practices, and they justly overthrew the Aztec empire. The practice virtually stopped overnight. That was one of the reasons that the Spanish were able to gain so much influence in the central American region. Many of the Aztecs and the neighboring tribes considered them heroes for destroying the empire that had been oppressing them and snatching them at will. The fact that this will be met with accusations of racism in our time shows just how stupid our times are. And it shows how deep and misguided our leftist leaders are, no matter how superior they think they might be.

I believe that our modern political establishment, if they had to face Socrates and his questions, would find a way to justify doing what the Greek Senate did. Socrates made the Greek Senate angry because he exposed their own lack of integrity, corruption, and hypocrisy. So, the Greek Senate democratically sentenced Socrates to death by a popular vote. His crime? 'Corrupting the minds of the youth' by introducing them to 'false gods.' Cruelly (and cowardly), the Senate imprisoned him and gave him a tincture of hemlock (a common deadly poison at the time). He was not given food or water, and so he would either starve to death or drink the poison to end his own life. It sounds like something out of a dystopian novel, but it is the actual historical account of how things went down. Before drinking the hemlock, he gave a final lecture on the immortality of the soul. We will get to the underlying teachings of Socrates that led to these accusations a bit later. For now, suffice it to say, he was onto something that the chosen people had received through revelation a few centuries before. Needless to say, Socrates' students (among them Plato and Aristotle) did not have a high view of democracy. Neither were our Founders who were students of these philosophical greats. Plato went on to create his own school in the 'theory of forms.' Aristotle went on to create his own school of 'realism.' Although there is much to glean from Plato, the writings of Aristotle lent themselves much more to the political philosophers who shaped the fate of the world when they came to America's shores.

There is a famous 1511 fresco painting by the Renaissance great Raphael called the 'School of Athens.' In it, Raphael captures the style of the Greek philosophical schools. Some people are seen reading deeply from the works of the greats that came before them. Small groups are discussing deep philosophical and scientific matters, parsing out the truth through dialogue. Others are walking the concourses, dialoguing with or lecturing students on matters of settled science and thought. Although it depicts many famous Greeks, such as Heraclitus, Pythagoras, and Archimedes, the center of the painting is a scene between Plato and Aristotle. Plato is seen pointing up toward the heavens in defense of his theory of forms. Aristotle's hand is flat, palm toward the ground, in defense of his theory of realism.

Both philosophers acknowledged the metaphysical reality that enveloped the material world and our existence here on this mortal plain. Plato argued that in this metaphysical reality, there existed the perfect form of every real thing that we see. It was the perfect embodiment of the imperfect reality that we interact with on a daily basis. As I said, there is a lot to glean from Plato as we already have in this book. But in the end, this overly idealistic thinking resulted in some very bizarre recommendations for politics. In Plato's Republic, he advocates for society to be run by a ruling class of "Philosopher Kings." He envisioned the Greek philosophical forum ruling over the people. They would continue to pursue truth, and the latest and greatest discoveries would dictate moral and social life. However innocuous or menacing that concept may sound, he believed that this kingly class would be sustained by the group engaging in absolutely open relationships so that the children would never know which one of their forebears was their real father. You can make the argument that they would be engaged in a weird form of collective marriage, but I think in the end, that creates far more divisions and wars than just knowing the real son of the king.

In my humble opinion, I think Plato, in his attempt to explain the theory of everything, made a claim that ultimately could not be tied back to reality. It also fell prey to having to rely on the claim of the theory itself to explain things rather than trying to make sense of new phenomena and evidence. He fell victim to the philosopher's paradox: to make sense of the world through Plato was to become so esoteric that it no longer comports with the reality of the human condition.

Aristotle, on the other hand, approached things from the opposite point of view. What is it that we can know? Let us define that and grow a philosophy out of it instead of trying to create an ultimate framework around the universe and trying to fit all our discoveries and revelations into it. Aristotle's framework lends itself to the humble pursuit of truth, which is why he became an outsized influence on the scholastics. The scholastics forged the natural law and influenced the social and political philosophers who came after them. And these political philosophers, when they came to the shores of America, were the ones who brought this entire tradition of the natural law into political reality.

The Founders knew their Aristotle, and it is very obvious in their writings, our national charter, and our Constitution. In the modern narrative, many people try to discredit the Christian heritage shared by many of the Founding Fathers. The argument is often made that they were not Christians, that they were 'theist rationalists,' or 'deists,' or a myriad of other clever euphemisms. It is true that the Founders had a great diversity of opinions on faith and politics. However, this does not mean that a thousand disparate, contradicting opinions somehow came together to create a cohesive tapestry of political thought. In reality, the Founding Fathers were all philosophical intellectuals. Regardless of their religious creed, they spoke the same philosophical language. While they might have had differences of opinion on salvation, they all agreed that the human person must strive to live a good life as a pre-requisite to being a truly free person. They may have had differences of opinion on God's relationship to mankind, but none of them denied the existence of the Unmoved Mover. They might have even had a difference of opinion on the standards of morality and justice, but none of them denied that the nation would need standards in order to function properly.

Part of living in our schizophrenic age is that we are presented with a false dichotomy, and we cannot even see that it is fallacious. We are given a false narrative in the post-modern liberal world: that we have to choose between this false dichotomy. On one side are the old, superstitious, judgmental Christians (who did I mention are smelly and dumb too?). On the other side are the beautiful, beneficent, benevolent, blusterous, and (did I mention beautiful?) modern liberals. This false dichotomy claims that the modern liberals place life and freedom before you, and the Christians place darkness and deprivation before you. I can just hear the infomercial now: 'Choose the life you've always wanted through relativism! Abandon all your responsibilities your entire life; we promise it all works out in the end! Thanks, relativism.' This is an absolutely wrong way to view the world. It is a false dichotomy against a straw man of Christianity at that. There is a better way forward into a great shared humanity through this philosophical tradition. A vision that can speak to the human condition, right and wrong, good and evil, and the actions and steps to become a good person who contributes to a good society. We need only stop believing the lie that we must choose between a twisted handmaid's tale of warped puritanism or the equally evil inverse of Godless, moral less, barbaric relativism. There is a better way that has been tried—and proved—before.

The reality that the majority of the Founders were Christians, and yet even those Christian Founders did not want to create an explicitly Christian nation, seems to be a contradiction that proves the Founders weren't Christians. But the reality of the colonial period was that people were deeply philosophically aligned. This resulted in the secularists and the Christians speaking a common language through Athens, even if they did not speak a common language via Jerusalem. I remarked earlier that this might be the blunder of the Founders, to find it inconceivable that a future generation of Americans might be so stupid as to abandon that common human tradition. Yet here we are, watching reruns of Grease, Gilmore Girls, and Game of Thrones, thinking that this is the highest form of art, made by the highest form of civilization to ever walk the face of the earth.

The divide can be clearly seen in what looks like contradictory statements from John Adams. The Treaty of Tripoli was signed in 1797, which concluded the first American military campaign after the Revolutionary War. Whether it was a diplomat who penned it or a direct quote, these were Adams' thoughts regarding the treaty:

"As the Government of the United States of America is not, in any sense, founded on the Christian religion, as it has in itself no character of enmity against the laws, religion, or tranquility of Muslims – and as the said States never entered into any war or act of hostility against the Muslim nation, it is declared by the parties that no pretext arising from religious opinions shall ever produce an interruption of the harmony existing between the two countries."[37]

A year later, in October of 1798, Adams penned a letter to the Massachusetts militia in which he said,

"our Constitution was made only for a moral and religious people. It is wholly inadequate to the government of any other."[38]

There is a through line that connects these seemingly contradictory statements. It should first be pointed out that, like Jefferson, Adams gave far too much credence to the benevolence and good will of their political counterparts. He made a false equivocation out of his own benevolence between jihadist thuggery and Christian morality. The second thing that must be pointed out is that we were fighting the Barbary Pirates, who were using the clout of Islam and the fear of a holy war to terrorize merchant ships. At that time, there were far fewer diplomatic divides in northern Africa, and Adams was trying to avoid a holy war with the Caliphates, which, at the time, spread from Mecca to Morocco. But in a fair read of both quotes, how do we reconcile Adams' rejection that America is a Christian nation and that it is founded on a Constitution that can only function when operated by moral and religious people?

The simple answer is that the Colonial Americans shared a deep philosophical foundation for what it means to be a good and moral person. And that vision was argued from a secular position founded in philosophy first, before it ever entered the 'finishing school' of being reconciled to one's faith tradition. It is also proof that, even if the Founders formed their own unique religious views, they understood that the greatest protection of America was in the continued marriage of Athens and Jerusalem. Modern academics attempt to muddy the water on the tone and tenor of the Founding era to justify their agnosticism or downright atheism, but we have to face the facts. The American tradition is inextricably tied to the people who founded it. And we must follow in their footsteps if we ever hope to understand the inner workings of the Constitution. When we fail to do so, we produce disparate and relative outcomes that become the undoing of our great country. It is our task, in this current age, to rediscover the footpath in the wilderness that led the Founders to produce what they did. It is our only hope for reclaiming the greatest nation ever to exist on the face of the earth. And it is our only hope for defeating the barbarism of relativism that seeks to overtake and destroy us.

All humans think, and their thoughts are aimed at something higher than the animal's thoughts. Whether it be desire, passion, want, or need, we strive toward something in our thoughts. We are not striving toward harm or bad, but rather toward good. Good for ourselves, our clan, and our flourishing. We make choices based upon those choices being good, and thus we are oriented toward the concept of 'the good.' This basic orientation toward the good does not guarantee that we will indeed choose the good for ourselves. Our desire for 'the good' is not an adequate mechanism in and of itself to arrive at good decisions. So, what is needed in the pursuit of the good in order to actually achieve good ends? This, my friends, is where the power of human reason must kick in, and it can go very far in answering what is required for goodness.

There are many choices to be made in life, and it is obvious that our choices are not of equal gravitas. Some actions are simple and immediate; others are means to other ends; and some have implications that last a lifetime. In this, there is a hierarchy of goods through which one must navigate. This does not, however, answer the nagging question of what these goods are good for. If there is a hierarchy of goods, they are pointing back to an ultimate good. That ultimate good is the state in which man is striving for by seeking these goods in the first place. That state of being is what Aristotle called "happiness." But what is happiness? It is not to be merely satiated in the moment; we are far more complex than to be merely quieted by our basest desires and the most primal goods. This is obviously true, or the highest good that any human would reach for was to be addicted to drugs and in an addled, catatonic state. Since this is not how we define happiness, perhaps we should keep searching for the definition.

Within this complexity, there are many goods that make us happy: honor, health, wealth, and knowledge are among the primary ones that we all subconsciously strive for in our pursuit of happiness. There are a lot of dead and depressed celebrities who possess all these things materially. Let these examples stand as proof that these goods are ultimately not goods in and of themselves. There must be an underlying, much more human element we strive for that will make us happy. It is true that a well-fed person is happier than the person who is starving, but rather than look at the difference between satiation and deprivation, this searching for the good leads our thoughts up to think about the ideal. What would an idyllic, truly happy person look like? The one who had perfect happiness? This person would have far more than the respect of his fellow man, the virility of life, a full table, and a capable mind. He would exhibit that he has the capacity to achieve what all people pursue. He is able to think, to know, and to bring that knowledge into existence through discipline and action in pursuit of his happiness. Fools lean on the tools of success and say, 'I'm going to own the world someday.' Only the wise of mind and disciplined of habit can actually attain it because they are the ones who get to work.

Habits are acquired through repetition of acting in a certain way. These actions will, over time and with consistency, produce specific outcomes and results. The person who rises early to work on a project will finish his goal; the one who refuses to do so, even if he has the exact same vision, will never attain his goal. It takes a certain disposition—both thinking and acting—to attain the happiness we seek that is beyond the material goods of life that we are choosing between. This disposition is recognizing that certain behaviors and actions lead to lesser (or even bad) outcomes, and other actions lead to higher (and good) outcomes. In this, we don't have a clear dogmatic view of morality, justice, and virtue, but we clearly see that virtue and vice exist in the habits of individual humans, no matter how much that individual human loves or hates God. Virtue, then, in this philosophical sense, can be said to be the habit of long-term, sustained integration of the knowledge of happiness with the will to act in such a way to attain it. This begins to form a clear path of habit and disposition, regardless of which material goods one chooses from.

For example, the means of garnering honor and health might be very different paths in and of themselves, but the habits, discipline, and rigor required to achieve either end up looking quite similar. The clear path to achieving happiness is the path of virtue, the path of integrating the whole of the human intellect and will toward the right-ordered end of happiness. As with any path one is traveling down, you can stray from the path to one side or the other. Aristotle would describe walking the path of virtue as the Golden Mean, the path that is navigated by avoiding the pitfalls on either side of the road. Bravery, as the preeminent Aristotelian virtue, can only be achieved by avoiding the vices of rashness and cowardice. Leeroy Jenkins, as our preeminent modern example of rashness, shows that no matter how wildly entertaining a rash life can be, it will eventually end in defeat. Conversely, if we are unwilling to ever fight for ourselves, we will never be happy, no matter how many things we have.

Aristotle's philosophical virtues are bravery, temperance, generosity, high-mindedness, and good temper. With these, you can build out quite a national ethic. That is, if you know and habituate the virtues and know and avoid their corresponding vices. To achieve the virtue of temperance, one must avoid the vices of intemperance and insensibility. For generosity, one must overcome the bad habits of wastefulness and stinginess. To attain high-mindedness, one must form his habits away from vanity and low-mindedness. And to achieve a good temper, a man must meter his actions so as not to be corrupted by irascibility or inirascibility. Although we can see the virtues and the implications of a life lived in the vices, the simplistic walking of the straight and narrow path is a complicated endeavor. That is because life is complex. Perfect ethical adherence to the virtues is very difficult to attain because life and life's choices are a complicated dance toward happiness. It takes constant reinforcement of these virtues and the encouragement of their habituation in order for them to be learned by the individual. And, more importantly, to teach it to the next generation with any semblance of authority.

It is out of this concern that public education was created, not the wild absurdity of today's modern classroom and curricula. If you know yourself, you will know your proclivities and your favorite vices. In this, when we know that we might stumble to the right side of the road, we ought to hang to the left side, and vice versa. This will make each person's journey and path unique to them within the greater framework of the Golden Mean. It does not, however, make the meter or the scale of virtues and vices a relative exercise of 'my truth' and 'my lived experience.' In order to live a life habituated in virtue, it requires an act of knowledge followed by an act of will. We are responsible for our actions because we are the ones who commit them. Involuntary actions are physiological actions that affect the body's function and survival. Voluntary actions are the act of the will to affect change in reality and to attain goods through our choices. And eventually, through our right-ordered and virtuous pursuits, we will attain happiness.

It would logically follow that, although not all our actions carry moral weight, those voluntary ones do. Thus, the moral weight of our actions can be seen by the intention within us that drives us to the deliberative decision that we have made. Every choice begins with intention, and thus proper deliberation is the proper disposition when choosing. But these intentions of ours come from a more primal place that does not deliberate on the basis of virtue. This is our desire for something to be so. We desire our happiness before we ever intend to do anything about it. But merely wishing something so is neither a philosophical nor a virtuous exercise. All our thoughts, especially our desires, must be judged as leading to good ends (virtuous ones) or merely to apparent goods (which could be good or bad). In this way, all of our desires must be tempered through the lens of virtue, and this would drive us to habituate an action that provides us with a virtuous intention of heart.

This happens through gaining knowledge of virtues and of yourself, so that you can be your own wise council in deliberating your actions. Thus, learning virtue from vice is a necessary social act that all men must engage in for the good of themselves and society. A right-ordered society with proper intention will lead men to virtue and, thus, toward good. Conversely, a disordered society will lead men toward apparent goods, which might be good but are most of the time bad and evil. Even the apparent goods that are 'good' are the lesser goods that will not bring you to your highest form of happiness. This is why I am so insistent that liberal relativists, although they are not evil, are at least adjacent to evil by their indulgence in apparent goods and their refusal to acknowledge The Good.

In the end, even beyond the lessons society teaches us about virtue and vice, we are ultimately responsible for our own actions. Those actions that we took in our attempt to affect reality, attain goods (or apparent goods), and achieve happiness in the end, our lives will reflect how well we have tempered our wishes. Our lives will reflect our intentions, and we will be able to be judged as good or evil. Note that there are two ways to be evil. Either in your evil actions or the indecision of relativism that led to your life being defined out of existence in your ultimate nothingness. Over time, as these habits of virtue or vice are lived out by people, their societies can also be judged in a similar manner. But not in the personal way that we all must contend with in our hearts: our desires, the intentions we form, the actions we take, the habits we form, and the inevitable destiny that is produced. If we are responsible for our actions, then we can be judged by our actions. Our actions can be defined by one of three dispositions. On one side of the equation is the disposition toward virtue and good. On the other side are the dispositions toward relativistic or evil intentions that lead to vice.

If there is an action to be judged, it implies that there is a standard of justice with which to compare one action to the next. It also implies that the collection of our life's choices can be judged as good or bad. In making our choices, then, our deliberation of our intentions must be metered not only by our desired outcomes and intentions but also by whether or not these actions will lead to just or unjust ends. Aristotle describes the just man in two ways. The first description is that he is one who follows the law and forms his habits in accordance with justice. The second description is that a just man is one who is not grasping in his relationships with others. The unjust man, conversely, has the constant intention of grasping from others and his surroundings. Because of this, he disregards the law and the rights of his fellow man. The unjust man is one who 'gains by another's loss.' This overarching sense of justice, not only in our personal actions but also in our effects upon the world and our fellow man, pulls the conversation of virtues and vices into the realm of society and politics (politics being how men ought to function in society together). But justice does something else besides. The scales of justice do not function unless there is a central pillar upon which they sit. If we can reason that there is a standard of justice that exists outside of the two people in the courtroom, and it exists even outside of the courtroom itself (which is there because of our collective belief that justice can be reached), then we must ask what this pillar is and what foundation it sits on.

Governments attempt to exact justice and are often imperfect bearers of that justice. But if there is an ultimate standard upon which our actions can be judged, what is the source of this ultimate standard? It is not an apparent good but The Good; goodness itself. Plato was onto something with his forms; he just didn't go far enough to establish the ultimate form of being itself. The Greeks were polytheists, and the tradition of the gods was a long standing one in their culture. Socrates, again through philosophy, reasoned that there must be a first principle for everything. Aristotle referred to this entity as the Unmoved Mover. No matter what our thoughts are on what this entity is, we can rationally know that it is a singular entity; if it were a duality, there would need to be an explanation of what created the two seemingly omnipotent things we are seeing. Even the theory of eternal inflation for how the universe was formed requires an initial catalyst.

Not to get too off-topic, but consider the absurdity of reconciling infinity with the present moment. If it is the practice of the flower shop owner to count all his flowers before opening (digress through all of the moments preceding the present moment), the flower shop could open as long as it was a finite number. But if the flower shop owner has to count to infinity, the shop never opens; we never reach the present where we clearly know we are—because here we are, thinking about existing in the present.

One of the accusations leveled against Socrates at his trial was that he "taught false gods to the youth." It sounds a lot like the accusations that had to be contrived to put Jesus to death as well. I digress; it was an easy accusation by hypocrites who needed to make a moral case for why they should win. The Founders, through the teachings of Aristotle, held to the belief that people were made for much more than to obtain power and material goods. There was an intrinsic desire in people that transcended power and wealth. The success of attaining that desire rested on the order of justice and goodness. As a matter of fact, it is our solemn duty in creating a good society to strive for the good over our own selfish desires. It is why making an honest living is more satisfying than a dishonest one (and why we say the former is a 'good' thing and the latter is not a 'good' thing). It is why the human person desires a relationship with others—not one of give and take but one of love and mutual friendship. These aren't even moral concepts. They are just things we know to be true about ourselves. They are the norm by which we judge how well adjusted a person is. People who don't have empathy, view relationships in a transactional way, and do not adhere to moral norms are called sociopaths. They are, by definition, unwell.

The intrinsic desire for the order of justice makes us truly happy, not because it makes us feel good but because it makes us better human beings. We laud successful relationships, strong marriages, and just professionals. They themselves are good people and are ultimately happier than individuals who do not engage in good human interactions. Why? It goes beyond being a paradox of the modern narrative; it flat contradicts doing what makes you feel good. Any married person knows that the honeymoon stage wears off. Love stops being a feeling and becomes a choice. What relationship exists that does not carry with it trials and suffering? We suffer even in our relationships with ourselves and our own character. Modern culture has robbed us of a true sense of happiness and the tools with which to attain it. I hope that this book helps you reclaim, at least in some way, a path to happiness. If the modern thought paradigm is true and we are to do simply what feels good from one moment to the next, then going to the gym is self-destructive behavior. Loving someone is equally dangerous. In the modern paradigm, using the other person in a sociopathic way for your own gratification is the order of the day. That sounds harsh, and again, even hedonists would deny these principles, even if they are the logical conclusions of their own life philosophy.

The contention is that a rigorous and fast hold on one ideology or another is ultimately harmful. A balance must be struck. But what does that look like in practice? You can't half-love someone in your shallow attempt to merely sleep with them. You can't half-befriend someone to get access to what they have. And you can't tell someone that things are one way while believing in your heart that they are not that way. That is not higher thinking; that is living your own contradiction. That concept isn't paradigm-shifting; it is just honest. And when we are being honest with ourselves, we know that living with one foot in each world is an untenable way to live, which will inevitably result in a miserable life.

The happy person is a realist about life. There will not be continuous satiation on our journey. There will be hard battles and even harder consequences to swallow when pursuing the best version of ourselves. However, instead of bending to his basest desires, the happy person pushes through the challenges of life to reach a height the hedonist can only mock in jaded contention. In what I consider to be my educated opinion, the greatest desire of man is to stand equal in dignity before his fellow man, having afforded his neighbor the justice to which he is due. The truly happy man leaves no right ordered human quality ungiven. He stands vindicated before humanity by living justly and owning—and conquering—the mistakes of his past. That is the desire of the human heart. Being a good person has everything to do with adopting a heroic version of what it means to be a human and never abandoning that principle, no matter how many times we fail. No amount of sex, drugs, or rock and roll can pacify that desire in our hearts. In fact, those will only rob us of the true happiness that awaits us when we turn from such foolish things and start living for happiness in the truest sense of the word.

All the arguments in the section above came from philosophical arguments, even down to the recognition of the Unmoved Mover. Without having to point to a single religious dogma, classic Western philosophy can bring us ninety-five percent of the way through the Founders vision for America. The last piece of the puzzle is that the Founders went further in defining the Unmoved Mover as The Creator, invoking the language of the Torah in Genesis, and thus forever linking our philosophical vision from Athens to that of the theological vision handed down from Jerusalem. The Unmoved Mover, which can be rationally perceived, has revealed himself through his chosen people and their traditions. We know from the revelation of this tradition that this is a personal God who created us in His image. Our reason is endowed in us because it is a reflection (in an imperfect sense) of God's perfect intellect. In the same way, we come by our dignity and therefore our rights.

Therefore, to truly understand and round out the Founders' understanding of the American vision that they created, you have to put the one true, omnipotent GOD upon the throne of America. Zeus, the Flying Spaghetti Monster, or any other diminutive god cannot fill that position, and certainly not Satan or his demons. If you believe in an omnipotent God who can be known to you personally, you can see the American vision. You can disbelieve and still be an American, but atheists cannot see through the proper lens by which to make right judgments about the freedoms afforded to them in a nation that was built by a particular worldview, which happens to not be their own.

The relativist is also at a similar disadvantage. It takes a moral and religious people to make the connection between Athens and Jerusalem and to adhere to the philosophical principles of the Greeks and align them with the commands of Almighty God. This framework is in no way founded on the Christian religion. It is, however, not throwing the baby out with the bathwater like the relativist liberals want us to do. Do not fall for the false dichotomy. It is what causes millions of Americans to not want to believe in God because they see so many poor examples of 'religious people.' And it is what makes millions more religious people believe the lie that we are not to bring our faith and our God into the political sphere. And, most perniciously, it creates the illusion that the moral dogmas of religion are impositions on your happiness and that a life devoid of impositions will lead you to true liberality and therefore true freedom. When comparing modern relativistic liberalism to Christianity in its moral demands, you tell me which one is more in alignment with the virtues required to achieve true human happiness and flourishing.

Believing in God, as understood as the first principle of all that exists, is a rational position. God, not as a limited being but as being itself—the very essence of existence and reason for all that is. It does take an act of faith to believe what the Jewish tradition reveals about God, which is that He is truth itself, goodness itself, and beauty itself. Understand the Creator in the Declaration of Independence to be this God who is truth itself, goodness itself, and beauty itself. This will take humility on your part, but that is the only noble thing in all the world that you should rightly humble yourself before. This God is the source of the virtue that Aristotle and our Founders were able to find through their reason. The Founders have asked us to trust the fact that the God who revealed himself to the Israelites is indeed the Unmoved Mover from whom our desire for happiness springs. If we move toward Him in our virtue, we will surely find that happiness, both in this life and the one to come.

In the book of Exodus, the chosen people of God are freed from slavery by a series of wonders and miracles. The sequence of events that took place for their liberation is no mistake. What happened next was neither a mistake nor a coincidence of the storyline. Right after they are set free from Pharaoh, God gives them the Ten Commandments. Yes, he imposes the law on them as a pre-requisite for them to maintain and embrace their freedom. In this way, Aristotle was seeing God as his Unmoved Mover. Without revelation, Aristotle could see God as you might see someone on the other side of opaque glass; you can make out the shape of someone there even if you can't see him face-to-face. This fundamental marriage of Jerusalem and Athens is the fundamental premise from which the Founders were operating. It was sternly stamped upon the hearts of every American living in the colonies, and it pervaded the colonial spirit. This became the animating spirit of the government that they founded, and that government was blessed because of it. It can become blessed by God's Providence again if we have the courage to rally behind the Founders' vision.

For thirteen years, the colonists ostensibly lived without a government. It was not until 1789 that we had a truly unified country under the Constitution. Of course, there were the Articles of Confederation, but there was no real federal mechanism of law and order. There were only local laws, and people abided by them. It takes a people with exceptional moral fortitude to live in freedom like that without descending into chaos. It is a testament to the American people and to the Founders who gave them the vision far before they gave them a country. This is the vision that we must carry into the future. If we cannot, our country will descend into chaos. Disjointed people with disjointed visions and disjointed philosophical understandings will descend into the throes of whatever strong man will arise. The liberals will give way to the progressives, who will give way to the collectivist doctrines, which will become the animating soul of this country. And in the end, we will be at each other's throats when the leaders of the WEF come to claim their prize and herd us all into the cave.

We need to come together, each in our own religious traditions (or lack thereof), and understand the immense power that comes from the vision the Founders set forth. We need to read the Athenian philosophers and adhere to the rationally perceived virtues in the context of the revelation divined from Jerusalem. That a personal God endows us with our reason, our rights, and the ability to know the path to freedom and finding true happiness. The true dichotomy is not one of rigor or liberality. The true dichotomy is the one between God and relativism; it is, as it always has been, a simple dichotomy between good and evil. There is no way to escape the rigors and hardships of life without consequence. There is no way to live life worshipping other idols without having to reap the consequences of doing so. God pulled no punches with His chosen people. After giving them the law, he laid out the consequences of following His commandments and the consequences that would come from not following them. I will let the text speak for itself. This is the Offer of Life and Death that God gives His people in the book of Deuteronomy, chapter thirty:

> *"Now what I am commanding you today is not too difficult for you or beyond your reach.*
> *No, the word is very near you; it is in your mouth and in your heart so you may obey it.*
> *See, I set before you today life and prosperity, death and destruction.*
> *For I command you today to love the Lord your God, to walk in obedience to him,*
> *and to keep his commands, decrees and laws; then you will live and increase ...*
> *But if your heart turns away and you are not obedient,*
> *and if you are drawn away to bow down to other gods and worship them,*
> *I declare to you this day that you will certainly be destroyed ...*
> *This day I call the heavens and the earth as witnesses against you, that I have set before you life and death, blessings and curses. Now choose life, so that you and your children may live."*[39]

Today is a time for choosing.
Today is the day that you choose life or death;
Today you choose blessings or curses.
What will you have for yourself, your children, and your nation?

CHAPTER 14

What Can I Do? And What Must Be Done

> *"Truth will ultimately prevail where there are pains to bring it to light."*[340]
>
> —George Washington

The number one thing that political pundits get asked by their audiences is, 'What can I do?' What is it that I can do to affect change in this world? If you are still reading this book, you are the person asking that question, and I commend you. You are courageous enough to realize that something needs to be done, and you are a noble enough soul to volunteer as tribute. In utmost sincerity, I salute you, and I stand with you in this fight. We will need many, many brave souls to come together if we want to win this battle. When it comes to political activism, there is a lot that we can do. It has been a challenge for me, but I have not gotten into policy with this book. I wanted to get outside of political tactics and write a book that helped you understand the why behind the what. My goal was not to give you a roadmap; it was to give you a 3D rendering of the terrain that you must travel. It is to help us reclaim our direction and recalibrate our final destination.

Ultimately, I want you, in your own capacity, to reclaim the true answer as to what freedom, liberty, and happiness are for. Also, to show you the pitfalls along the way and the temptations that might befall you. I wanted the readers of this book to be not merely soldiers but tacticians themselves. I want you to find relativism in your daily life, in the materials that you read, and in the political arguments that you engage in. I want to give you the tools to see clearly and thus clearly convey the truth about our national politics. Especially to those friends and family of yours that are in the great disaffected middle. I do not want to tell you what to say to leftists; I want you to be able to cut right through their argument with your own perspective and wisdom.

We are no longer in the days of Rush Limbaugh and his legacy, where one powerful voice on the right was enough to keep the left from going too far too often. Firstly, we need to abandon the legacy of trying to maintain a pseudo-status quo. We can no longer be willing to tolerate leadership on the right that negotiates with the left and meets them in the middle. It is going to require more than just a few smart people with shows and podcasts to cut through this haze and move from defense to offense. It is going to take all of us being b.s. meters to the lies of relativism, liberalism, and global collectivism. It is going to take all of us rejecting the convenient arguments of relativism in our own lives and daily experiences. It is going to take all of us becoming better and better versions of ourselves until we are a people strong enough to win this ideological war. The political activism that we do has to begin with deep foundational principles, and that is what I hope to bring to the fight.

There is a common expression that says 'anger is the Devil's cocaine,' meaning that, in the face of injustice, it is very easy to blur the lines of justice when it comes to our personal anger and hurts. This makes it very easy to improperly respond in turn. It spills into a warped sense of grievance, from which unjust vengeance pours forth. And, of course, each overstep must be met with a grander display from the other side. Thus begins the endless cycle of perpetual grudges and violence, each trying to outdo the other in their pursuit of something that—whatever it is now—abandoned justice a long time ago. We cannot be hooked on the Devil's cocaine if we hope to defeat our declared enemy, who has waged war on us. We can't—and most assuredly do not want to—beat the left and the globalists with their tactics. We don't want to be nastier, more brutish, and shorter than our enemies. But we do have to be ready and willing to do what is necessary to win. We have to be able to look evil dead in the face and have the courage to both reject it and defeat it. But in this inside-out world of ours, we are also going to have to discern the whispers of evil when they don the face of goodness in order to defeat us. And we are going to have to learn to contend with evil on its own claimed territory without resorting to evil's tactics. But how can we do such a thing? How are we to save the nation and keep the integrity of our souls at the same time? But we must be able to do it. It is what we can do, and it is what must be done.

If we go out and start creating skirmishes with the left without knowing what we are ultimately fighting for, we are going to end up fighting them on their terms with their tactics. Believe me—that is what they want! They want you to show up on their turf and fight them on their terms. They want to make sure you both snorted a line before you entered the fight. That way, it is just power vs. power, and it justifies their power grab. They want a situation where just two sets of hypocrites are trying to prove which one is the worse sinner. Because in the court of public opinion, the hypocrite with the better marketing team is going to win every time. That dynamic is not going to change anytime soon, so we have to choose a better tactic. That tactic will require a great deal of political activism, and you will be required to step up. As much fun as it is to see the 'man-on-the-street' viral videos, we cannot be islands unto ourselves out there in the fray.

We have to be unified in our vision and move policy and positions forward together. I fight anger in my heart every single day. I am preaching now to myself just as much as I am giving you advice. People trapped in anger and fear can defend, but they cannot create. You will have to do both for us to win in the end. When the Founders signed the Declaration of Independence, Franklin was credited with saying, "We must hang together, or, most assuredly, we shall all hang separately."[41] If we can't rally around the Founders' vision and take the country back, we are going to meet the latter fate. If you can't see the vision, then you are incapable of seeing where you fit into it. We will all have a role to play in bringing about our own Great American Rebirth. Ultimately, we need to find a way that we can feed the vision of the Great Rebirth. You will need to know what that is in your life. And, by the end of this book, you will know how.

There is only one benefit to chaos, and that is the clarifying effect it has on good and evil. We live in a very chaotic time, a cacophony of voices, distractions, false flags, and gaslighting at every turn. And still, the only thing that becomes clearer and clearer by the day is the divide between the truth seeker and the relativist. As I have said before, there are only two fundamental orientations that we can choose from. No matter how complicated things are, they always come back to good and evil. One leads to life, the other to death. It is our task in this age to choose life and be ready to defeat those who have chosen death before they kill us all. But we cannot do that without recognizing the great divide in this country right now. It is not left and right; politics will make strange bedfellows in the coming decade because the camps will come down to the people who have oriented themselves toward the good and those that would go in the opposite direction and use everyone else's good will to grow their power.

Choose the better path. Strive for maximal goods, leaving all other lesser goods behind. You will be driven and inspired by the fruit of your decisions. You will, because of your discipline, leave lesser things behind in pursuit of greater and greater visions, dreams, and goals. Your confidence will increase, and your capacity will continue to expand. Each new precipice is an inspiration, and you can see the next summit. But you are committed now; the discipline required to reach the next level has paled in comparison to your determination. When you are no longer captured by bad habits and vices, you discover that you are a truly free person. You will be acting on your own volition instead of the promptings of your favorite temptations and debased habits. In your relationships, you will be able to give each other what they are due. You will no longer be emotionally conflicted or stunted in your ability to deal with controversy. You will attract like-minded people and repel those who are not on the same path. You will be an inspiration to those around you, and people will follow your leadership.

This path of growing and becoming is a path of continuous learning and improvement; that should go without saying. Because this is not about being a savant of this obscure art or that academic study. It is becoming a savant of life itself. When you do so, you are not arriving; you are rising. Others cannot pull you down, people cannot enslave you, and you become ungovernable. Not because you are impervious to error, but rather because your life is held to a higher standard that is above the law. Not in its flaunting, but in its authentic character. When you and I reach that pinnacle, we will be a people who can inspire the great disaffected middle to leave this generation's obsession with the soma of relativism and modern liberalism. We will be able to take our country back. And it will happen far quicker than you might think.

The left has gone mad. Now, their madness is boiling over the thin veneer of modern liberalism that has, for these many decades, hidden their nefarious plans under its surface. As the madness of the left implodes in on itself and our country, the T.O.D.s are going to force the hand of the world. They are counting on us being wholly unprepared and still arguing amongst ourselves about who the real enemy is. They expect us to be fighting the battle of the cacophony when they arrive. They are counting on the fact that we will be addicted to relativism and modern liberalism when they come. They hope to find people who want soma more than freedom. They fully expect to step into the breach during the manufactured cataclysm and have us march willingly into their brave new world. They are the ones that have set the date, they are the ones that have declared war on us, and they are forcing us closer and closer to this inflection point. There is only one thing that the Davos thrones fear at this point. It is the fact that you can dethrone them. That is, if you can untangle the web woven to deceive you, see your declared enemy for who they are, and be personally courageous enough to be the person who can unseat evil.

What they fear the most from us is what they cherish the most in themselves. They fear our disobedience; they fear the words 'non-serviam' being said back to them. We must have the personal courage to stand up and say we will not serve the WEF, and instead we will preserve our freedom. Even if their reaction is war, death, and carnage. We will still have our freedom and the right to fight for it to the death. I pray that we do not have to go to kinetic war, and I cannot stress how much we should all be avoiding it. That is the desperate ground on which we would fight, and we must do everything we can in this moment to keep that from happening. If you want peace, prepare for war, but our moment is far more hopeful than that. With a majority of our countrymen behind us, we can just say 'no.' Then the entire game is up.

Don't get me wrong, there will be much work in the coming decades to rebuild what has been destroyed. But that is a vision beyond the Great American Rebirth that must be decided by a future age. We are required in this age to face the moment, stare our enemy in the face, and have the courage to believe that pursuing the good will give us far greater freedom and flourishing than anything that they have to offer. It is our duty and our sacred honor to say no to the WEF, its regime of collectivist overlords, and the evils of relativism as their means to control us. If we can do that, we will have met our moment and stopped a one-thousand-year reign of darkness upon the face of the earth.

Our time, our moment, is a moment of course correction. It is not in going back; we are going to have to be a kind of progressive ourselves, moving to our intended destination. There is no escaping this fact, nor is there escaping the fact that we will have one destination or another. Too often, people on the right are categorized as 'conservative.' This has practically become a mainstream media trope, and it is always followed with a disdainful sentiment about how conservatives are troglodytes who want to take us 'back in time.' We aren't going back, baby! We can't go back; we can't 're-establish the old ways,' or look at some past time as a 'golden age' when we got things right. But we can, as a nation, stop being evil adjacent relativists. We could choose to orient ourselves toward the maximal good instead, so that we will be walking forward on that path and contending with our modern problems. At least we will be dealing with them in the realm of truth and life instead of lies and death.

There are two visions placed before us, and in choosing one, we must turn our back on the other. We will be relying on the principles of our Founding in the Great American Rebirth, and we will be moving forward on the path of light and truth. That involves solving problems that the Founders never anticipated. We have a chaotic and schizophrenic culture that suffers from not only an identity crisis but a crisis of morals as well. The Great American Rebirth will not cure our ills overnight. Taking back the mantle of the soul of America will be a long process. But if we, as a society, can see the divide clearly, we can do the most truly progressive thing. That is, to recognize that we are on the wrong road and have the courage to stop, turn, and then march in the right direction.

I began this book with the teachings of Sun Tzu in The Art of War, and from there we journeyed through many writers, ideas, and concepts. Now, as the pages grow short in your right hand, we have arrived at the teachings of Aristotle and the Offer of Life and Death from the Torah. Whether you are traveling north to south or east to west, you will come full circle if you are willing to travel far enough. Such is life; those who cannot travel the distance and those unwilling to journey are equally lost. Only those willing to go the distance, and return forever changed, can fearlessly overcome any obstacle in front of them. There is one last bridge that links that full circle that we must walk in this age and in our time. It is what we can do to fix our modern age, and it is what must be done if we want our children to journey forward in freedom. And that is to realize that this bridge is the one that connects our last destination back to the first. In doing so, it gives us a complete picture of our age and what we must do. And it cannot be a bridge too far for us. The closing of this age will decide the fate of the age to come. It is a bridge too far for weak men who have no reason, no control over their wills, and a lack of vision that would cause them to fall off the path to the right or left and into the chasm that must be bridged.

Our world has been corrupted against us; this realization is the first plank of the bridge. We have been lied to about freedom and told that we will find it in the satiation of our basest passion instead of reaching for higher goals that make us human. If we are oriented in the school of modern relativistic liberalism from step one, we are going to be warped right back into the power struggle of the progressives. The second plank of the bridge is realizing that our society will be a reflection of what we are oriented toward. Do we believe that truth only extends to the gratification we can extract from others? Or do we believe in a maximal good and ultimate truth that speaks to who and what we are as human beings? This leads directly to the third plank: to recognize and accept that there are only two default positions of viewing the world, we have to choose between relativism and the truth. There is no middle position; perhaps in comfortable times you can stall that decision. But in the end, there is no avoiding it. The fourth plank is choosing the truth. Conflicted men with conflicted hearts cannot make brave soldiers who can battle those who have chosen evil. The fifth plank is to be dedicated to it and to never stop in our growth in and pursuit of the truth. The sixth plank is rejecting relativism personally. This one is going to be the hardest part, my friends. But we have to break our addictions to social media, screens, and the enslavement that we are in by virtue of being attached to the digital matrix.

We have to be able to conquer the coaxing lie of liberalism that we can do as we please and never suffer the consequences of our debasement. If we cannot do it, those who come after us will only find a way to push the example that we give them even further. They will believe the lies of transhumanism and walk into a brave new world of further neglecting their humanity in the search for godlike power. The seventh plank is rejecting it in society and in our politics. We have to have a strong platform of truth and justice to win over the great disaffected middle. And we will need a clear vision for the new party of truth, which our new politicians can step into and represent. The eighth plank is raising the next generation in the knowledge that this is the harder path—but it is the only one that leads to true human flourishing. We all know the famous line from Reagan that 'freedom is just one generation away from extinction.' That sounds ominous, but it is the simple reality of free societies. Which is why it is so incumbent upon us to teach our children to cherish that one generation of freedom over all other alternatives. They must know that anything besides freedom is slavery. The ninth plank is to enshrine it in the laws of our land and, in justice, hold all accountable to the law. This will also be hard, my friends, because the left will not easily let go of power. They have proven that they will use lawfare at every turn to achieve their ends. We have to outmaneuver them with simply worded legislation, clear definitions, and principled laws rather than legalistic ones. Define collectivism as treason. Declare that using one freedom to abuse another is unconstitutional. Officially recognize religion as the Founders would have done so: as a monotheistic religion where the God of all gods is in the place of The Creator. And lastly, we have to reverse every single ruling of the Supreme Court that ruled in the name of modern liberalism.

The tenth plank is to teach the next generation to repeat steps one through nine. The tools of rising to one's freedom must be given to each new generation, with enough knowledge that they might do the same to the generation that comes after them. This is not a bridge 'back' to some distant place or time that we might perceive as a golden age. This is not the bridge of nostalgia, but the bridge beyond to a new and heightened America. It is a bridge to the future, where we can take the timeless wisdom of the ages to heights that the Founders could not imagine. Please be a part of that American future by doing the unglamourous work of reading Aristotle's Nicomachean Ethics, by doing the boring and oftentimes seemingly thankless work of forming yourself into a habit of virtue. If you can, you can rightly demand that from others and from every level of leadership in this country. Be brave enough to defend this orientation toward the good—even to the death—and ensure that it is passed down to future generations. If we can do this, we will live to see those who have declared war on us crumble under the weight of their own destruction. Their empire of lies will collapse, and it will have been you that was the power that Dethroned Davos.

Believe me, I wish the maximal goods in life were both fast and easy to obtain. I wish we could pull some lever to cure our ills. I wish it were as simple as defeating this current batch of progressives at the next election. And wouldn't it be nice if we could simply outlaw bad things and, by virtue of outlawing them, they would be erased from the face of the earth? But that is not how we are going to win in the end. We will not wish for foolish things. We will envision greatness and then go about achieving it. We are going to achieve our Great American Rebirth by knowing our enemies and how to defeat them, but we can only know that because we first know ourselves.

The vision of taking the country back must be instilled within us, and we all have to know what we are fighting for and progressing toward if we want to be victorious. The quiet part that no progressive says out loud is that people must have an aim and destination in mind that they are 'progressing' to if they want to be "progressive." If the progressives told the American people their full vision, they would never work in Washington again. But that is because the destination they are 'progressing' to is a global dictatorship that preaches collectivist rhetoric for the sake of complete hegemonic control by whatever means necessary. And the truth is, we are well on the way to their intended destination.

By now, you might have come to the realization that I am not going to provide an infomercial-style solution to sorting your life out. The $19.99 version isn't what you really need or want anyway. Nor am I providing a step-by-step policy proposal or political platform. But what I am giving you is the vision required to build it. Because, make no mistake, the world is changing. The world will be a radically different place in ten years. We will either have built the bridge to freedom or the WEF will have built their empire. We need to have a Great American Rebirth in this country in order to build that bridge and be able to cross over the chasm that has been built to swallow us up. Achieving that vision is a both-and approach; good people make good societies. Bad people cannot make good societies because they are, by definition, oriented away from goodness. Good people can make free societies because they are oriented toward the good and move themselves, their families, and their country toward what is true, good, and right. Thus, they have chosen life.

Relativists cannot make free societies because, in their worship of their own power, they cannot see that they are orienting themselves away from all that is good. In the end, we become what we orient ourselves toward. In this age, we don't have to answer every single question about policy or morals. Our time, our moment, is a decision of monumental bravery: we have to defeat the globalists and reject the modern liberalism that has ushered them in. Our society is a culture of death, oriented toward evil. We have to be courageous enough to say 'no more.' We have to be able to boldly choose to orient ourselves to a truth that many of us have little relationship with. And let me tell you, at first, we are all going to really suck at it. Having been raised in this relativistic mess for more than sixty years, we are at a great disadvantage in seeing truth clearly. But we don't have to be perfect; we just have to be on the path of choosing the good; that is the only way our children and grandchildren will be able to raise our society even higher in the years to come. In order for us to raise our society out of the pit, we must be on the path that acknowledges and seeks truth and goodness. As long as we can do that, we are not relativistic hypocrites going in the opposite direction to a different end entirely. And once you have chosen life, it will become clear to you how you can contribute to bringing that into a flourishing life. Not only for yourself, but for your nation.

We must become a people that can choose truth and maximal goods, and we must be a people strong enough to reject those that will not. The rejection comes from winning politically and enshrining the pursuit of the good into our laws. We definitely cannot do this as long as the relativism of evil abounds in our society. But neither can we do so as long as the relativism of modern liberalism is still around to poison the well. We have been taught by modern liberalism that we can do as we please and there will never be a negative consequence. Liberty is argued to be a mere license, and it is a blessing of liberty that Americans can abuse their freedoms in the name of freedom. **But one cannot use his freedom to abuse personal or societal freedom.** It is a tragic time when this is bolded in an American political work as a profound truth. Yet here we are. You can't use your freedom of expression to burn the symbol of the country that recognizes that right. The only country in the world that acknowledges, and therefore refuses to inhibit, your God-given right to speech and expression. At least, not without negative consequences and the denigration of your freedoms. No more than you can use your freedom to sin and expect your life to continue to move in a positive and righteous way. Again, if the Founders blundered, it was in failing to imagine a future relativistic age that was so stupid that it could not understand this basic premise.

The people who don't understand that freedom of speech cannot be used to preach hatred of the country to its youth are not serious people. The people who think that evil is protected by the freedom of religious expression are not the adults in the room. The people who have welcomed our doom by tolerating every voice, even the anti-American progressives, do not deserve to be a part of the conversation on how to rebuild after we have won. I don't care how nice, tolerant, and charming they are; they are misguided, and we cannot follow that path again if we ever want to live in true freedom. We have to recognize that our freedoms have withered away in a fading light. That is because modern liberalism turned our orientation away from the light of truth that gave us freedom in the first place. We aren't 'going back' to the way things were; we are going forward by turning back toward that light of truth and leaving evil behind. All we have to do is start walking. As long as we are on that path, walking toward the good and away from the evils of relativistic hypocrisy, we will have left a future for our children. A future that will be illuminated and elevated, upon which future generations will reach even higher.

When World War II broke out in 1939, Carol Wojtyla was in college. He and his friends were part of an informal, underground theater group. To fight the Germans who had invaded their country of Poland, some members of this group wrote articles critical of the Nazis. Others made underground plays that could demonstrate the bad ideological ends on the stage. Others joined the military and fought the Nazis on the battlefield. Some stayed home in protest of violence but ran society and provided the materials necessary to feed and care for the troops on the front lines. But they all contributed to the war and, in doing so, shaped its outcome. Carol went to seminary, where he became a Catholic priest. Although the Nazis were the first to invade Poland, their ideological brothers came to stay for another fifty years after the war was over.

One of the key contributing factors to the fall of the Soviet regime was that priest's return to Poland in 1979, having been away in Vatican City, becoming Pope John Paul II. Returning to his country of origin and the outpouring of the Polish people toward God and His Church were unmistakable witnesses. In open defiance, too, of the Godless Soviet regime. It was a PR nightmare that the Soviets never recovered from, haunting them until their collapse thirteen years later. Even then, in the radicalism of the sexual revolution, the hollowing out of the Western Churches, and the collapse of our moral framework, relativism could not hide its ugliness from the world when light shone upon its darkness. Some of us will be asked to be JPII-type figures; some of us will be asked to argue; and some of us will be asked to teach. Some of us will be asked to expose relativism through art, movies, or plays. Others will be asked to simply be good parents to their children and to bring them up in the ways that they are to go.

Some of us will go our entire lives thinking that we have never contributed much to anything. But you will shape the future in some way. You might have a conversation with someone that changes the course of their lives, and that conversation changes the course of the world. Your son or daughter might, by virtue of their upbringing, be a very bright light to the world. Most of us will lead very unglamourous lives that contribute only to the stability of our community and our society. But in so doing, we become the salt of the earth. We become the glue of society that holds everything together. In doing so, we will drive our country upward because that type of society demands ever-better leadership and policy.

Either way, we will be called in our own way to see relativism for what it is, to recognize the pernicious personal and political ideologies it produces, and to seek to eradicate it from our lives. That is the vision for the Great American Rebirth: to recognize and reject relativism as a utopian nowhere place that leads to death. It leads to personal death through bodily destruction, eternal death through sin, and the death of the nation that adopts it by making everyone exactly equal in their misery and discontent. We must reject the enticements of evil and seek the good if we ever want to be truly free and for our society to flourish. Any other lesser good sought after will orient us away from the good, and in our adjacent state, we will orient the world toward evil, and evil will continue to advance until it wins. We cannot feed that vision if we are struggling to envision ourselves—as right-ordered selves. People who are asking, 'What can I do?' while shaking their spears in anger are capable of quite a lot. But they are not capable of being the type of people that can defeat the other side; who are equally angry, shaking their spears with equal vigor. Because in the end, if we defeat the left by taking vengeance into our own hands, we will not have defeated them; we will just have become them. We will simply replace the tyrants whose vision is only one of personal power. We wouldn't have defeated them; we simply will have replaced them as Satan's class pet.

To launch a proper counteroffensive, we will need a united front doing what we are, in our virtue, being called to do. Whether that is to write books or articles, have shows and podcasts, or even do mainstream interviews. Most of us, whether content creators or not, will be in the political know and sharing this information out as much as possible. If that group of people takes the vision to heart and can point to the bad arguments and b.s. in our own ranks, it will make the content that is being produced even better. And in my opinion, that is far more important work than being the talking head. Most importantly, the ability of the grassroots to hone people in media or political leadership means that we get better and more unified candidates running for office. We get people who aren't trying to fill us with platitudinous phrases and slap us on the back. Right before they go to Washington and get blindsided by, and then corrupted by, the system.

However, it takes more than being a keyboard warrior. You have to know who your delegate is for the Republican Party in your area. They need to hear from every Republican and every rational person who is clued into what the left is doing. They need to be shamed into standing up for the voters who are opposing the other party, whether we consider ourselves Republicans or not. They need to know that you stand on the side of good, and if they won't become that mechanism for change, we will replace them—and we'll bring eighty percent of their voter base with us. We have to be poll watchers, and very vocal and active members of our local political parties. Those are the local institutions that are often providing the pool of volunteers that physically do the work of conducting elections. We also need to know who our chief election official is for our state, what rules are allowed, and what is not allowed. Our election process is so corrupted that, sometimes, it gives me a sense of hopelessness. But if we are not in that space doing the work, it certainly will not get better.

If this is your particular calling, please begin learning today how you can be involved at your local polling place. But those are just a few examples of the countless ways you can get involved; the only person who knows how and where to get involved is you. There are great organizations in the arena today; one that I have great respect for is Turning Point USA. Their outreach is to younger audiences and doing events on college campuses. They are always actively looking for volunteers and people to start local chapters on their high school and college campuses. If this isn't your particular calling, you'll need to find an organization that caters more to your talents. Make sure they are as on fire and as on vision as TPUSA, and you will not be led astray.

Life in the last century was one of dereliction of duty, in the wake of an enemy that has sought our country's ruin. We go to one of two places from here. 1. In the next decade, we can be victorious in this great ideological war and reclaim our country. Or 2. The next decade will be the fruition of the WEF vision, the destruction of America, and the subjugation of the world under a one-world rule. We will be subjugated by materialist transhumanists, who will further rob our humanity, our dignity, and our freedom through their continued denial of our shared humanity. But it doesn't have to end that way. If the globalists win, they will install regimes preaching communism throughout the world to do their bidding. It will be at least a thousannd-year struggle to regain any sense of freedom, autonomy, or self-determination. If we win, I cannot guarantee an equally long millennium of peace. I can guarantee you only one generation of that—a century at best. It is an uphill battle to preserve human freedom upon the face of the Earth, but it is noble work that you must do today, here in our age. And this must become your legacy that you pass along to the next generation.

We are in the great decade that will decide the fate of the world. It is our metal, our fortitude, that is going to be tested, and it will be our actions that determine our fate and the fate of our children in the tenth and twentieth generations. It all comes down to what we choose: will we have peace, prosperity, and life? Or will we have slavery, darkness, and death? The communists, the WEF, and the rulers of this world have declared war on your freedom, your sovereignty, and your way of life. Now, they are here to claim their prize, which will result in slavery, darkness, and death for you. You can no longer deny these declared enemies their war. There is no way out but through, for there is nowhere to run if they are victorious. I have said that we must build a bridge to cross a chasm. The chasm is the trap that has been set for us; call it the cave or any other analogy. Descending into it is the inevitable conclusion of doing nothing and letting their plans come to fruition. In order to win, we must learn how to defeat them—and then have the metal to do it. We will have to be the people who can build that bridge and then be able to cross it.

We need a philosophical revolution in this country to understand the modern divide. To be able to see clearly enough to know the way out of this madness. Bringing clarity to chaos is not for the faint-hearted, nor for the hearts of the conflicted. We must remain lovers of peace while we are forced by our enemy to become wagers of war. We must be a people who are not afraid to wield the sword but wise and metered enough to know when to put it down. Weak, misguided, and confused people cannot do this. It is a narrow bridge that we must navigate, and there will be many chances to fall off to the right and the left. I pray that we do not come to an open, kinetic civil war in this country. I hope that we don't have to go to war as a country against other countries captured by the WEF. I have been using the language of war throughout this book because I see the tactics of our enemy. There is no other way to describe the machinations of a force that requires your destruction for the sake of its power. If you allow the left to trap us in that same dynamic, we will not be worthy of taking up the mantle of America, and God's Providence certainly will not return to our country upon our victory.

The vision of the Great American Rebirth is for us to see the divide between good and evil in this current age and choose life for ourselves and our children. Not to always choose the harder path or the more depriving habit. No, it is to choose the right thing. The just way and the maximal good, regardless of our temptations to choose lesser goods. That takes personal discipline and societal cohesion, but your personal commitment is the prime mover in that equation. If we can do this, we will become the type of people who can attract the great disaffected middle at the very time when the left goes mad. We must also recognize that the divide between good and evil will create strange alliances, and we must be prepared to give quarter to anyone who would be willing to defect to our side in service of the good. Our protection against treachery will be our abandonment of modern liberalism. Usurpers will not be able to hide their evil intent in a world that no longer accepts duplicity. Even the quietest lie cannot hide in a crowd of truth seekers. And lastly, it is to clearly identify those who are seeking evil and give them neither mercy nor quarter. And hear me clearly: I am referring to the T.O.D.s who have founded the WEF and any of their lesser political and cultural 'elite' who defend them. I do not refer to any private citizen, no matter how sincere their indoctrination.

Those who have for a century set up mechanisms to destroy us are the ones deserving of no mercy and no quarter. Those who have been their ideological useful idiots and shaped the progressive vision for this country deserve no mercy and no quarter. And anyone who would rather burn the world down to reign over the ashes—who can see nothing but a power struggle and would never turn from their seeking of power—deserves no mercy and no quarter. This is an extremely important point; there should never be a future moment where anyone associated with the WEF gets to 'apologize' and 'rejoin the efforts to rebuild' the society for which they have such utter contempt. I am not calling for anyone's head on a pike or for torture or anything like that. I am just saying that, when we defeat them, they will pivot. And if we are not prepared to tell them that they can pivot to St. Helena, then they will just burrow in and wait us out again.

A just society would rightly treat the T.O.D.s and their useful idiots like the pariahs that they are, force their hand at every turn, and expose them as wretched souls. Vengeance for their actions is not ours to wield, but we are perfectly within our rights to expose them for what they are and deal with them justly. They deserve to be called evil to their faces, be put on their backs, and attempt to justify how they are good. They deserve to fumble over themselves to explain how their particular brand of evil is good. There is nothing more powerful than forcing evil to speak plainly. They deserve to admit they would see all of us die for their wretched power. Then, if justice requires it, they must be tried and punished for their crimes.

We have to be ready at every turn to do what is necessary to see our side win. Serving the good will take on many forms along the way. It will be a complex tapestry of choices, personal and political policies, habit formation, and growing in our knowledge of the maximal good. That starts by rejecting the ways that have brought us to the brink of this chasm and not falling into the final trap. Rather, it means that we have to build a bridge over it and walk to the other side, where we can begin rebuilding a new society that is wise enough to continue marching toward the good and not fall off the path to the right or left when the temptations of relativism come along. Andrew Klavan, author and podcaster, speaks of a concept that he refers to as the "Great Speculation."[42] This concept, he says, is an act of faith in which we must believe that another person's inner life and pursuit of happiness is just as important to them—as our own pursuit of happiness is to us.

This is the primal reasoning behind why we would treat each other as equals. The second that we stop, we move from the realm of good will into the realm of a struggle for power. In order for us to treat each other as equals, we must acknowledge that there is a source of truth that exists outside of us, and thus it becomes our duty, personally and societally, to pursue that truth as the good that will lead to our own flourishing and the flourishing of society. This is the good that we must form our consciences in above any other pursuit of our own power. That is our challenge. If you honor the fact that we are equal before the truth, you will have chosen life. If you reject this, you will find yourself stealing another's life for your power.

We must be a people of life and true freedom, and a people of right-ordered governance. We will be the ideological victors over the great disaffected middle if we can become this people, and we will stand strong enough for whatever our declared enemies throw at us. If you approach life assenting to and orienting yourself toward the idea that we can know the truth and that knowing the truth will lead to good ends, you will be able to take this country back. If you are not, you will orient yourself away from the truth and simultaneously away from good. There is no iffy middle position, no matter how much modern liberals have insisted there is. Vacillating back and forth can, at best, only produce lesser goods.

If this is the status quo that we carry forward into the world, we will show that we are on the side of good will. We can find common ground with people oriented toward the good, even if we don't align on all things moral. That is your calling, here at this time and in our age. We do not have to solve the world's problems, just the problems that are in front of us. We have to have the courage to see the problem clearly, even when it is deeply lodged in our own hearts.

Most of all, we have to be a people of high character and discernment. Only then will we be able to see the enticements of relativism clearly and reject them. By doing this, your enemies cannot overcome you. Because, in your adherence to the truth, you can see and reject even the smallest lie. People like this, united in vision, can create a truly great society. We must become these people. We can do it. And it is what must be done.

CHAPTER 15

In Conclusion: Reset Wisely

So, here we are. We are at the end of an age, just as sure as we are at the end of this book. There will be a new world order. As to what that new world order will look like, well, that depends. My advice for surviving the inevitable chaos that is to come? Be a good person—someone who acknowledges that there is a truth and that we can seek it in good faith with our fellow man. To stand as a lover of the good and the peace that it brings. What a letdown, huh? Where's the call to arms? Where is all the war talk from earlier? You need not fear that your declared enemy will bring the fight to your door. And if you are not prepared to respond properly, you will lose by either being a pushover or becoming a bully yourself.

Being a good person, capable of discernment, is the foundation from which we must enter the battlefield. That is why it is my first piece of advice. In order for us to establish a good world order, we must be able to recognize the divide of our age. So, my second piece of advice is to be a wise person—one who can stand against the forces of evil and defeat them without replacing evil with evil. Only a person who is aligned with the good can do this. People who are not conflicted in their own hearts as to who they are. Not conflicted about what is owed to their fellow man, nor conflicted about what is owed to God. I do not know what form that might take for you. And it will look different for each and every one of us. I will leave it to the pundits and political class to give the Braveheart speeches before the battles. What I can give you is the vision and the foundation from which to build the future. You can accept it or deny it. Either way, there will be a new world order, and we will get exactly what we deserve.

This is the event horizon. The event horizon describes the point where the gravity well of a black hole will pull anything into its power; its gravity is far too great for even light to escape. We are in the final days of orbit around the chasm; things are moving rapidly, and the very laws of normalcy and decency that we have relied upon for centuries are being warped to a breaking point. Not unlike the laws of physics around an immense gravitational anomaly. We are quickly approaching the point of no return, but we are not reclined to fall into the WEF's chasm. There is an inevitable change on the horizon, and we must be prepared for it. Today is not the day for standing still; we cannot remain where we are or revert back to where we were. We are going to be launched into a great new unknown, one that we can assist in shaping.

If we stand still or allow ourselves to become part of the problem through any lesser defeat, we will fall into the darkness that has been shaped for us. In order to escape this event horizon and pull ourselves out of the clutches of the WEF and their plan for humanity's future, we need to first recognize that we are in an ideological struggle for the future. We need to realize that this war has been raging since the beginning of time and that this particular campaign within that struggle was waged well over a century ago. We must be able to equip ourselves with the tactician's armor and fight for the good against the forces of evil. For those who have chosen death, the WEF, and their useful idiots, they get no mercy and no quarter; we must command control of the current age so that future generations can build a future worth having.

The WEF and their useful idiots have declared themselves your enemies and will, without remorse, trade your life for their power. We must be about the business of constantly pulling back the veil and showing their evil for what it is. That will take many forms. It is a gentle conversation with your family and friends in the great disaffected middle, even when they are spouting the words of the enemy. To anyone that you can impact, you must bring truth, light, and a love of the good to them. And it will look like sternness of character in our daily lives, committing ourselves daily to orienting ourselves to the good and teaching by example. It will look like shrewdness in politics and crafting policy, drawing the clear distinction between those seeking the truth and those seeking their own power. And it will even take the form of rebuking—and even shunning—bad-faith actors who would slit your throat before you knew you were bleeding. If we are successful, we will be hated by the world and the modern narrative. We will be vilified by those whose power is jeopardized by our pursuit of the good. This is often referred to as being "over the target." If you are not viewed by your enemy as a demon of utopia, you aren't doing it right.

This book has walked through the battle on its surface. We have explored the material and economic sources of our enemy's power. We have explored their political tactics and how they are using the very mechanisms of political discourse to destroy us and set up centers of power around the world that only have allegiance to them. And we have discovered the ultimate, underlying theology that drives them and makes the other two possible. Seeing their plans at every level is how we can truly understand our enemy. And it is also how we can come to know ourselves, and how we are being called to serve the good in the ultimate battle between good and evil. The conflict will be decided by who commands control of the conflict in the end. We can control this conflict if we can first control ourselves. To be disciplined enough to say no to the enticements that evil offers. If we can do that, we can win. I want to close this book out by telling you how you can do just that.

First, let me introduce you to the wrong way. We are not going to win by white knuckling our way through this event horizon, grinding and grinding at our moral characters without knowing if it will make a difference in the end. People abandon their New Year's resolutions before the end of January not because they don't have the capacity to be disciplined but because their discipline is not motivated by a vision of what they actually want to accomplish. The vision can't be that you want to lose fifty pounds. The vision can't even be that you want to fit into that old pair of jeans. The vision has to be far deeper than that to be lasting and motivating. The vision has to be that you want to be the kind of person who strives to be healthy and maintain your health because it makes you a happier person. You have more energy and can contribute more to your family and friends, because you are a higher functioning person who doesn't have joint pain, soreness, or a cycle of fatigue and depression. You have to know who you want to be and then strive toward that.

Envision that new you and become familiar with who he or she is. Imagine what that person says, what they do, and how they act. Imagine what they eat, how metered they are, and how they are the type of person who has long ago abandoned the lie of gluttony and the false promises it dangles in front of them. Know that person well, and most importantly, know that you can—and that you will—become that person. And then start living into that person and their image every single day.

Your very identity will change, and you will become what you desire. That is a motivating vision that will not only help you get to your ideal weight but also stay there and never want to go back. Weight is the easy one. What about our society's addiction to pornography? First of all, I want to give you, me, and everyone in this degenerate age some grace. It is not a stretch at all to say that we were groomed by our modern narrative into this porn addiction. Hollywood groomed us through the entertainment that they put out. They showed us things that should have never left the bedroom. Modern liberalism grooms us in the name of liberality and freedom, breaking every sexual taboo in our culture. Now, we are contending with sexual proclivities that are so unnatural that we celebrate genital mutilation as an expression of the authentic self. By the way, if you support genital mutilation as a solution to something, you're evil. (There is no middle ground where you can be kind and loving to someone while you irreversibly hack their perfectly healthy body apart.)

We were groomed by a wicked generation that sold us sexual pleasure as the height of freedom. And now we are a society enslaved to our sexual desires. I did not break my habit by just wanting to stop. It took years of struggling with it, like some people do with gaining and losing weight. Eventually, what stopped it was recognizing that I had been groomed to think this was normal and that I had to create a vision of a new normal if I ever wanted to be free from it. I had to see a vision of myself—to envision a version of me that wasn't just strong enough not to but was the kind of man that porn would not even tempt. Once I believed that I could become this man, that motivated my discipline, and I began chasing him. That motivated me to seek good and edifying entertainment. That motivated me to avoid spending alone time with me and my little portal to hell (my smart phone). That motivated me to seek out the reasons why I should not be looking at porn in the first place and seek solace in that extracurricular activity that goes along with it (as Woody Allen describes it, "having sex with someone you love").[43]

As long as you are ensnared by your favorite vices, you will not be the kind of person who overcomes them, no matter how much you love to hate yourself for having them. We have to break the cycle of modern liberalism if we hope to make lasting change, and that is both an internal and external exercise. And it begins with not hoping that we can be better, nor complaining about the modern ills while still being wed to them in our own minds and hearts. The vision that we need to defeat the WEF and stop their implementation of their new world order has to be one that motivates our discipline. Once we have the vision, we will then be motivated to become the people that we need to be. Where we fit into this battle for the soul of our nation will become clear. It begins with a vision that is larger than wanting the madness to stop.

Without a motivator, we will not have the strength to win. Who is the ideal you? It is not the person strapped to the metaverse in his or her pod who will remain satiated as long as they are obedient.

Although we are fast approaching this almost unimaginable extreme, it is still just a pointed example of what modern liberalism is slowly doing to us: depriving us through depravity. What we must do today and in the years to come is recognize that we are living smaller versions of this extreme—just littler versions of the hell that we as a society are oriented toward. We have to recognize that we are being led through the manipulation of our normalcy bias to think that all is well, just like the meme of the dog drinking coffee while the house burns down. Most of the time, people have to hit the wall and have no place to go before they are motivated to change. We don't have that luxury. You have to be someone of vision and make a change before your enemy's plans become inevitable and swallow us all. Let us strive to reset the world to something better, envision what ought to be, and let that motivate your discipline so that it will become reality.

There is a reason that Canadian psychologist and author Jordan Peterson is public enemy number one. It is a strange world that vilifies a man who tells other young men to make their beds. But he is a threat because he gives people vision for their lives and extols discipline. I would not consider him to be a 'motivational speaker,' but he is in the loose sphere of people who are in the business of wanting their fellow man to succeed. It is by design that you have to type their names into the search bar of your social media apps, but the 'free the nip' videos and the videos of drunk people doing stupid stuff are at the top of the feed. That is the normal that we have been raised in. Jordan Peterson and others like him are asking you to take stock of your life. To overcome your weaknesses, your excuses, and your demons and seek to be a better person. This is a grave threat to the people who want us to become their subjects, not their fellow citizens. When you question the narrative, you are deciding for yourself who you want to be. You are here, reading this, because you question the narrative. I hope that I have done you justice by helping you navigate the fray outside of the narrative. I hope that I have helped you see clearly what we are dealing with, what is coming, and what we must do. The last thing that I want to do is give you hope in the face of what seems like an insurmountable foe.

I can't give you that hope by telling you the Convention of States is going to save us. Or that supporting one candidate or the other will save us. Or that we will be saved by your adoption of some policy point. It is by first seeing the divide clearly and helping you to choose to be a seeker of truth over a seeker of power. Then, it is to help us all stand united in a vision that will help us reset wisely. The last is to ask you to shift your mindset in these final days of this age—to shift your thinking into envisioning a good world order and letting that motivate you in your life, your politics, and your future. Some of you have gotten to the point where you know it is in your best interest to do exactly the opposite of what the narrative is telling us. Some of you are still on the fence, although I hope you are ready to come down after what I've had to say. When the moment comes, in whatever form it takes, it will no longer be sufficient to say 'no' to the machine because the machine will be gone. We will have to think for ourselves, and if we are not ready to do so, we are doomed to repeat this cycle all over again.

It is this vision, this 'yes' that will echo into the future and shape the new world that will be born from the ashes of this age. If it is just a puritanical vision of aesthetic denial and white knuckling, we will have doomed future generations to repeat the past's mistakes. We will even be doomed to repeat the errors that were adopted when we founded this great nation. Our victory cry at the end of this conflict must be that great 'yes.' A 'yes' that we assent to the good and the pursuit of an ever more perfect union. That is the hope that we can give this country, a hope that will ring far into the future and inform other generations as they identify and contend with the evils of their age.

This is the only practical advice directly about politics that I want to give. All Americans should read Aristotle's trilogy: Nicomachean Ethics, Politics, and Metaphysics. It is best to do this with a commentary as a guide. Although not an exhaustive treatise on the Founders inspiration, this is the philosophy that underlies the Founders' understanding of the country that they founded. It is neither a Christian text (obviously) nor an apologetic work on theology. It deeply comports with Christian teaching and is a necessary read for all Americans, Christian or not. All people of good will are going to have to link arms. We might be in separate militias, but we cannot hold separate camps. Reading these books will help to expose one of the most pernicious lies of the modern liberal movement: that fundamentalism and Christian asceticism are the source of 'the old order' that they claimed to have overthrown. Although Christianity was displaced in the process, it was our common humanity that was usurped by the relativists who came preaching modern liberalism.

The second piece of advice is this: no matter who you think you are in this world, you do not have rights if you do not think they are divinely instituted by God. No other country in the world has the ability to claim what we claim through our Declaration of Independence: "That we are endowed by our Creator with certain unalienable rights, among those the right of life, liberty, and the pursuit of happiness."[44] Remember that the government does not give us our rights, and they can only remain just if they uphold the rights of the sons of the King. Every other person in the world is a subject of their country. We are the only true citizens in the world; we are co-equal members of We The People of this great nation. Again, I want to stress this fact: I pray that kinetic war never breaks out in this country, either through civil war or engagement with another country captured by the WEF. However, we are in an ideological war with an enemy who seeks to radically redefine this paradigm, and if you are not ready to accept that challenge and see it clearly for what it is, you will be completely hopeless in navigating your way to victory. Our rights come from our divine sonship through the Creator, King of America. And there is no power on earth that has the right to take them from us, not even the government instituted in America in 1789.

My third piece of advice is this: understand that being oriented toward the good gives you a litmus test to discern good political policy from bad political policy. The freedom that comes from the rights endowed by our Creator can never be used in service of usurping any other freedom. We live in a world of leftists using their freedom of speech to try to eradicate the Second Amendment. They abuse the 'freedom of expression' to preach hatred of the country. They champion bureaucracy that robs us of our autonomy and state sovereignty. It is a sad age that has to 'protect' this basic, common-sense premise. But we are going to have to enshrine this into our laws. And we are going to have to be brave enough to repeal every bad precedent that violates this simple premise. Lastly, if this premise comes into question in any policy, that is a question that the federal government cannot answer. That needs to be handed over to the lowest subsidiary government to decide at the community or state level.

And that brings me to my last piece of advice: we will not have true freedom until we eradicate the fourth branch of government, the bureaucratic state. This includes the disbanding of the intelligence agencies. Over the past century, Congress has slowly derelicted their lawmaking duties into these agencies. They have also made the water even muddier by putting them under the tutelage of the president. Until the government consists only of the President and Cabinet, the Congress, and the Supreme Court, we will never be able to break the stranglehold that the WEF has on our government. There, that's my hot take.

There is a very famous short radio address from Paul Harvey that was written and read over the air in 1965. It is called 'If I Were the Devil,' and it turned out to be a deeply prophetic work. Paul Harvey could see the radical shift all those years ago and could articulate the great ideological divide that was introduced during that radical time. The piece began:

> *"If I were the devil ... If I were the Prince of Darkness, I'd want to engulf the whole world in darkness. And I'd have a third of its real estate, and four-fifths of its population, but I wouldn't be happy until I had seized the ripest apple on the tree — Thee. So I'd set about however necessary to take over the United States. I'd subvert the churches first — I'd begin with a campaign of whispers. With the wisdom of a serpent, I would whisper to you as I whispered to Eve: 'Do as you please.'"*[45]

Harvey would then go on to describe how the Devil would use that simple relativistic phrase "Do as you please" to destroy the culture. Starting with the young, the Devil would convince the people that religions were no different than mythologies. And that any semblance of God was a human construct. Paul Harvey also prophesied that the Devil would become a political organizer as well as promote promiscuity in entertainment so that everything else that came before would be boring by comparison. He also predicted the drug epidemic that would come in the decade of its airing. We have the same problem today, except some drugs are legally prescribed by doctors, and they have all become more normalized. Harvey could also see the communist underpinnings of the Devil's message, saying that the Devil would soon have families, churches, and communities all at war with each other. Although he does not say the words "critical theory," he does point out the end of the Devil's tactics: "... until each in turn was consumed." He even predicts the media fanfare and the relativism of people who seek to call their emotions 'my truth.' Harvey predicted that, in the end, even the churches would substitute religion, morality, and discussions about God and the Devil for psychobabble and the deification of science. Paul Harvey concludes his address by saying:

> *"If I were the devil I'd take from those who have, and give to those who want until I had killed the incentive of the ambitious. ... I would caution against extremes and hard work, in Patriotism, and in moral conduct. I would convince the young that marriage is old-fashioned, that swinging is more fun, that what you see on the TV ... is the way to be. ... In other words, if I were the devil, I'd just keep right on doing what he's doing."*[46]

He was not far off the mark. The only thing that could be said in criticism is that his prophecies were too conservative to account for just how crazy things have gotten! Or perhaps he thought the level of madness he described would spell the end of the country. I am not going to attempt to carry his prophecy forward, primarily because there aren't another sixty years of chaos and destruction ahead of us in order to attempt a guess at. I think you know we are in an unsustainable time and that we cannot continue like this for much longer. There is not a material known to man that can bend as far as America has without breaking, and we live in the moment of the breaking. We are being pressed into a paradigm-shifting event by our declared enemy. Whatever the catastrophe, it will be a planned chaos, a forced emergency. Whatever form it takes, one thing is for sure: the purpose will be to motivate you through fear and trembling to give up your freedoms, your sovereignty, and your self-reliance for the semblance of security. And if you are not prepared—in your heart and in your mind—you will bend and break before your declared enemy.

I personally believe that this will happen in the next ten years and that the use of the year 2030 by the WEF is no mistake. And if we are just slightly successful in taking back the reins of power in our country, that will only delay their plans by a few years. I want to conclude by comparing two visions: the vision of the good world order that will motivate us into right-ordered discipline versus the 'normal' that has been set by the new world order. And I want to also compare what each vision thinks about the human person, human flourishing, and human freedom.

The WEF, through their useful idiots, have been engaged in ideological warfare for a long time, so we can see how their normal has played out in the culture that we have. This was a culture that was never meant to be sustainable, because it was a culture that was never meant to last. It was a transitory means of achieving their ends.

That is why we spend into oblivion and call that just. That is why our culture celebrates the most debased members of our culture and has come to think that the government's role is one of handing out benefits, favors, and even rights. It is also the source of anger and division in this country. The establishmentarian right and left are the only ones defending it; the purple octogenarians cannot let go of their power because they cannot let go of the lie of modern liberalism: that relativism will set us free.

The soft relativism of modern liberalism has been rejected by those who will decide the future. All that is left is to battle it out and see which side will command control of the conflict in the end. The left has chosen their side. They will see 'the revolution' out to the end and serve the WEF in their utopian visions. You will decide if they win by seeing the vision beyond the immediate defeat and allowing that to propel you forward. Forward to do the hard work that lies ahead—in your heart and in the country. You know your enemy, and now you know where the divide is in the culture. It is the same one that runs through every human heart. I want to compare the way that these competing world orders will view the human person. As I do, keep in mind the words of Paul Harvey. I will present my concluding arguments in a similar vein. He is right in recognizing the heart of the conflict. He is also correct in identifying the general, who, even if only through the madness of his broken ideology, is marshaling our declared enemy. If you were given a century to wage ideological warfare on a people before you ever had to challenge them on the battlefield, what would you do to demoralize the people?

If I were a relativist, I would befuddle the people. You see, in ambiguity, I would draw my power. I could bewitch the reasonable, confound the just, and make those prone to emotion completely irascible. I would erase all distinctions except one: do whatever you please. I would convince people of this truism and thus guarantee that no moral principle, no limiting principle, and no cultural taboo would ever become a roadblock to their pursuit of hell, which I have by my lies convinced them is happiness. I would denigrate people in the health of their bodies and minds. I would convince parents that the natural disposition of their children is unnatural, and then I would convince them that it is right and just to give those children state-approved drugs to solve their 'ills.' Every year after, I would diagnose every twinge of emotion and stinging of the conscience as a sickness as well, not to be cured by making the soul healthy but by the euphoria of drugs and pretending that the soul does not exist. Once filled with my soma and unable to deal with themselves or heal themselves, I would go about corrupting the people through their minds. I would dull their consciences until they railed for their satiations and demanded them over their own self-reliance. I would make sure that they extolled the virtues of 'niceness' and 'tolerance.' That way, if ever my game was exposed, I could shut them up quickly.

If I were a relativist, I would denigrate their relationships until every one of them ultimately warped into serving me. Then I would force them into isolation, taking away their humanity and the semblance of what it means to have human connection. I would make sure that the people were afraid to speak plainly and felt the awkwardness of doing so even when what needed to be said was not even that controversial. I would destroy the art of crafting true relationships; I would accuse men of being 'womanish' for having substantive relationships with their fellow man. I would create so many sources of division and distraction among women that they could never sincerely connect either. I would make courtship into dating, and then dating into casual sex. I would pit men and women against each other as primal enemies. That is, of course, until I reach the point of my game where I would attack the distinction altogether.

If I were a relativist, I would seek to destroy the notion of true value and warp people into serving mammon. I would enslave them into a system where the flow of money came to me. And, if they obeyed my every whim and caprice, I would allow some to flow back to them to cover the cost of their final days. I would twist their sense of security in their wealth and in their contribution until they were serving my ends, thinking that they served themselves. In other words, I would take over the global economy, form the WEF, fund the progressive movement, and watch the tangled web that I have woven destroy the people until they beg me to solve their problems.

In short, if I were a relativist, I would implement humanism, collectivism, scientism, atheism, occultism, modern liberalism, the Great Society, progressivism, feminism, the sexual revolution, drugs, spiritualism, modern monetary theory, Marxism, critical theory, critical race theory, modern gender theory, transhumanism—and whatever else I could possibly throw at them to destroy them. Because the point ... well, it was never the point. Winning my game was the point. And oh, how I will win in the end; and steal every ounce of your life for my power. That is, as long as you never realize that life and death are the stakes of my game. But you never will, as long as you believe my lies. And believe that you are the king of your own little universe in the relativist trap I have set for you. No, you will find yourself my subject, either in my utopian nowhere place on earth or in my nowhere place called Hell, and you will have volunteered to do so, all the while pursuing a hell that I have convinced you is happiness.

The way out of the trap of relativism is a narrow path, one that we must walk in a single file line. That is because we cannot hide behind affiliations and the organizations that we are part of. It is because each of our hearts must be judged worthy to walk across that narrow bridge to freedom. That is the primary disposition, the freedom of the self, that produces a free society. Free people are not free to simply do whatever they please. People are free because they do not need to steal their neighbor's life in service of their own power. They are free because they have defined happiness not in the lies of relativism but in the humble pursuit of The Truth.

When happiness is defined not by my satiation from one moment to the next but rather by my fulfillment as a person, I am free. When happiness is defined not by my survival but rather by my flourishing, I am free. This freedom comes with great responsibility, and thus it is easily lied about by relativism. The relativist loves to drag people off the narrow path, convincing them that the rigor required to truly be free will never be worth it. That the juice is not worth the squeeze. Many times, we will give into this temptation. But as long as we remain resolute in our vision, we can always course-correct and rejoin our fellow truth seekers on the narrow path to freedom. However, if ever our minds are clouded by relativism, we will come to voluntarily abandon that path and live in the pit with the hypocrites, degrading themselves and serving their own power at the cost of their souls. And that is what is lost in the end: your soul. Your self-identity, your self-sovereignty, and the capacity to hold the good in your heart, mind, and soul are utterly lost, as is your desire for them.

The narrow path is the way to freedom, as long as that thin ray of hope is alive in your heart. If it is, step up to the challenge. Take stock of your physical and mental health. Strengthen your mind with good things and strengthen your body until it is powerful enough to heal itself. Take stock of your relationships and ensure that you are showing goodwill to everyone you are in a relationship with. Have the strength to push away anyone who is abusing your good will. Have true friendships, people who you can rely on in good times and in bad, and seek to have complementarity in your marriage. And take stock of your ability to be self-reliant. Whatever pathway of wealth and contribution you choose, make sure that you are not beholden to the state for your family's future. All of that will take work on your part, but even if it is a life that seems like hell on earth, it is the only path to true happiness.

The way out, my friends, is to become a people who are ungovernable by your declared enemies. We do that by being people who do not need a governess. Be smarter than those who would have you adopt their worldview, their satiations, and the way of life that will lead you to death. You must instead adopt a mindset of growth—a mindset of true liberation, true freedom, and true self-determination. If you asked me to define this mindset, I would have a hard time putting that definition into a Merriam-Webster format. There are several moving parts, each affecting the other parts, and it affects the whole in a way that a bumper sticker slogan just can't quite stick to. This mindset is not stasis; it is unlocking a way of seeing, interacting with, and becoming in the world. It is the flipping of a switch in your mind, an 'activation' of your mind that requires daily growth and furtherance of being. The 'unlocking' of this growth mindset is this: recognizing that you can do more than 'nibble around the edges of your life.' It is a realization that you can both transform your life and affect the outcome of your existence. It is the scales of past biases and lies coming off your eyes, so you can see that almost everything about your current life is up for debate, improvement, and change, no matter how closed, damaged, or dark it is.

This mindset looks to heal the body and the mind, not run from the problems and mistakes of the past. Call it ownership, accountability, empowerment, etc.; the growth mindset starts you on the journey to radical transformation, which starts in the mind and can only come to full effect through the accordance of the will. Action is the real mover in the growth mindset, although it cannot happen, of course, without that primary movement of the mind into the growth mindset space. And you will never find the value of doing so without first envisioning the person you will become. See your future self, the one who knew what time it was and was part of the dethroning of Davos. They are a fearsome thing to behold. How do you become that person? By adopting the mindset that will help you grow into the person who can defeat your declared enemies.

From revelation to continuous mind growth to continuous life transformation, the cycle of the growth mindset expands your existence until you are ready to receive the next, larger revelation that you would have been unable to fathom without the mental work and action of the first cycle. On and on, larger and larger the cycle grows; your growth expands your capacity, your mental ability, your relational and emotional IQ, and your potential for reaching, influencing, and helping others. This is the pathway to true change, and I hope you join me on this journey. Because we all must reset wisely, my friends. If you want to be ungovernable by your declared enemy, become someone who is continually growing into a more formidable foe every single day. Become a force of reason that can destroy their arguments, not only in your own heart but in the court of public opinion.

Orient yourself toward the maximal good, motivated by who you are in the fullness and flourishing promised by God, because you have chosen life. Give life to all who give life, and never allow those who have chosen death to foist it upon you. If you do this, we will endure, and our children will live to see the freedom that our declared enemies almost stole from us. That is the story I want to tell my children; what about you? So go forth! We The People have a brand-new country to forge—one that can stand up and declare that it has become a more perfect union in the face of defeat. We will do so only if we are a nation of people clear-eyed in our pursuit of The Truth. And, of course, if we can expand into the people that can choose it, attain it, and come to live a life defined by it. Only then will we possess the only thing that can truly set us free. Can you see the vision?

You are free in the days after the fall of the empire of lies. And you are free because, first, you became a person worthy of their freedom. You let go of the lies and trained your mind in the search for truth. You sought maximal goods and rose ever higher in your pursuit. You gave each what they were due and left no right-ordered virtue untouched. You stood in the face of evil and did not break under its temptations. You were firm in your victory over your declared enemies—and just in sentencing them for their crimes. You chose life, and freedom was your reward. In the days after the empire's fall, you bask in true friendships and deep familial connections. You are a person of integrity, not easily swayed by temptations and lesser ends. You are in control of your destiny because nothing is in control of you. You enjoy a country worthy of the Providence that oversees its prosperity. You now live in a cohesive America where the division wrought by the collectivists has withered away as liberty and justice for all blossom in their place.

There is no duplicity in this society that you have helped to construct. Liars and power-hungry fools are pushed to the edge of the realm and are not tolerated by you and your fellow citizens. The ominous deep state, the fourth branch of government, no longer reigns over your life and the lives of your fellow Americans like a tyrannical governess. There is no need for red tape, regulation, or calls for accountability amongst people who are accountable to God and their fellow man. It will not be a perfect future; no one is claiming that we can make a utopia. But it is one where you could leave your door unlocked. A world where you smile, look a passerby in the eye, and say hello. A world where standard economic policy dictates that the burdens of work cannot rob you of your family. A world where you have community and belonging, people are counting on you in the same way that you are counting on others to make the world go around. You do not live in fear of crime; you do not live in fear of corrupting influences on your children. You live among people who deal in good will and honesty, and society is blessed because of it. And it was you who did it. You became like George Washington, who could dethrone King George without building a throne of your own. You brought down the inapparent kings of the world because lies cannot stand in the face of truth and win. Your goodness prevailed in the face of evil. And after you dethroned Davos, your goodness was the mechanism by which the world was made new.

Now close your eyes and imagine yourself and who you are in this world. What is that future-state you doing as a means of fulfilling work? How do you dress? How do you talk to people? How do you treat your family members and your children? Where do you live? Imagine yourself in the quiet moments of the day. What do you do for leisure? How do you contribute to your family and community? Imagine the home of that best self. What does it look like? What furniture does that highest you have? What are their style choices? Sit on your porch and imagine being that person and what you are doing in your spare time. Imagine what that person thinks about as well as your disciplines and habits. Imagine every part of daily life and how inspiring it is.

You must be a fearsome thing to behold, as we all are when we are at the height of what we were created to be. See that maximal you in your mind; think about them often, as often as you can. Know that you can become that person; you already are that person. It is only a matter of understanding how to unlock your potential. I hope that this book has at least pointed you in the right direction. I hope I have done something to bring clarity to your life in this modern madness. And I hope that I have given you the proper motivation to pursue the you that you are meant to become. Now the only thing left to do is become the best version of yourself. Let nothing stand in your way or dissuade you from the pursuit—and attainment—of your true happiness. Let that motivate your discipline in becoming your best self. Because no less is being demanded of you at the end of this age and in the forging of the future to come. The fate of the world is in your hands, and the future hangs in the balance. No matter what you are called to do or where you find yourself in the final battle for the future, there is but one rallying cry on the side of those of us who have chosen life. Do whatever it takes to make sure that you have a place at the victor's banquet table. There, may we raise a glass to that hard-won freedom. I pray that I have the courage to do the same, and I hope to see you there, my friend.

Stay in touch

Follow T.G. Pierce on X: twitter.com/TeddyP1776

For book updates, merch, related articles and more, visit: dethronedavos.com

Connect with and keep in touch with fellow patriots at the all-new website: therighteousten.com

Notes:

1: Sun Tzu, *The Art of War*, trans. Ralph D. Sawyer (Boulder, CO: Westview Press, 1994).

2: Sun Tzu, *The Art of War*, trans. Ralph D. Sawyer (Boulder, CO: Westview Press, 1994).

3: Sun Tzu, *The Art of War*, trans. Ralph D. Sawyer (Boulder, CO: Westview Press, 1994).

4: Orwell, George. *Nineteen Eighty-Four.* London: Secker & Warburg, 1949.

5: 8 Predictions for the World in 2030. 2020. YouTube. Uploaded by World Economic Forum, November 11, 2020. https://www.youtube.com/watch?v=2gmBN7N5pPM.

6: 8 Predictions for the World in 2030. 2020. YouTube. Uploaded by World Economic Forum, November 11, 2020. https://www.youtube.com/watch?v=2gmBN7N5pPM.

7: 8 Predictions for the World in 2030. 2020. YouTube. Uploaded by World Economic Forum, November 11, 2020. https://www.youtube.com/watch?v=2gmBN7N5pPM.

8: Thomas Paine, *Common Sense* (Philadelphia: W. and T. Bradford, 1776).

9: Thomas Paine, *Common Sense* (Philadelphia: W. and T. Bradford, 1776).

10: Adams, John. Letter to the Officers of the First Brigade of the Third Division of the Militia of Massachusetts. October 11, 1798. Founders Online, National Archives. https://founders.archives.gov/documents/Adams/99-02-02-3102

11:Madison, James. 1788. "Federalist No. 51." Independent Journal, February 6, 1788. Founders Online, National Archives. https://founders.archives.gov/documents/Madison/01-10-02-0262.

12: US Congress. 1776. The Declaration of Independence. July 4, 1776. America's Founding Documents. National Archives. https://www.archives.gov/founding-docs/declaration.

13: Newton, Isaac. 1675. Letter to Robert Hooke, February 5, 1675. Historical Society of Pennsylvania. http://www.livesandletters.ac.uk/papers/FOR_Display.php?id=6.

14: G.K. Chesterton, Orthodoxy (New York: John Lane Company, 1908).

15: Thomas Jefferson to Edward Carrington, 16 January 1787, National Archives, Founders Online, https://founders.archives.gov/documents/Jefferson/01-11-02-0047.

16: Kundera, Milan. The Book of Laughter and Forgetting. Translated by Aaron Asher, HarperCollins Publishers, 1999.

17: John Milton, Paradise Lost (London: Peter Parker, 1667).

18: Sun Tzu, The Art of War, trans. Ralph D. Sawyer (Boulder, CO: Westview Press, 1994).

19: Alexander Solzhenitsyn, The Gulag Archipelago 1918-1956: An Experiment in Literary Investigation, trans. Thomas P. Whitney, vol. 1 (New York: Harper & Row, 1973).

20: Reagan, Ronald. Quoted in Lou Cannon, "President Rejects Notion of Talks; Defends TWA Response," The Washington Post, July 5, 1985, A7.

21: Alexander Solzhenitsyn, The Gulag Archipelago 1918-1956: An Experiment in Literary Investigation, trans. Thomas P. Whitney, vol. 1 (New York: Harper & Row, 1973).

22: Wilson, Woodrow. Congressional Government: A Study in American Politics. Houghton Mifflin, 1885.

23: Dutschke, Rudi. "On Anti-authoritarianism." Speech at the 22nd Congress of the German Socialist Student Union in Hanover, June 17, 1967. Translated by Marianne Herzog and published in Robert Holt, Rudi Dutschke: Revolutionary Theory, Political Practice (Westport: Lawrence Hill, 1973).

24: Pelosi, Alexandra, quoted in Susan Page, "Daughter Unlocks Nancy Pelosi," USA Today, July 25, 2006, https://usatoday30.usatoday.com/news/washington/2006-07-24-pelosi-main_x.htm.

25: Machiavelli, Niccolò. The Prince. Translated by W. K. Marriott, Floating Press, 2009.

26: Hilaire Belloc, as quoted in: Frank Sheed, Sidelights on the Catholic Revival (New York: Sheed & Ward, 1932).

27: Alexander Solzhenitsyn, The Gulag Archipelago 1918-1956: An Experiment in Literary Investigation, trans. Thomas P. Whitney, vol. 1 (New York: Harper & Row, 1973).

28: Saul Alinsky, Rules for Radicals (New York: Vintage Books, 1971).

29: John Milton, Paradise Lost (London: Peter Parker, 1667).

30: Chesterton, G. K. "The Drift from Domesticity." The Thing: Why I Am a Catholic, Macmillan and Co., Limited, 1929.

31: Shakespeare, William. Hamlet, Act 1, Scene 5. The Tragedy of Hamlet, Prince of Denmark, Simon & Schuster, 2004.

32: Jesus Christ, quoted in Bible. English Standard Version, Matthew 12.30. Accessed [02/21/24].

33: Franklin, Benjamin. The Works of Benjamin Franklin, Volume 10. Edited by Jared Sparks, Hilliard, Gray and Co., 1840.

34: Descartes, René. Discourse on the Method of Rightly Conducting One's Reason and Seeking Truth in the Sciences. Translated by Ian Maclean, Oxford University Press, 2006.

35: Franklin, Benjamin. The Works of Benjamin Franklin, Vol. 10. Edited by Jared Sparks, Hilliard, Gray and Co., 1840.

36: Augustine, Confessions, book 11, chapter 14, translated by Henry Chadwick (Oxford: Oxford University Press, 1991).

37: Adams, John. "Treaty of Peace and Friendship between the United States and the Bey and Subjects of Tripoli of Barbary." 1796-1797. Treaty, U.S. National Archives and Records Administration, Washington D.C.

38: Adams, John. Letter to the Officers of the First Brigade of the Third Division of the Militia of Massachusetts. October 11, 1798. Founders Online, National Archives. https://founders.archives.gov/documents/Adams/99-02-02-3102

39: The Holy Bible, New International Version, Biblica, 2011, Deut. 30:11-19.

40: Washington, George. Letter to Charles M. Thruston. 10 Aug. 1794. Manuscript/Mixed Material. Library of Congress, Washington D.C.

41: Franklin, Benjamin. "Speech at Signing of the Declaration of Independence." Speech, July 4, 1776, Philadelphia.

42: Klavan, Andrew. "The Great Speculation." Speech, Values Voter Summit, Washington D.C., September 14, 2007.

43: Allen, Woody. "Having Sex with Someone You Love." From an interview in The Observer, September 5, 2004.

44: US Congress. 1776. The Declaration of Independence. July 4, 1776. America's Founding Documents. National Archives. https://www.archives.gov/founding-docs/declaration.

45: Paul Harvey, "If I Were the Devil," Paul Harvey's The Rest of the Story, ABC Radio Networks, April 3, 1965.

46: Paul Harvey, "If I Were the Devil," Paul Harvey's The Rest of the Story, ABC Radio Networks, April 3, 1965.